Maldives

James Lyon

LONELY PLANET PUBLICATIONS
Melbourne • Oakland • London • Paris

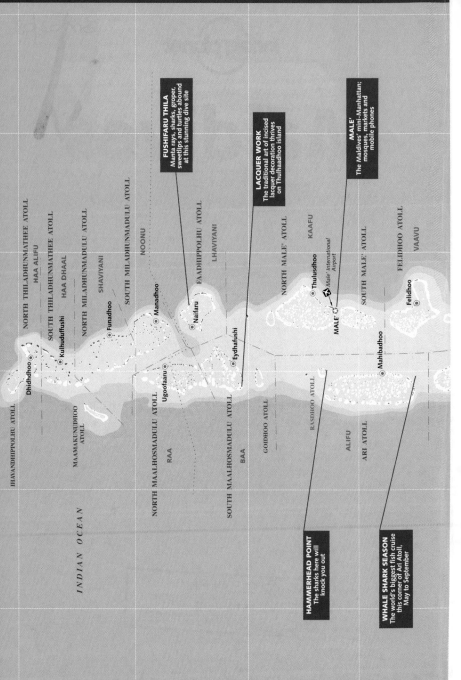

FUSHIFARU THILA
Manta rays, sharks, groper, sweetlips and turtles abound at this stunning dive site

LACQUER WORK
The traditional art of incised lacquer decoration thrives on Thulhaadhoo island

MALE'
The Maldives' mini-Manhattan; mosques, markets and mobile phones

HAMMERHEAD POINT
The sharks here will knock you out

WHALE SHARK SEASON
The world's biggest fish cruise this corner of Ari Atoll, May to September

INDIAN OCEAN

HUVANDHIPPOLHU ATOLL

NORTH THILADHUNMATHEE ATOLL
HAA ALIFU

SOUTH THILADHUNMATHEE ATOLL
HAA DHAAL

NORTH MILADHUNMADULU ATOLL
SHAVIYANI

SOUTH MILADHUNMADULU ATOLL
NOONU

FAADHIPPOLHU ATOLL
LHAVIYANI

NORTH MALE' ATOLL
KAAFU

SOUTH MALE' ATOLL

FELIDHOO ATOLL
VAAVU

MAAMAKUNUDHOO ATOLL
RAA

NORTH MAALHOSMADULU ATOLL

SOUTH MAALHOSMADULU ATOLL
BAA

GOIDHOO ATOLL

RASDHOO ATOLL

ALIFU
ARI ATOLL

Dhidhdhoo

Kulhuduffushi
Funadhoo
Manadhoo
Naifaru
Eydhafushi
Ugoofaaru
Thulusdhoo
Male' International Airport
MALE'
Mahibadhoo
Felidhoo

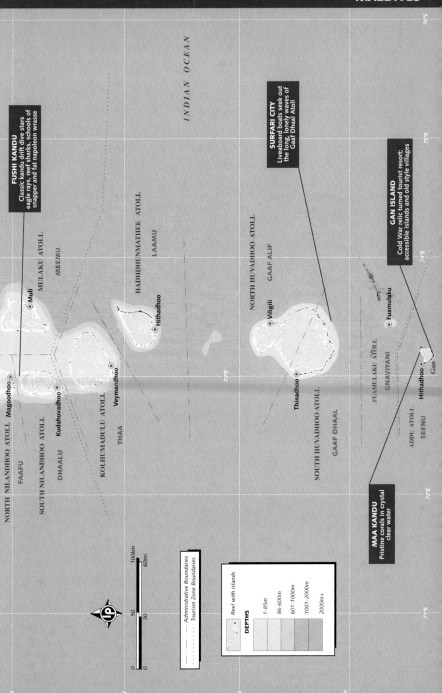

MALDIVES

INDIAN OCEAN

FUSHI KANDU
Classic kandu drift dive stars eagle rays, reef sharks, schools of snapper and fat napoleon wrasse

SURFARI CITY
Liveaboard boats seek out the long, lonely waves of Gaaf Dhaal Atoll

GAN ISLAND
Cold War relic turned tourist resort; accessible islands and old style villages

MAA KANDU
Pristine corals in crystal clear water

NORTH NILANDHOO ATOLL — Magoodhoo
FAAFU
SOUTH NILANDHOO ATOLL
DHAALU — Kudahuvadhoo
KOLHUMADULU ATOLL
THAA — Veymandhoo
MULAKU ATOLL — Muli
MEEMU
HADHDHUNMATHEE ATOLL — Hithadhoo
LAAMU

NORTH HUVADHOO ATOLL
GAAF ALIF — Viligili
SOUTH HUVADHOO ATOLL — Thinadhoo
GAAF DHAAL

FUAMULAKU ATOLL — Fuamulaku
GNAVIYANI
ADDU ATOLL
SEENU — Hithadhoo — Gan

Administrative Boundaries
Tourism Zone Boundaries

DEPTHS
Reef with islands
1-85m
86-600m
601-1000m
1001-2000m
2000m+

0 50 100km
0 30 60mi

3°N
2°N
1°N
Equator

71°E 72°E 73°E 74°E 75°E 76°E

Contents – Text

Contents – Maps

MAP INDEX

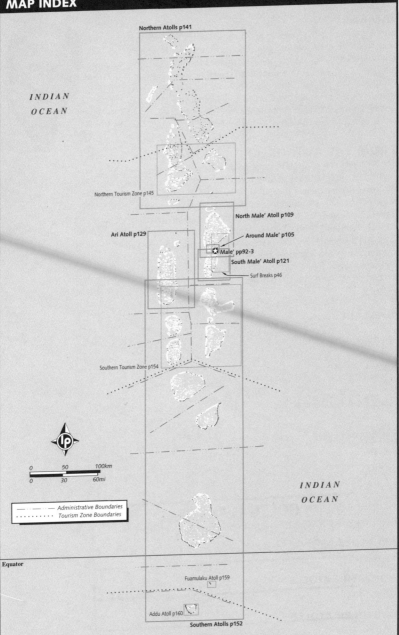

INDIAN
OCEAN

Northern Atolls p141

Northern Tourism Zone p145

North Male' Atoll p109

Around Male' p105

Ari Atoll p129

Male' pp92-3

South Male' Atoll p121

Surf Breaks p46

Southern Tourism Zone p154

INDIAN
OCEAN

| 0 | 50 | 100km |
| 0 | 30 | 60mi |

— — — Administrative Boundaries
· · · · · · Tourism Zone Boundaries

Equator

Fuamulaku Atoll p159

Addu Atoll p160

Southern Atolls p152

The Author

JAMES LYON

James worked for five years as an editor at Lonely Planet's Melbourne office, then 'jumped the fence' to become a researcher and writer, and has since worked on guides to Bali, California, Mexico, Maldives, South America and the USA, sometimes travelling with his wife and their two sons. He finds the Maldives' unique geography and devotion to Islam especially intriguing, and he's always amazed at the richness of the underwater world, just a snorkel's length below the surface.

FROM THE AUTHOR

The Maldives is a difficult destination to research. You can't just walk up to a hotel and ask to see a room – not unless you can walk on water. Many people helped me to get around the country, supplied me with information and provided new perspectives. I am especially grateful (in no particular order) to Ibrahim Abdulla; Naseer, Xain and Firaq at Inner Maldives; Maldivian Air Taxi; Gert and Shahina at Sea Explorers; Trans Maldivian Airways; Tim Godfrey; Tony and Zulfa Hussein; Ian Lyon and Pauline (as ever).

Thanks also to Aishath Velezinee, who contributed the section on Women in the Maldives.

This Book

Robert Wilcox researched and wrote the first edition of *Maldives & Islands of East Indian Ocean*, Mark Balla updated the second edition and James Lyon updated the third edition, which concentrated solely on the Maldives. James updated the fourth and fifth editions.

FROM THE PUBLISHER

This fifth edition of *Maldives* was produced in Lonely Planet's Melbourne office and coordinated by Melissa Faulkner (editorial), Daniel Fennessy (mapping) and Yvonne Bishofberger (layout design). Editing and proofing assistance was provided by Barbara Delissen, Stefanie Di Trocchio, Cecilia Thom and Simon Williamson. Janine Eberle was the commissioning editor and Chris Love the project manager.

Thanks to Quentin Frayne for editing the language chapter, Wendy Wright for designing the cover, Brendan Dempsey for the cover artwork, and Pepi Bluck for the illustrations. Photographs were provided by Lonely Planet Images.

THANKS

Many thanks to the following travellers who used previous editions of *Maldives* and wrote to us with helpful hints, useful advice and interesting anecdotes about travelling in the Maldives.

Anthony & Angharad Dew, Pamela Barr, Christine Briggs, L Burt, Robert Chatfield, Ian Chicken, Connie Chrisafic, Perry Clark, Wendy Clark, LK Collier, Martin Cripps, John Dale, David Davies, Wendy Davies, John Devlin, Philip Drury, Bronwen Fallens, Ansgar Felbecker, Joco Freitas, Anne Froger, Claire Fryer, Kurt Goergen, Rea Ivanek, Sue & Ray Jones, Annelie Jung, Adam Mansfield, David Nash, Kathleen Ng, Lee O'Donovan, Alison Park, Lincoln Siliakus, Irene Smith, Robert J Stagg, Mrs Sullivan, Paul Sutton, Paul Thatcher, Dianne Thomas, Meera Vyas, Peter Watson, Chien Wei.

Foreword

ABOUT LONELY PLANET GUIDEBOOKS

The story begins with a classic travel adventure: Tony and Maureen Wheeler's 1972 journey across Europe and Asia to Australia. There was no useful information about the overland trail then, so Tony and Maureen published the first Lonely Planet guidebook to meet a growing need.

From a kitchen table, Lonely Planet has grown to become the largest independent travel publisher in the world, with offices in Melbourne (Australia), Oakland (USA), London (UK) and Paris (France).

Today Lonely Planet guidebooks cover the globe. There is an ever-growing list of books and information in a variety of media. Some things haven't changed. The main aim is still to make it possible for adventurous travellers to get out there – to explore and better understand the world.

At Lonely Planet we believe travellers can make a positive contribution to the countries they visit – if they respect their host communities and spend their money wisely. Since 1986 a percentage of the income from each book has been donated to aid projects and human rights campaigns, and, more recently, to wildlife conservation.

Although inclusion in a guidebook usually implies a recommendation we cannot list every good place. Exclusion does not necessarily imply criticism. In fact there are a number of reasons why we might exclude a place – sometimes it is simply inappropriate to encourage an influx of travellers.

UPDATES & READER FEEDBACK

Things change – prices go up, schedules change, good places go bad and bad places go bankrupt. Nothing stays the same. So, if you find things better or worse, recently opened or long-since closed, please tell us and help make the next edition even more accurate and useful.

Lonely Planet thoroughly updates each guidebook as often as possible – usually every two years, although for some destinations the gap can be longer. Between editions, up-to-date information is available in our free, monthly email bulletin *Comet* (W www.lonelyplanet.com/newsletters). You can also check out the *Thorn Tree* bulletin board and *Postcards* section of our website which carry unverified, but fascinating, reports from travellers.

Tell us about it! We genuinely value your feedback. A well-travelled team at Lonely Planet reads and acknowledges every email and letter we receive and ensures that every morsel of information finds its way to the relevant authors, editors and cartographers.

Everyone who writes to us will find their name listed in the next edition of the appropriate guidebook. The very best contributions will be rewarded with a free guidebook.

We may edit, reproduce and incorporate your comments in Lonely Planet products such as guidebooks, websites and digital products, so let us know if you don't want your comments reproduced or your name acknowledged.

How to contact Lonely Planet:
Online: e talk2us@lonelyplanet.com.au, W www.lonelyplanet.com
Australia: Locked Bag 1, Footscray, Victoria 3011
UK: 72-82 Rosebery Ave, London, EC1R 4RW
USA: 150 Linden St, Oakland, CA 94607

Introduction

Relax. Cool your face with a moist, scented towel. Look out over the blue lagoon, and listen to the breeze rustling through the palm trees. Lose the shoes, and wriggle your toes in the sand floor of the lobby. Stroll on the powder-soft beaches, luxuriate in the warmth of the sun, and dip into the crystal-clear water. The Maldives has made its remarkable coral atoll environment into a tourist destination that fulfils all our fantasies of the perfect tropical island, and indulges us with abundant food, fine service and the most agreeable of entertainments and activities.

Maldives resorts have a unique sense of seclusion, of being away from it all. Each one is its own island, and exists only to pamper its fortunate guests. Even more secluded is a live-aboard boat, which you can hire for a week or two, cruising through blue lagoons and anchoring beside desert islands. You'll always be well looked after, with cold drinks, satisfying meals and accommodation that's very comfortable.

You'll be surrounded by water in any case, because 99% of Maldivian territory is below sea level. To explore that fantastic territory, you'll have to get wet. First-time snorkellers and hard-core divers will be amazed at the rugged submarine landscape – the cliffs, caves and canyons, the great visibility and

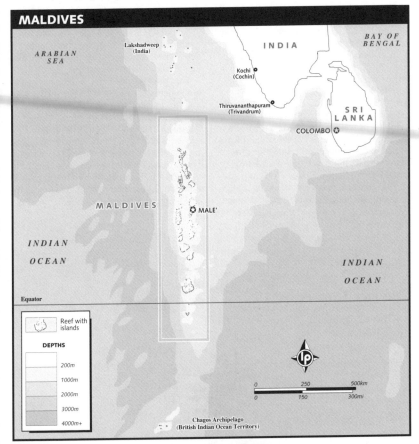

MALDIVES

ARABIAN SEA

Lakshadweep (India)

INDIA

BAY OF BENGAL

Kochi (Cochin)

Thiruvananthapuram (Trivandrum)

SRI LANKA

COLOMBO

MALDIVES

MALE'

INDIAN OCEAN

INDIAN OCEAN

Equator

Reef with islands

DEPTHS

200m
1000m
2000m
3000m
4000m+

0   250   500km
0   150   300mi

Chagos Archipelago
(British Indian Ocean Territory)

the zillions of fish. Over three-quarters of the world's reef-fish species can be found in the Maldives, and many can be seen just by snorkelling a short distance from the beach. For scuba divers the Maldives are world famous. As well as the beauty of the fish and soft corals, there is the thrill of diving with turtles, moray eels, manta rays, whale sharks and dolphins. There's new coral too, regrowing after the coral bleaching of the 1998 El Niño. The reefs are regenerating like a forest after a fire, and they'll continue improving if global warming can be averted.

For Maldivian people, managing the marine environment is paramount. The sea has been their food store for centuries, and now they are depending on its natural beauty continuing to attract tourists. Sustainable tourism is a national objective, and they'll use 21st-century technology to achieve it. Behind the back-to-nature ambience of an island resort is a well equipped microtown, with its own power, water and communications infrastructure, and its own extremely professional management. The latest resorts may look like the Swiss Family Robinson's house, but they all run like a Swiss watch. They're committed to providing creature comforts as well as preserving a pristine environment – the guests expect nothing less.

For guests who expect something more than lying on the beach, there's a lot to see and do above the water line. You can windsurf, kitesurf or catamaran across a lagoon, or paddle a canoe to an uninhabited island.

Surfers can ride perfect waves just minutes from the comfort of a five-star resort room, or take a fully appointed safari boat to some of the remotest surf breaks on earth. Fishing enthusiasts can catch their dinner on a morning trip, go big-game fishing on the open sea, or chase after tuna Maldivian style – with simply a hook and a line.

The Maldives is a stage setting for a romantic holiday, perfect honeymoon or second honeymoon, with its lush gardens, sparkling seas and starry skies. Lavish spa treatments, deep massages, body scrubs and aromatherapy are soothing and sensual, and resorts have rooms to match, with outdoor bathtubs, four-poster beds and private sea views.

If you want to see how Maldivians live, you can easily visit a fishing village. Walk through the tidy streets, watch a boat being built and see kids in white uniforms playing at school. Or you visit Male', the intriguing capital island, with its mosques, markets and maze-like streets; its modern bustle, new buildings and busy shops.

But mostly you'll be immersed in the ambience of a tropical island or relaxing on a safari boat cruising crystal-clear waters. If you want to simply enjoy food, accommodation or recreation, you'll be in the right place. But if you're an underwater ecotourist or water-sports enthusiast, a closet beach bum or a chronic romantic, you're in danger of atoll addiction. You might have to come back year after year to get another fix of Maldivian sea and sunshine.

Facts about the Maldives

The Republic of Maldives is a small Islamic nation of about 270,000 people with a history, culture and language all of its own. The country comprises some 1190 tiny islands, none of them more than a couple of kilometres across or more than a few metres above sea level. Traditionally a fishing and trading people, the Maldivians have been able to maintain their independence for centuries.

HISTORY

The history of the Maldives can be divided into two stages: before and after the conversion to Islam in 1153.

The latter, well-documented stage has passed through a series of sultanic dynasties to the recent birth and rebirth of the republic. The pre-Muslim period is full of hazy, heroic myths, mixed with conjecture based on inconclusive archaeological discoveries.

Early Days

Some archaeologists, including Thor Heyerdahl, believe that the Maldives were well known from around 2000 BC, and were a trading junction for several ancient maritime civilisations including Egyptians, Romans, Mesopotamians and Indus Valley traders. The legendary sun-worshipping people called the Redin may have descended from one of these groups.

Around 500 BC the Redin either left or were absorbed by Buddhists, probably from Sri Lanka, and by Hindus from northwest India. HCP Bell, a British commissioner of the Ceylon Civil Service, led archaeological expeditions to the Maldives in 1920 and 1922. Among other things, he investigated the ruined, dome-shaped structures called *hawittas*, mostly in the southern atolls, which he believed were Buddhist stupas similar to the dagobas found in Sri Lanka (Ceylon).

Conversion to Islam

For many years, Arab traders stopped at the Maldives en route to the Far East – their first record of the Maldive islands, which they called Dibajat, is from the 2nd century AD. Known as the 'Money Isles', the Maldives provided enormous quantities of cowry shells, an international currency of the early ages. (The cowry is now the symbol of the Maldives Monetary Authority.)

Abu Al Barakat, a North African Arab, is credited with converting the Maldivians to Islam in 1153. According to the legend, young virgin girls in Male' were chosen from the community and left alone in a temple as a sacrifice to Rannamaari, a sea jinni. One night Barakat took the place of a prospective sacrificial virgin and drove the demon away by reading from the Islamic holy book, the Quran. The Maldivian king at the time was sold on Islam, and ordered that the whole country convert.

A series of six sultanic dynasties followed, 84 sultans and sultanas in all, although some did not belong to the line of succession. At one stage, when the Portuguese first arrived on the scene, there were actually two ruling dynasties, the Malei (or Theemuge) dynasty and the Hilali.

The Portuguese

Early in the 16th century the Portuguese, who were already well established in Goa in western India, decided they wanted a greater share of the profitable trade routes of the Indian Ocean. They were given permission to build a fort and a factory in Male', but it wasn't long before they wanted more from the Maldives.

In 1558, after a few unsuccessful attempts, Captain Andreas Andre led an invasion army and killed Sultan Ali VI. The Maldivians called the Portuguese captain 'Andiri Andirin' and he ruled Male' and much of the country for the next 15 years. According to some Maldivian beliefs, Andre was born in the Maldives and went to Goa as a young man, where he came to serve the Portuguese. (Apart from a few months of Malabar domination in Male' during the 18th century, this was the only time that another country has occupied the Maldives; some argue that the Portuguese never actually ruled the Maldives at all, but had merely established a trading post.)

According to popular belief, the Portuguese were cruel rulers, and ultimately decreed that Maldivians must convert to Christianity or be killed. There was ongoing resistance, especially from Mohammed Thakurufaanu, son of an influential family on Utheemu Island in the northern atoll of Haa Alifu. Thakurufaanu, with the help of his two brothers and some friends, started a series of guerrilla raids, culminating in an attack on Male' in which all the Portuguese were slaughtered (see the boxed text 'The Legend of Thakurufaanu').

This victory is commemorated annually as National Day on the first day of the third month of the lunar year. There is a memorial centre on the island of Utheemu to Thakurufaanu, the Maldives' greatest hero, who went on to found the next sultanic dynasty, the Utheemu, which ruled for 120 years. Many reforms were introduced, including a new judicial system, a defence force and a coinage to replace the cowry currency.

Protected Independence

The Portuguese attacked several more times, and the rajahs of Cannanore, South India, (who had helped Thakurufaanu) also attempted to gain control. In the 17th century, the Maldives accepted the protection of the Dutch, who ruled Ceylon at the time. They also had a short-lived defence treaty with the French, and maintained good relations with the British, especially after the British took possession of Ceylon in 1796. These relations enabled the Maldives to be free of external threats while maintaining

The Legend of Thakurufaanu

As the man who led a successful revolution against foreign domination, and then as the leader of the newly liberated nation, Mohammed Thakurufaanu (sultan from 1573 to 1585) is the Maldives' national hero. Respectfully referred to as Bodu Thakurufaanu (*bodu* meaning big, or great), he is to the Maldives what George Washington is to the USA. The story of his raid on the Portuguese headquarters in Male' is part of Maldivian folklore and incorporates many compelling details.

In his home atoll of Thiladhunmathee, Thakurufaanu's family were known and respected as sailors, traders and *kateebs* (island chiefs). The family gained the trust of Viyazoaru, the Portuguese ruler of the four northern atolls, and was given the responsibility of disseminating orders, collecting taxes and carrying tribute to the Portuguese base in Ceylon. Unbeknown to Viyazoaru, Thakurufaanu and his brothers used their position to foster anti-Portuguese sentiment, recruit sympathisers and gain intelligence on the Portuguese. It also afforded the opportunity to visit southern India, where Thakurufaanu obtained a pledge from the rajah of Cannanore to assist in an overthrow of the Portuguese rulers in the Maldives.

Back in Thiladhunmathee Atoll, Thakurufaanu and his brothers built a boat in which to conduct an attack on Male'. This sailing vessel, named Kalhuoffummi, has its own legendary status – it was said to be not only fast and beautiful, but to have almost magical qualities that enabled it to elude the Portuguese on guerrilla raids and reconnaissance missions.

For the final assault, they sailed south through the atolls by night, stopping by day to gather provisions and supporters. Approaching Male', they concealed themselves on a nearby island. They stole into the capital at night to make contact with supporters there and to assess the Portuguese defences. They were assisted in this by the local imam, who subtly changed the times of the morning prayer calls, tricking the Portuguese into sleeping late and giving Thakurufaanu extra time to escape after his night-time reconnaissance visits.

The attack on Male' was carefully planned and timed, and allegedly backed by supernatural forces – one story relates how a coconut tree mysteriously appeared in the Portuguese compound, which provided cover for Thakurufaanu as he crept close and killed Andiri Andirin with a spear. In the ensuing battle the Maldivians, with help from a detachment of Cannanore soldiers, defeated and killed some 300 Portuguese. Most versions of the story have the Portuguese drinking heavily on their last night, making it a cautionary tale about the evils of alcohol.

The Thakurufaanu brothers then set about re-establishing a Maldivian administration under Islamic principles. Soon after, Bodu Thakurufaanu became the new sultan, with the title of Al Sultan-ul Ghazi Mohammed Thakurufaanu Al Auzam Siree Savahitha Maharadhun, 1st Sultan of the 3rd Dynasty of the Kingdom of the Maldives.

internal autonomy. Nevertheless, it was the remoteness of the islands, the prevalence of malaria and the lack of good ports, naval stores, or productive land that were probably the main reasons neither the Dutch nor the British established a colonial administration.

In the 1860s Borah merchants from Bombay were invited to Male' to establish warehouses and shops, but it wasn't long before they acquired an almost exclusive monopoly on foreign trade. The Maldivians feared the Borahs would soon gain complete control of the islands, so Sultan Mohammed Mueenuddin II signed an agreement with the British in 1887 recognising the Maldives' statehood and formalising its protected status.

The 20th Century

In 1932 the Maldives' first constitution was imposed upon Sultan Shamsuddin. The sultan was to be elected by a 'council of advisers' made up of Maldivian elite, rather than being a hereditary position. In 1934, Shamsuddin was deposed and Hasan Nurudin became sultan.

WWII brought great hardship to the Maldives. Maritime trade with Ceylon was severely reduced, leading to shortages of rice and other necessities – many died of illness or malnutrition. A new constitution was introduced in 1942, and Nurudin was persuaded to abdicate the following year. His replacement, the elderly Abdul Majeed Didi, retired to Ceylon leaving the control of the government in the hands of his prime minister, Mohammed Amin Didi. Amin Didi nationalised the fish export industry, instituted a broad modernisation program and introduced an unpopular ban on tobacco smoking.

When Ceylon gained independence in 1948, the Maldivians signed a defence pact with the British, which gave the latter control of the foreign affairs of the islands but not the right to interfere internally. In return, the Maldivians agreed to provide facilities for British defence forces.

In 1953 the sultanate was abolished and a republic was proclaimed with Amin Didi as its first president, but he was overthrown within a year. The sultanate was returned, with Mohammed Farid Didi elected as the 94th sultan of the Maldives.

British Bases & Southern Secession

While Britain did not overtly interfere in the running of the country, it did secure permission to re-establish its wartime airfield on Gan Island in the southernmost Addu Atoll. In 1956 the Royal Air Force began developing the base, employing hundreds of Maldivians and resettling the Gan people on neighbouring islands. The British were informally granted a 100-year lease of Gan which required them to pay £2000 a year.

When Ibrahim Nasir was elected prime minister in 1957, he immediately called for a review of the agreement with the British on Gan, demanding that the lease be shortened and the annual payment increased. This was followed by an insurrection against the Maldivian government by the inhabitants of the southern atolls of Addu and Suvadiva (Huvadhoo), who objected to Nasir's demand that the British cease employing local labour. They decided to cut ties altogether and form an independent state, electing Abdulla Afif Didi president.

In 1960 the Maldivian government officially granted the British the use of Gan and other facilities in Addu Atoll for 30 years (effective from December 1956) in return for the payment of £100,000 a year and a grant of £750,000 to finance specific development projects. Later, Nasir sent gunboats from Male' to quash the rebellion in the southern atolls. Afif fled to the Seychelles, then a British colony, while other leaders were banished to various islands in the Maldives.

In 1965 Britain recognised the islands as a completely sovereign and independent state, and ceased to be responsible for their defence (although it retained the use of Gan and continued to pay rent until 1976). The Maldives were granted independence on 26 July 1965 and later became a member of the United Nations.

The Republic

Following a referendum in 1968 the sultanate was again abolished, Sultan Majeed Didi retired to Ceylon and a new republic was inaugurated. Nasir was elected president. In 1972, the Sri Lankan market for dried fish, the Maldives' biggest export, collapsed. The first tourist resorts opened that year, but the money generated didn't benefit many of the people. Prices kept going up and there were revolts, plots and banishments as Nasir clung to power. In 1978, fearing for his life, Nasir stepped down and skipped across to Singapore, reputedly with US$4 million from the Maldivian national coffers.

A former university lecturer and Maldivian ambassador to the United Nations, Maumoon Abdul Gayoom, became president in Nasir's place. Gayoom's style of governing was much more open, and he immediately denounced Nasir's regime and banished several of the former president's associates. A 1980 attempted coup against Gayoom, involving mercenaries, was discovered and more banishments occurred.

Gayoom was re-elected in 1983 and continued to promote education, health and industry, particularly tourism. He gave the tiny country a higher international profile with full membership in the Commonwealth and the South Asian Association for Regional Co-operation (SAARC).

The 1988 Coup

In September 1988 51-year-old Gayoom began a third term as president, but only a month later a group of disaffected Maldivian businessmen attempted a coup, employing about 90 Sri Lankan Tamil mercenaries. Half of these soldiers infiltrated Male' as visitors, while the rest landed by boat. The mercenaries took several key installations, but failed to capture the National Security Service headquarters.

More than 1600 Indian paratroopers, immediately dispatched by the Indian prime minister, Rajiv Gandhi, ended further gains by the invaders who then fled by boat towards Sri Lanka. They took 27 hostages and left 14 people dead and 40 wounded. No tourists were affected – many didn't even know that a coup had been attempted. The mercenaries were caught by an Indian frigate 100km from the Sri Lankan coast. Most were returned to the Maldives for trial, several were sentenced to death, but reprieved and returned to Sri Lanka.

Growth & Development

In 1993 Gayoom was nominated for a fourth five-year term, and confirmed with an overwhelming referendum vote. Recent years have been characterised by modernisation, a very high rate of economic growth, and improvement in most social indicators. The main contributors to this growth have been the fishing industry, tourism and foreign aid.

At the same time, the Maldives is experiencing many of the problems of developing countries, notably rapid growth in the main city, the environmental effects of growth, regional disparities, youth unemployment and income inequality. There is concern that the economy is too vulnerable to external factors, such as variations in the price of tuna and events which impact on international tourism.

The 1998 El Niño event, which caused coral bleaching throughout the atolls, was detrimental for tourism and it signalled that global warming might threaten the existence of the Maldives. When Gayoom began a fifth term as president in 1998, the environment and sea-level rises were priorities for him.

The whole country is now linked with a modern telecommunications system. Over 90% of the people have electricity; hospitals and higher secondary schools centres have been established in outer atolls; and Male' is protected by a sea wall. A new island has been built near the capital, to accommodate a growing population an extra metre or so above sea level. The economy has grown more or less steadily, though not everyone enjoys the benefits of economic growth – 15% live below the World Bank's poverty level. The key tourism industry suffered a setback in 2001, but achieved record numbers in 2002.

Expectations have risen too, as more Maldivians are educated, and more travel abroad. The Internet and satellite TV have opened the country up to the world, and created demands for similar transparency at home. The government is firmly established in power. The Maldives is acutely aware that any appearance of instability could be disastrous for its tourist industry, and it guards its reputation as a safe, secure and healthy destination with an unspoiled environment.

GEOGRAPHY

The Maldives is about 600km southwest of the tip of India. The national territory comprises about 1190 small, low-lying coral islands and innumerable reefs forming 26 atolls that are the natural geographic regions of the country – the word 'atoll' actually derives from the Maldivian word *atolu*.

The atolls stretch out across the Indian Ocean in a vertical strip about 850km long and 130km wide. The total territorial area is 115,300 sq km, but only 298 sq km of this is dry land, less than 0.3% of the country. The Maldives claims an exclusive economic zone in the adjacent areas of the Indian Ocean, with a total area of 859,000 sq km. There are no hills or rivers, and none of the islands rises more than about 3m above sea level, depending on the tide, or is longer than 8km. Generally, the islands are infertile and support only a limited range of flora and fauna.

The number of islands has been estimated variously from 1300 to 13,000, but the government determines that there are 1192, of which only 202 are inhabited. Counting the islands may seem a simple matter, but it's almost impossible to distinguish between a reef that is just below the surface, and a sandbank that is just above it – the situation may change with the next high tide. An obvious sandbank can be swept away in the next big storm, or be divided into two separate islands.

Officially, it's a matter of vegetation – an island means a vegetated land area, but even this is not definitive. Some sandbanks sprout a small patch of scrub while others feature a single coconut palm, like the desert island of the comic-strip castaway. The bigger

Rise & Rise of the Atolls

A coral reef or garden is not, as many people believe, formed of multicoloured marine plants. It is a living colony of coral polyps – tiny, tentacled creatures that feed on plankton. Coral polyps are invertebrates with sack-like bodies and calcareous or horny skeletons. After extracting calcium deposits from the water around them, the polyps excrete tiny, cup-shaped, limestone skeletons. These little guys can make mountains.

A coral reef is the rock-like aggregation of millions of these polyp skeletons. Only the outer layer of coral is alive. As polyps reproduce and die, the new polyps attach themselves in successive layers to the skeletons already in place. Coral grows best in clear, shallow water, and especially where waves and currents from the open sea bring extra oxygen and nutrients,

Charles Darwin put forward the first scientific theory of atoll formation based on observations of atolls and islands in the Pacific. He envisaged a process where coral builds up around the shores of a volcanic island to produce a fringing reef. Then the island sinks slowly into the sea while the coral grows upwards at about the same rate. This forms a barrier reef, separated from the shore of the sinking island by a ring-shaped lagoon. By the time the island is completely submerged, the coral growth has become the base for an atoll, circling the place where the volcanic peak used to be.

This theory doesn't quite fit the Maldives though. Unlike the isolated Pacific atolls, Maldivian atolls all sit on top of the same long, underwater plateau, around 300m to 500m under the surface of the sea. This plateau is a layer of accumulated coral-stone over 2000m thick. Under this is the 'volcanic basement', a 2000km-long ridge of basalt that was formed over 50 million years ago.

The build-up of coral over this ridge is as much to do with sea-level changes as it is with the plateau subsiding. When sea levels rise the coral grows upwards to stay near the sea surface, as in the Darwin model, but there were at least two periods when the sea level actually dropped significantly – by as much as 120m. At these times much of the accumulated coral plateau would have been exposed, subjected to weathering, and 'karstified' – eroded into steep-sided, flat-topped columns. When sea levels rose again, new coral grew on the tops of the karst mountains and formed the bases of the individual Maldivian atolls.

Coral grows best on the edges of an atoll, where it is well supplied with nutrients from the open sea. A fringing reef forms around an enclosed lagoon, growing higher as the sea level rises. Rubble from broken coral accumulates in the lagoon, so the level of the lagoon floor also rises, and smaller reefs can rise within it. Sand and debris accumulate on the higher parts of the reef, creating sandbars on which vegetation can eventually take root. The classic atoll shape is oval, with the widest reefs and most of the islands around the outer edges.

Test drilling and seismic research has revealed the complex layers of coral growth that underlie the Maldives. The evidence shows that coral growth can match the fastest sea-level rises on record, some 125m in only 10,000 years – about 1.25cm per year. In geological terms, that's really fast.

An Alternative Geography

The Maldives has appeared in the Guinness Book of Records as the world's flattest country, with no natural land higher than 2.4 m above sea level – but you can look at it from another angle.

The Maldives is one of the most mountainous countries in the world. Its people live on peaks above a plateau that extends 2000km from the Lakshadweep Islands near India to the Chagos Islands, well south of the equator. The plateau is over 5000m high and rises steeply between the Arabian Basin in the northwest and the Cocos-Keeling Basin in the southeast.

Mountain ranges rise above the plateau, and the upper slopes and valleys are incredibly fertile, beautiful and rich with plant and animal life. The entire plateau is submerged beneath the Indian Ocean and only scattered, flat-topped peaks are visible at the surface. These peaks are capped not with snow, but with coconut palms.

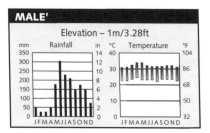

islands have thick bush, mangroves and towering trees.

To locals, the more important distinction is between inhabited and uninhabited islands. Inhabited means inhabited by Maldivians. The 90 or so islands used for resorts are officially 'uninhabited', as are those used for factories, airfields or agriculture, but which don't have a village or a mosque. The biggest inhabited island is Gan, in Hadhdhunmathee Atoll (not the one in Addu), at 5.16 sq km (about 7km long, 1.5km wide at one end), with 2244 people. The smallest inhabited island is Maduvvari, in Mulaku Atoll, at 0.0031 sq km (about 80m long and 40m wide), with 451 people. The least populous island, according to the census, has three people (all females).

CLIMATE

Generally, the year is divided into two monsoon periods – the northeast monsoon or *iruvai*, from December to March, which are the drier months; and the southwest monsoon or *hulhangu*, from May to November, which are wetter months with more storms and strong winds. Transitional periods, in mid-April and late November, are supposed to be calm with exceptionally clear water.

Maldivians further divide the year into 27 *nakaiy*, each about two weeks long, with a characteristic weather pattern. Each *nakaiy* has its place in the cycle of fishing, planting and harvesting, and its significance for personal and family fortunes.

The average maximum temperature is remarkably consistent throughout the year, ranging from 30° to 31.8°C, while nights are between 25.1° and 26.3°C. Sea temperatures remain pretty constant at around 27°C. Almost continual sea breezes keep the air moving and make life quite bearable, but you can't always count on the weather patterns. Heavy rain can fall at any time in the dry season, and you can have clear sunny days in the middle of the wet.

ECOLOGY & ENVIRONMENT

As a small island nation in a big ocean, the Maldives had a way of life which was ecologically sustainable for centuries, but certainly not self-sufficient. The comparatively small population survived by harvesting the vast resources of the sea and obtaining the other necessities of life through trade. The impact on the limited resources of their islands was probably minimal.

Now the Maldives' interrelationship with the rest of the world is greater than ever, and it has a high rate of growth supported by two main industries, fishing and tourism. Both industries depend on preservation of the environment, and there are strict regulations to ensure sustainability. To a great extent the Maldives avoids environmental problems by importing so many of its needs. It could be asked whether this is environmentally friendly or whether it just moves the environmental problems offshore.

Fisheries

Ocean Fishing Net fishing and trawling is prohibited in Maldivian waters, which include an 'exclusive economic zone' extending for 320km beyond the atolls. All fishing is by pole and line, with over 75% of the catch being skipjack or yellowfin tuna. The no-nets policy helps to prevent over-fishing and protects other marine species, such as dolphins, from being inadvertently caught in nets.

The local tuna population appears to be holding up despite increased catches, and Maldivian fisheries are patrolled to prevent poaching. But the tuna are migratory, and can be caught without limit in international waters using driftnets and long-line techniques.

Reef Fishing A problem with reef fisheries is the sudden surges in demand for particular species, which can cause a big depletion in stocks before authorities recognise and deal with the problem. Lobster numbers declined rapidly around Male' when resorts began serving them, and they are now protected in that area. Sea cucumbers were over-fished, but a ban on scuba divers collecting them should allow regeneration in deeper waters. Giant clams were much more common before commercial divers began collecting them – export of clam meat was banned in 1991.

There has been a decline in shark numbers at some popular dive sites in recent years, especially when the price for shark fins rose to US$70 per kg. The large and handsome Napoleon wrasse seemed in danger of extinction when it was selling for US$50 per kg. The government has now banned all exports following protests from many dive operators and tourism interests. Collecting tropical fish for the aquarium trade is a growth industry and quotas have now been imposed on the export of various species.

Tourism

Tourism development is strictly regulated and resorts are established only on uninhabited islands that the government makes available (see the boxed text 'Quality Tourism Strategy' in the Choosing a Resort chapter). Overwhelmingly, the regulations have been effective in minimising environmental costs – the World Tourism Organization has cited the Maldives as a model for sustainable tourism development. In 2002 the number of tourist arrivals was 484,500 – 1.7 times the Maldives' own population – but away from the capital, the airport and the resorts, tourists and tourist facilities are barely noticeable.

Construction and operation of the resorts does use resources, but the vast majority of these are imported. Large amounts of diesel fuel are used to generate electricity and de-salinate water. The demand for hot running water and air-conditioning has raised the overall energy cost per guest.

Sewage must be effectively treated on the resort island itself – it cannot be pumped out to sea. Efficient incinerators must be installed to dispose of garbage that can't be composted, but many resorts request that visitors take home plastic bottles, used batteries and other items which may present a disposal problem.

When the first resorts were developed, jetties and breakwaters were built and boat channels cut through reefs, without much understanding of the immediate environmental consequences. In some cases natural erosion and deposition patterns were disrupted, with unexpected results. More structures were built to limit the damage and sand was pumped up to restore the beach. This was expensive and it marred the natural appearance of the island, and now developers are more careful about altering coasts and reefs. Environmental studies are required before major works can be undertaken.

Rubbish

Traditionally Maldivians have thrown their rubbish from boats or beaches into the sea. When this stuff was biodegradable it wasn't a problem, but with increasing use of products and packaging made of metal and plastic, rubbish can now be found washed up on beaches or accumulating on reefs. You won't see it on resorts, where the beach is cleaned every morning, but it's there on other islands. There are steps to raise awareness and educate the people, but it will take time. If the operator of a boat or resort does dispose of rubbish irresponsibly, a letter of complaint to the Ministry of Tourism can be very effective.

Reef Mining

Coral has long been mined in the Maldives, to make cement and to use in coral-stone walls. With new resorts being built, rapid growth in Male' and greater affluence on many islands, the amount of mining and the extent of damage increased. The government has now banned the use of coral as a building material, and concrete bricks are being used instead.

Growth in Male'

Nearly all the problems of rapid growth in the Maldives have been concentrated in Male'. As in many developing countries, there has been a population movement from regional areas to the main city. People come to continue their education, to find employment or to join family members who have already moved. Male' is absorbing nearly all the country's population growth.

The resultant problems include housing shortages, overbuilding, traffic congestion, unemployment and depletion of the natural ground-water supply. Bore water in Male' smells horrible and is scarcely useable for gardening, much less for washing or drinking. Urban sprawl is not an option – the island is full to the edges.

Solutions are being sought. Schools and facilities are being developed in the outer atolls, so young people will have less reason to move to Male'. The neighbouring island of Viligili is being developed as a satellite community, as will be the new island of Hulhumale' (see the Male' chapter). In the longer term, the country needs to limit its population growth. A family-planning education program is under way, but in the outer atolls the average woman still has six children.

Global Warming

The environmental consequences of global warming are far from certain, but so potentially catastrophic that they can't be ignored, especially in the Maldives. Predictions are that global warming might result in average sea-level rises of between 5mm and 10mm per year. At that rate it would take one or two centuries to submerge most of the country, but this is not the real danger. The combination of big storms, high tides and rising sea levels can cause a major catastrophe, as in 1987 when much of Male' was flooded and recently reclaimed land was washed away.

Energy

With its relatively small number of private cars and lack of industry, the Maldives is not a very energy-hungry nation. Most people and goods move between the islands and atolls by slow boats, which are quite an energy-efficient form of transport.

Tourist resorts, however, use surprisingly large amounts of fuel to run the generators supplying power for water desalination, air-conditioning, lighting and so on – a big resort will use several thousand litres a day. Some new resorts are being built with energy-conserving features such as solar hot-water systems.

Marine Environment

A high proportion of visitors come principally for diving and snorkelling – underwater ecotourism. Preserving the underwater world in a pristine state is a high priority for the government, the tourism industry and the vast majority of visitors. The dive operators at resorts have taken a leading role in promoting environmentally sensitive diving practices. Anchors are not used over reefs, spear fishing is forbidden, garbage is kept on boats, it's 'not done' to touch fish or coral and even wearing gloves is discouraged. Some feel that the sheer number of divers could become a problem, though this is more a threat to the quality of the diving experience than the environment.

The government has designated 25 Protected Marine Areas, mostly popular dive sites in tourism zones, and fishing is now banned in these areas.

FLORA & FAUNA
Flora

Most islands have poor, sandy soil and vegetation ranges from thick to sparse to none at all. The vegetated islands have mangroves, breadfruit trees, banyans, bamboo, pandanus, banana, heliotrope, caltrop, hibiscus, tropical vines and numerous coconut palms. Larger, wetter islands have small areas of rainforest.

Sweet potatoes, yams, taro, millet and watermelon are grown. The most fertile island is Fuamulaku in the extreme south, which supports a wider variety of crops, including mangoes and pineapples. Lemons and limes once grew all over the islands, but a fungal disease killed them off, and virtually all citrus fruit is now imported.

Fauna

Giant fruit bats or flying foxes are widespread on many islands; you'll see them cruising past at dusk. Colourful lizards are quite common and there is the occasional rat. The 'palm squirrel' and the 'Maldivian hamster' are both euphemisms that resort staff might use for rat.

The mosquito population varies from island to island but tends to be less bothersome in Male' and the villages. There are ants, centipedes, scorpions and cockroaches, but they're not problematic.

Local land birds include crows, the white-breasted water hen and the Indian mynah. The rose-ringed parakeet is introduced. There are migratory birds, like harriers and falcons, but waders like plover, snipe, curlew and sandpiper are more common. Thirteen species of heron can be seen in the shallows and there are terns, seagulls and two species of noddy.

Marine Life

Seaweeds and hard coralline algae grow on the reefs, but are continuously eaten by various herbivores. As well as the many types of coral, there are various shells, starfish, crustaceans and worms inhabiting the reef. There are more than 700 species of fish in the Indian Ocean, which can be divided into two types: reef fish, which live inside the atoll lagoons, on and around coral-reef structures; and pelagics, which live in the open sea, but may come close to the atolls or into channels for food. These include some large animals, such as turtles and cetaceans, which are very popular with divers.

Coral These are coelenterates, a class of animal that also includes sea anemones and jellyfish. A coral growth is made up of individual polyps – tiny tube-like fleshy cylinders, which look very much like anemones. The top of the cylinder is open and ringed by waving tentacles (nematocysts), which sting and draw any passing prey inside. Coral polyps secrete a calcium-carbonate deposit around their base, and this cup-shaped skeletal structure is what forms a coral reef – new coral grows on old dead coral and the reef gradually builds up.

Most reef-building is done by *hermatypic* corals, whose outer tissues are infused with zooxanthellae algae, which photosynthesise to make food from carbon dioxide and sunlight. The zooxanthellae is the main food source for the coral, while the coral surface provides a safe home for the zooxanthellae – they live in a symbiotic relationship, each dependent on the other. The zooxanthellae give coral its colour, so when a piece of coral is removed from the water, the zooxanthellae soon die and the coral becomes white. If the water temperature rises, the coral expels the algae, and the coral loses its colour in a process called 'coral bleaching'.

Polyps reproduce by splitting to form a colony of genetically identical polyps – each colony starts life as a single polyp. Although each polyp catches and digests its own food, the nutrition passes between the polyps to the whole colony. Most coral polyps only feed at night; during the daytime they withdraw into their hard limestone skeleton, so it is only after dark that a coral reef can be seen in its full, colourful glory.

Hard Corals These *Acropora* species take many forms. One of the most common and easiest to recognise is the staghorn coral, which grows by budding off new branches from the tips. Brain corals are huge and round with a surface looking very much like a human brain. They grow by adding new base levels of skeletal matter and expanding outwards. Flat or sheet corals, like plate coral or table coral, expand at their outer edges. Some corals take different shapes depending on their immediate environment.

Soft Corals These are made up of individual polyps, but do not form a hard limestone skeleton. Lacking the skeleton that protects hard coral, it would seem likely that soft coral would fall prey to fish, but they seem to remain relatively immune either due to toxic substances in their tissues or to the presence of sharp limestone needles. Soft corals can move around and will sometimes engulf and kill off a hard coral. Attractive varieties include fan corals and whips. Soft corals thrive on reef edges washed by strong currents.

Molluscs Invertebrate creatures that inhabit shells are all in the group *Mollusca*, although not all molluscs have visible shells. The three groups of molluscs include all the sea shells, octopus, sea slugs and even garden snails.

The gastropods, or univalves, include most of the shells of interest to observers, including the cowry, noted for its gently rounded shape, beautiful patterns and glossy surface. Living examples are mainly seen at night, when they come out in search of food. The shell-less sea slug is also a gastropod.

The bivalves group includes all the creatures with a two-part shell, such as oysters, clams and scallops. Some bivalves embed themselves in rocks, but most live in mud or sand. Giant clams are a common sight on reef flats in the Maldives. Stories of divers being trapped when a huge clam snaps shut are mythical – the clams shut slowly and none too tightly. Their adductor muscles are certainly strong, however, and persuading a closed clam to reopen is not easy.

Finally there are cephalopods, which include octopus, squid, the pearly nautilus and cuttlefish.

Echinoderms Starfish, urchin fish, feather stars and sea cucumbers are all echinoderms. The crown-of-thorns starfish has appeared on Maldivian reefs, but is not in anything like plague proportions.

Crustaceans This group includes shrimp, lobsters and crabs. The most interesting shrimp are the cleaners, which have a symbiotic relationship with larger fish, removing parasites from moray eels, starfish and other reef fish. Lobsters live in small reef crannies and are nocturnal (lobster harvesting is banned in the Male' area). Hermit crabs live in old sea shells, and these shells can often be seen scurrying across the sand. Other crabs are common on the shoreline, often wonderfully camouflaged with fascinating patterns, and are well worth looking for. Underwater, crabs are also common, but even harder to spot.

Reef Fish Hundreds of fish species can be spotted by anyone with a mask and snorkel. They're easy to see and enjoy, but people with a naturalist bent should buy one of the field guides to reef fish, or check the attractive posters which are often displayed in dive schools. You're sure to see several types of butterflyfish, angelfish, parrotfish and rock cod, unicornfish, trumpetfish, bluestripe snapper, Moorish idol and oriental sweetlips. For more on fish see the 'Fish-Spotter's Guide' in the Snorkelling & Diving special section.

Sharks The white-tip reef shark is a small, nonaggressive, territorial shark rarely more than 1.5m long and is often seen over areas of coral or off reef edges. Grey reef sharks are also timid, shallow-water dwellers and often grow to over 2m in length.

Other species are more open-sea dwellers, but do come into atolls and especially to channel entrances where food is plentiful. These include the strange-looking hammerhead shark and the whale shark, the world's largest fish species, which is a harmless plankton eater. Sharks are not a problem for divers in the Maldives – there's simply too much else for them to eat.

Stingrays & Manta Rays Rays are cartilaginous fish, like flattened sharks. Stingrays are sea-bottom feeders, equipped with crushing teeth to grind the molluscs and crustaceans they sift out of the sand. They are occasionally found in the shallows, often lying motionless on the sandy bottom of lagoons. A barbed and poisonous spine on top of the tail can swing up and forward, and will deliver a very painful injury to anyone who stands on a stingray.

Manta rays are among the largest fish found in the Maldives and a firm favourite of divers. They tend to swim along near the surface and pass overhead as a large shadow. They are quite harmless and, in some places, seem quite relaxed about divers approaching them closely. Manta rays are sometimes seen to leap completely out of the water, landing back with a tremendous splash. The eagle ray is closely related to the manta, and often seen by divers.

Endangered Species

Local populations of some marine animals have suffered severe declines at times and the government has usually responded with effective restrictions, which have prevented total extinction (see Fisheries earlier in this chapter).

Turtles Most turtle species are endangered worldwide. Four species are known to nest in the Maldives: green, olive ridley, hawksbill and loggerhead. Leatherback turtles visit Maldivian waters, but are not known to nest. Turtle numbers have declined in the Maldives, as elsewhere, but they can still be seen by divers at many sites. The catching of turtles and the sale or export of turtle-shell products is now totally prohibited.

Turtles are migratory and the population can be depleted by events many miles from

Coral Bleaching – Death on the Reef

In March 1998, the waters of the Maldives experienced a temporary rise in the sea temperature associated with the El Niño effect. For a period of about two weeks, surface-water temperatures were above 32°C, resulting in the loss of the symbiotic algae that lives within the coral polyps. The loss of this zooxanthellae algae causes the coral to lose its colour ('coral bleaching'), and if the algae does not return, the coral polyps die. Coral bleaching has occurred, with varying degrees of severity, in shallow waters throughout the Maldives archipelago. When the coral dies, the underlying calcium carbonate is exposed and becomes more brittle, so many of the more delicate branch and table structures have been broken up by wave action. Mainly hard corals have been affected – soft corals and sea fans are less dependent on zooxanthellae algae, are less affected by the sea temperature changes and recover more quickly from damage.

Some corals, particularly in deeper water, recovered almost immediately as the symbiotic algae returned. In a few places the coral was not damaged at all. In most areas, however, virtually all the old hard corals died and it will take years, perhaps decades, for them to recover. Some of the biggest table corals may have been hundreds of years old. Marine biologists are watching this recolonisation process with interest. (See 'Back from the Bleaching', in the Snorkelling & Diving special section.)

The Maldives' dive industry has adapted to the changed environment, seeking places where the regrowth is fastest and where there are lots of attractive soft corals. There's still a vast number and variety of reef fish to see, and spotting pelagic species, especially mantas and whale sharks, is a major attraction. Some long-time divers have become more interested in the very small marine life, and in macrophotography.

Many other coral reefs around the world were also affected by the 1998 El Niño, including those in Indonesia, Thailand, Papua New Guinea and Australia's Great Barrier Reef.

There is evidence that coral bleaching has occurred previously, and that the reefs have always recovered eventually. The fear is that El Niño events are becoming more severe as a result of human-induced global warming. El Niño is believed to be a seven-year cycle so the next one is due in 2005, well before the reefs have recovered. Maybe the 1998 event was exceptionally severe for reasons that had nothing to do with global climate change – sunspot activity for instance. It's a question of whether coral bleaching is a natural process, a natural disaster, or a man-made disaster.

their home beach, such as accidental capture in fishing nets, depletion of sea-grass areas and toxic pollutants. Widespread collection of eggs and the loss of nesting sites are problems that need to be addressed. The consequences do not show up in the adult turtle population for 10 to 20 years.

Turtle eggs are a traditional food and used in *velaa folhi*, a special Maldivian dish. Development of resorts has reduced the availability of nesting sites. Artificial lights confuse hatchling turtles, which are instinctively guided into the water by the position of the moon. Beach chairs and boats can also interfere with egg laying and with hatchlings. Some attempts are being made to artificially improve the survival chances of hatchlings by protecting them in hatching ponds.

GOVERNMENT & POLITICS

The Maldivian parliament, the Majlis or Citizens' Council, has 50 members. Male', which is the capital island, and each of the 20 administrative atolls have two representatives each, elected for five-year terms. All citizens over 21 years of age can vote. The president chooses the remaining eight parliamentary representatives, has the power to appoint or dismiss cabinet ministers and appoints all judges.

The Majlis considers candidates for the presidency for each five-year term and makes a nomination, which is put to a national vote. Only one candidate is put forward, so the vote is not so much an election as a national referendum – a strong vote of support for the president is seen as a show of loyalty to local political leaders and the country as a whole. In recent votes, the current president Mr Gayoom has always received over 90% support.

In 1998, for the first time, any adult male was eligible to put himself up to the Majlis as a presidential candidate, and several people did so. There was no doubt that the Majlis would nominate Gayoom again, but the candidates were making themselves known on the political scene, and using the chance to express alternative points of view. Some of them were later sanctioned for speaking out, indicating that the Maldives is still some way from multiparty politics and complete freedom of political expression. Mr Gayoom was re-elected with another huge vote. The main constraints on his power are the conflicting demands of business on government policy, and Muslim fundamentalists keen to maintain traditional values. Poverty is not visible because begging and living on the streets are not permitted.

Nearly all the food is imported and agriculture accounts for less than 3% of GDP; this proportion has declined over the last decade. Manufacturing and construction make up 15% of GDP: small boat yards, fish packing, clothing and a plastic pipe plant are modern enterprises, but mostly it's cottage industries producing coconut oil, coir (coconut-husk fibre) and coir products such as rope and matting. Some of the new industrial activities are on islands near Male' while others, like fish-packing plants, are being established in the outer atolls.

Fishing

Fishing, the traditional base of the economy, is still a big export earner, but is declining in relative importance. It now accounts for around 14% of GDP, employs 22% of the labour force, and contributes nearly 40% of export earnings. Skipjack tuna is the principal catch, followed by yellowfin tuna, little tuna and frigate mackerel.

Government policies have helped to mechanise the fishing fleet, introduce new packing techniques and develop new markets. Nevertheless, the fishing industry is vulnerable to international market fluctuations.

Most adult males have some experience in fishing, and casual employment on fishing boats is something of an economic backstop. Men are unlikely to take on menial work for low pay when there is a prospect that they can get a few days or weeks of relatively well-paid work on a fishing dhoni.

Tourism

It was an Italian tour operator, George Corbin, who saw the tourism potential of the Maldives when he visited the islands in 1971. The following year, he brought a group of travel writers to the country for a promotional tour. They were enthusiastic, but experts from the United Nations Development Program (UNDP) warned that tourism could never succeed in the Maldives – there was no infrastructure, no cultural attractions, no local supplies of suitable food, it was too remote and the people had no experience.

Kurumba Island opened as a resort in 1972 with 30 huts made of local materials. Visitors came on a side trip from Sri Lanka, and they loved it. The word spread around Europe and other islands close to Male' were turned into resorts. In 1978 there were 17 resorts and nearly 30,000 visitors. President Gayoom came to power that year, determined to make the industry generate real benefits for the country. He introduced the bed tax of US$6 per night (which was an immediate boon to the treasury) and adopted a strategy of 'quality tourism'. The average cost of developing a resort, per bed, was US$900 in 1979, US$33,000 by 1993 and US$67,000 for the big Sun Island resort in 1998.

The rate of tourism growth has been stunning. The annual number of visitors was 1097 in 1972, 74,400 in 1982, 235,800 in 1992 and 484,600 in 2002. The industry accounts directly for 32% of GDP and provides over 60% of export earnings.

Most of the tourists (77%) are Europeans, especially Italians (24%), British (17%), and Germans (13%). The Asian market was the fastest-growing sector in the mid-1990s, but growth stalled with the Asian economic 'meltdown', and the proportion of tourists from Asian countries dropped from a peak of 27% in 1992 to 20% in 2002. An expansionist tourism strategy encouraged the opening of more than a dozen new resorts in the late 1990s, but when demand slowed after 11 September 2001, a number of new projects were postponed, so supply would not exceed demand.

POPULATION & PEOPLE

The most recent census, in 2000, put the population at 270,101, with 74,000 in Male'. The annual rate of population growth is about 3%. There is a family planning program but some couples still have large families and the youthful population means a high proportion are of child-bearing age.

Also, Maldivians have their families at a young age, accelerating the rate of increase. Life expectancy is about 63 years.

It is thought that the original settlers of the Maldives were Dravidian and Sinhalese people who came from south India and Ceylon. There has also been a great deal of intermarriage and mixing with people from the Middle East and Africa.

You can address Maldivians by their first or last name. Since so many men are called Mohammed, Hassan or Ali, the surname is more appropriate. In some cases an honorary title like Maniku or Didi is used to show respect. Among friends and family, many Maldivians have a nickname, for example, an Ibrahim is often called Ibbie or Ibbay.

EDUCATION

There are a few preschools or kindergartens, but many children start learning the Quran in neighbourhood classes from about the age of three. There are government primary schools *(madrasa)* on every inhabited island, but some are very small and do not go past fifth grade. For grades six and seven, children may have to go to a middle school on a larger island. Atoll capitals have an Atoll Education Centre (AEC) with adult education and secondary schooling to grade 10 (British GCE 'O level'). Children must often move to another island to continue their education.

Officially, 90% of students finish primary school, and the adult literacy rate is 98%. English is taught as a second language from grade one and is the usual teaching language at higher secondary school – Maldivians with a secondary education speak excellent English.

The best students can continue to a free-of-charge higher secondary school which teaches up to the British GCE 'A level' – there's one in Male', one in Hithadhoo, in the country's far south, and one in Kulhuduffushi, in the far north. Students coming to Male' to study generally take live-in domestic jobs, affecting their study time: girls are often expected to do a lot of housework.

The Maldives College of Higher Education, also in Male', has faculties of health, education, tourism-hospitality and engineering. For university studies, many young Maldivians go abroad, usually to Sri Lanka, India, Britain, Australia or Fiji.

There is a system of bonded labour under which people must work for the government at a meagre wage for a period which depends on the length of their education in government schools. For many this means a period in the National Security Service or in a government office. They may pursue another occupation part time to establish their career or to make ends meet. Many people in Male' have a second job or a business interest on the side.

ARTS

Though performances of traditional music and dance are not everyday events, contemporary Divehi culture is strong and adaptive, despite foreign influences which range from martial arts and Hindi movies to Eminem and Muslim fundamentalism.

Western and Indian fashions, pop music and videos are highly visible, but on public occasions and festivals the celebrations always have a Maldivian style. Three daily newspapers and several magazines are published in the unique national language and rock bands sing Divehi lyrics. It's remarkable that such a tiny population maintains such a distinctive culture.

Song & Dance

Bodu beru means 'big drum' and gives its name to the best-known form of traditional music and dance. It is what tourist resorts put on for a local culture night and it can be quite sophisticated and compelling. Dancers begin with a slow, nonchalant swaying and swinging of the arms, and become more animated as the tempo increases, finishing in a rhythmic frenzy. In some versions the dancers enter a trance-like state. There are four to six drummers in an ensemble and the sound has strong African influences.

This is also the entertainment at private parties, where a few guys will play the drums and everyone else dances, more and more frenetically as the night goes on.

Local modern rock bands often perform at resorts where they do credible covers of old favourites. They may incorporate elements of *bodu beru* in their music, with lots of percussion and extended drum solos when they're in front of a local audience. Two popular bands are Mezzo and Zero Degree – cassettes and CDs from these, and quite a few other bands, are sold in Male' music shops.

Literature

Despite a unique script which dates from the 1600s, most Maldivian myths and stories are from an oral tradition and have only recently appeared in print. Many are stories of witchcraft and sorcery, while others are cautionary tales about the evils of vanity, lust and greed, and the sticky fates of those who transgressed. Some are decidedly weird and depressing, and don't make good bedtime reading for young children. Novelty Press has published a small book called *Mysticism in the Maldives*, which is still available.

Architecture

A traditional Maldivian village is notable for its neat and orderly layout, with wide streets in a regular, rectangular grid. Houses are made of concrete blocks or coral-stone joined with mortar, and the walls line the sides of the streets. Many houses will have a shaded courtyard in front, enclosed by a chest-high wall fronting the street. This courtyard is an outdoor room, with *joli* and *undholi* seats, where families sit in the heat of the day or the cool of the evening. A more private courtyard behind, the *gifili*, has a well and serves as an open-air bathroom.

At intersections, the coral walls have rounded corners, which considerably soften the streetscape. These corners are seemingly designed to facilitate turning vehicles, but they are like this in small island villages that never see a vehicle. The same style is used in Male', where it does make turning easier for cars and trucks. On the upper floors of a modern building, the rounded corners are more for appearance than practicality, and seem to be a deliberate adaptation of a traditional feature.

The architecture of resorts is eclectic, imitative of anything from a Balinese *bale* to an African rondavel or an American motel. The most identifiably Maldivian feature is the open-air bathroom, a delightful feature popular with guests.

Visual Arts

There's no tradition of painting but it has been developing in recent years – many Maldivians do seem to have a talent for graphic design, which is most often seen in advertising, printed matter and locally designed websites.

Some islands were once famous for wood and stone carving – elaborate calligraphy and the intricate intertwining patterns are a feature of many old mosques and gravestones. A little of this woodcarving is still done, mainly to decorate mosques. The facade of the new Majlis building in Male' is decorated with intertwined carvings.

Crafts

Mats Natural-fibre mats are woven on many islands, but the most famous are the ones known as *tundu kunaa*, made on the island of Gadhdhoo in Gaaf Dhaal Atoll. This may have been an endangered art form, but interest has been growing in the last few years. A Danish researcher in the 1970s documented the weaving techniques and the plants used for fibre and dyes, and noted that a number of traditional designs had not been woven for 20 years. Collecting the materials and weaving a mat can take weeks, and the money that can be made selling the work is not much by modern Maldivian standards. Some fine examples now decorate the reception areas of tourist resorts, and there's a growing appreciation of the work amongst local people and foreign collectors.

Lacquer Work Traditionally, lacquer work, or *laajehun,* was for containers, bowls and trays used for gifts to the sultan – some fine examples can be seen in the National Museum in Male'. Different wood is used to make boxes, bowls, vases and other turned objects. Traditionally the lathe is hand-powered by a cord pulled

Sitting in the Maldives

The Maldives has two unique pieces of furniture. One is the *undholi*, a wooden platform or a netting seat that's hung from a tree or triangular frame. Sometimes called a bedboat, the *undholi* is a sofa, hammock and fan combination – swinging gently creates a cooling movement of air across the indolent occupant.

The *joli* is a static version – a net seat slung on a rectangular frame, usually made in sociable sets of three or four. They were once made of coir rope and wooden sticks, but steel pipes and plastic mesh are now almost universal – it's like sitting in a string shopping bag, but cool.

round a spindle. Several layers of lacquer are applied in different colours which then hardens, then the design is incised with sharp tools, exposing the bright colours of the underlying layers. Designs are usually floral motifs in yellow with red trim on a black background (most likely based on designs of Chinese ceramics). Production of lacquer work is a viable cottage industry in Baa Atoll, particularly on the islands of Eydafushi and Thuladhoo.

Jewellery Ribudhoo Island in Dhaalu (South Nilandhoo Atoll) is famous for making gold jewellery, and Huludeli, in the same atoll, for silver jewellery. According to local belief, a royal jeweller brought the goldsmithing skills to the island centuries ago, having been banished to Ribudhoo by a sultan. It's also said that the islanders plundered a shipwreck in the 1700s, and reworked the gold jewellery they found to disguise its origins.

SOCIETY & CONDUCT
Traditional Culture
Fishing villages away from the tourist resorts rarely experience personal contact with foreigners, although most villages now have telephones, radio and TV. Young people may leave the island for education or employment, and men may leave for fishing or trading, but most of the people don't travel and few travellers have any reason or opportunity to visit. But satellite TV and the Internet may bring changes.

Fishing is the main economic activity and fish is traded for other necessities at the nearest big island. Attending the mosque is the main religious activity, and on smaller islands it's probably the main social and cultural activity as well.

Within the tourism zone, access to island villages is limited to daytime trips with resort-based excursions. Souvenir shops burst into activity when a tour group arrives but the quiet, traditional lifestyle resumes as soon as the tourists leave.

Social Class & Status
Not so long ago, the sultans and their families were the aristocracy, courtiers and local chiefs were the upper classes, and everyone else was part of a peasantry. Though the country is now a republic, and business can

be a source of wealth and status, there is still a sense of social hierarchy, but it's nothing like a Hindu caste system.

The upper class of privileged families is called the *befalu* and often have names like Manik or Didi. At the other end of the scale are the Giraavaru people, descended from early settlers from southern India. They are the Maldives' aborigines and only a small community survives in Male' (they were moved from their home island of Giraavaru when their numbers fell below the 40 adult males required for a functioning mosque).

The traditional social structure can be reflected in business and government, where it's important to know the right people and have the right connections. Organisations are often hierarchical and those down the ladder don't make decisions.

RELIGION
Islam is the religion of the Maldives and those who practise it are called Muslims. Islam shares its roots with Judaism and Christianity, and its teachings correspond closely with the Torah, the Old Testament and the Gospels. Adam, Abraham, Noah, Moses and Jesus are all accepted as Muslim prophets, but Jesus is not recognised as the son of God. According to Islam, these prophets all received the word of Allah (God), but only Mohammed received the complete revelation.

All Maldivians are Muslims of the Sunni sect, as opposed to the Shi'ia sect. No other religions or sects are permitted.

The Maldives observes a liberal form of Islam, like that practised in India and Indonesia. Maldivian women do not observe purdah, though they may wear a headscarf. Children are taught the Arabic alphabet and learn to read and recite the Quran.

Most mosques are of simple, unadorned design, but some of the older mosques have intricate wood carvings inside and elaborate carved gravestones outside. The Islamic Centre in Male' is especially imposing, with soaring ceilings and big carved wood panels and screens.

The Prophet Mohammed
Mohammed was born in Mecca (now in Saudi Arabia) in AD 570 and had his first revelation from Allah in 610. He began to preach against idolatry and proved to be a powerful and persuasive speaker. His

Women in Society

In the 14th century, long before the call for equality took momentum, the Maldives were ruled by women. Three queens reigned; one, Sultana Khadija held the throne for 33 years from 1347 to 1379. The shift from monarchy to a constitutional republic barred women from the post of President, and this fundamental clause is retained in the 1997 Constitution.

Traditional lifestyle, especially in the islands away from the capital dictated gender-specific roles for women and men. Women tended to their children and the household duties during the day, and cooked fish in the evenings. Men spent the day fishing and then rested in the evenings. Modernisation and development changed the traditional way of life and conferred a double burden on many women – income generation plus domestic responsibilities. More opportunities and better education mean that more women are ready to join the workforce or take up income-generating activities at home. This has become a necessity rather than a choice for most women living in Male', as rising expenses and changing lifestyles demand a dual income to meet basic family expenses.

In Male' women work in all sectors, but mainly in teaching, nursing or administrative/secretarial positions. The Government, which is the major employer of women, employs fewer than 5% women at policy level. Less stereotypical jobs such as the police force also recruit women and offer equal opportunities. With no childcare facilities available, and little help from husbands on the domestic side, working mothers depend heavily on the efforts of other women in the extended family – grandmothers, aunts, sisters etc. While movement of women from domestic roles to paid employment has been rapid, there is very little progress in getting men to pour their own water, let alone share in domestic work.

On the outer islands, with little opportunity for formal employment, women tend to be self-employed, but with little financial gain. Markets are limited by geography, demography and the lack of regular and reliable interisland transport. Women on islands close to the tourism zones grow fruits and vegetables for sale to resorts. They also weave coconut-leaf matting (cadjan) and make rope and other products from coir. On remoter islands women make dried fish, a product that can withstand the long boat journey to the market. At least a few women on each island are experts at sewing and most women do home-gardening for consumption. Some island girls get an education and train as teachers and health workers, but most prefer to stay on Male' where there are wider career choices, rather than return home. Recent appointments of a few women to the posts of atolu verin (atoll chief) and kateeb (island chief), till now the realm of men alone, opens new opportunities for educated women.

Marriage is seen as a must for all Maldivian women, and fewer than 1% of those over 30 have never married. Marriage and divorce have always been casual, giving a woman no security within a marriage. Until recently, she could be divorced on the whim of her husband, without reason or compensation. Divorce carries no stigma, and early marriage, divorce and serial marriages are the norm. A woman retains her own name after marriage – this is sensible as she could be Mrs X, Mrs Y and Mrs Z in the space of a single year.

teachings appealed to the poorer levels of society and angered the wealthy merchant class.

In 622 Mohammed and his followers were forced to migrate to Medina, 300km to the north. This migration, known as the *hejira*, marks the start of the Islamic Calendar: AD 622 became year 1 AH. By AD 630 Mohammed had gained enough followers to return and take Mecca.

Within two decades of Mohammed's death, most of Arabia had converted to Islam. The Prophet's followers spread the word, and the influence of the Islamic state soon extended from the Atlantic to the Indian Ocean, south into Africa and east to the Pacific.

The Five Pillars of Islam

Islam is the Arabic word for submission and underlies the duty of all Muslims to submit themselves to Allah.

Shahada, the profession of faith that 'there is no God but Allah and Mohammed

Women in Society

In an effort to strengthen family and bring down the high divorce rate (which was once the highest in the world), the first-ever codified Family Law came into force on 1 July 2001, raising the minimum age of marriage to 18 and making unilateral divorce illegal. Prenuptial contracts registered at the court can strengthen a woman's position within the marriage as she can stipulate her rights. Where once a man could divorce his wife merely by telling her that she was divorced, now both partners must go through the court to initiate divorce, and it is permitted only when all reconciliation attempts fail. While the divorce rate has gone down, questions remain as to whether fewer divorces mean a better life for women. Polygamy is legal, and men can have up to four wives at a time, although it is not common practice to have more than one wife.

Traditionally, a woman could choose a suitor and name a bride-price *(rhan)*. The bride-price is paid by the husband to the wife, at the time of marriage or in instalments as mutually agreed, but must be paid in full if there's a divorce. Young women today quote higher bride-prices, reflecting higher expectations, and perhaps a scepticism about the fairytale happy-ever-after marriage. The wedding itself is a low-key affair, but is often followed by a large banquet for all family and friends, who can easily number in the hundreds.

Women in the Maldives can, and do, own land and property but, as in the rest of the world, women have a fraction of the property that men do. While inheritance generally follows Islamic sharia' law in the Maldives, land is divided according to civil law, whereby a daughter and son inherit equal shares of land.

There is little overt discrimination between the sexes. Though it's a fully Muslim society, women and men mingle freely and women enjoy personal liberty not experienced by women in most Muslim societies. However, Islam is used as a tool by some patriarchs to counter gender equality, even as they proclaim that Islam grants equality to women and men. Local discourse tends to say that the factors limiting gender equality are cultural rather than Islamic, and therefore it is possible to change them.

Movement of women is not officially restricted, but women's mobility is limited by factors such as domestic responsibilities and societal attitudes as to what is a woman's place. Home is where 'good girls' are. Although physical assaults against women are very unusual, women on streets and other public spaces can be harassed.

Most women in the Maldives go bareheaded though many are adopting a headscarf, a sign of growing commitment to Islam. The government has banned face coverings to limit the appearance of radical religious ideas. Gyms and fitness centres attract Maldivian women as do hair and beauty salons. Formal functions require women to wear one of the officially sanctioned 'national dresses', which includes the traditional *libaas* (dress) and *dhiguhedhun* (traditional full-length dress with long sleeves and a wide collar) as well as a Malay-style skirt and blouse with *libaas*-style neck embroidery. For everyday wear, young women dress in T-shirts, tank tops, flimsy blouses, fashionable jeans, pants and short skirts. The more self-conscious choose Indian-style *shalwar kameez*, or loose blouses and pants. Older women wear the traditional *dhiguhedhun* and *libaas*.

Aishath Velezinee, Maldivian writer, researcher and women's rights advocate

is his prophet', is the first of the Five Pillars of Islam: the tenets guiding Muslims in their daily life.

The second pillar, *salath*, is the call to prayer, and Islam decrees that Muslims must face Mecca and pray five times each day. In the Maldives, *salath* is also called *namadh*.

The third pillar is *zakat*, the act of giving alms to the needy. Some Islamic countries have turned this into an obligatory land tax which goes to help the poor.

The fourth pillar is the fast during the day for the month of *Ramazan*, the ninth month of the Islamic calendar.

The fifth pillar is the haj or pilgrimage to Mecca, the holiest place in Islam. It is the duty of every Muslim who is able, to make the *hajj* at least once in their life.

Prayer Times

The initial prayer session is in the first hour before sunrise, the second around noon, the third in midafternoon around 3.30pm, the fourth at sunset and the final session in the early evening.

The call to prayer is delivered by the *mudhim* or muezzin. In former days, he climbed to the top of the minaret and shouted it out. Now the call is relayed by loudspeakers on the minaret and the *mudhim* even appears on TV.

Shops and offices close for 15 minutes after each call. Some people go to the mosque, some kneel where they are and others do not visibly participate. Mosques are busiest for the sunset prayers, and at noon on Fridays.

Ramadan

Called Ramazan in the Maldives, this is the month of fasting, which begins at the time of a new moon and ends with the sighting of the next new moon. The Ramazan month gets a little earlier each year because it is based on a lunar calendar of twelve 28-day months (see Public Holidays & Special Events in the Facts for the Visitor chapter).

During Ramazan Muslims should not eat, drink, smoke or have sex between sunrise and sunset. Exceptions to the eating and drinking male are granted to young children, pregnant or menstruating women and those who are travelling. It can be a difficult time for travel outside the resorts, as tea shops and cafés are closed during the day, offices have shorter hours and people may be preoccupied with religious observances or the rigours of fasting. Visitors should avoid eating, drinking or smoking in public, or in the presence of those who are fasting. After a week or so, most Muslims adjust to the Ramazan routine and many say they enjoy it. There are feasts and parties long into the night, big breakfasts before dawn and long rests in the afternoon. Kuda Eid, the end of Ramazan, is a major celebration.

Local Beliefs

In the islands people still fear jinnis, the evil spirits that come from the sea, land and sky. They are blamed for everything that can't be explained by religion or education.

To combat jinnis there are *fandhita*, which are the spells and potions provided by a local *hakeem* or medicine man, who is often called upon when illness strikes, if a woman fails to conceive or if the fishing catch is poor.

The *hakeem* might cast a curing spell by writing phrases from the Quran on strips of paper and sticking or tying them to the patient or writing the sayings in ink on a plate, filling the plate with water to dissolve the ink and making the patient drink the potion. Other concoctions include *isitri*, a love potion used in matchmaking, and its antidote *varitoli*, which is used to break up marriages.

Facts for the Visitor

HIGHLIGHTS

If your idea of paradise is a simple holiday on an unspoilt tropical island, then strolling on soft white sand, sitting under a coconut tree and swimming in a sapphire-like lagoon will be all the highlights you'll need. The brilliant blue of the water is exceptional.

For many, the highlights are underwater, especially the amazing range of fish of fantastic shapes and lurid colours. It's like swimming in an aquarium.

For scuba divers accustomed to these delights, there is the larger marine life – turtles, napoleon wrasse, mantas and morays, whale sharks, nurse sharks, hammerheads and rays.

Another underwater highlight is the shipwrecks, such as the *Maldive Victory,* which are alive with new coral growth, and a home to trevally, snapper, squirrelfish and cod.

For something different, take a flight over the atolls and watch the free-form patterns of sea, sandbank, reef and island.

Visit Male', the capital and mini-Manhattan, as a day trip from nearby resorts, or a short stop at the start or end of your trip.

Finally, for the Maldives' most elusive highlight, find a small fishing village and walk back between the white-coral walls, where children play and old people smoke a hookah in the shade of a breadfruit tree.

PLANNING

Most visitors to the Maldives will be looking for a holiday in an island resort – see the Choosing a Resort chapter following. A substantial minority will be taking a trip through the islands on a live-aboard boat – see the section on Safari Cruises later in this chapter. In both cases, people usually make all their arrangements in advance through a travel agent at home.

When to Go

If you're looking for a few extra hours of sunshine then you should go between December and April, which is the dry season, with less rain and lower humidity. February to April is the hottest time and the most popular, when resorts can be fully booked and prices are higher. Mid-December to early January is peak season and prices are even higher. Easter and the holiday week in

August also attract peak prices at some resorts, especially the Italian-oriented resorts.

From May to November is the period when storms and rain are more likely. It's still warm, but skies can be cloudy and the humidity is higher. This is the low season, with fewer people and lower prices, but August can be more expensive because many Europeans take their holidays then.

There are amazingly complex descriptions of Maldivian weather patterns (see Climate in the Facts about the Maldives chapter) and the pricing patterns of the tourist resorts are equally complex.

Maps

Maps of the Maldives look pretty confusing. There's much more water than land, and on most maps it's hard to distinguish the islands among the reefs. It can also be hard to match names with which tiny spots of land. One problem is scale – the country is over 800km from north to south, but the largest island is only about 8km long. Some of the best maps are the 1:300,000 British Admiralty charts. At this scale, the whole country covers 3m of paper while Male', the capital, is only 6mm long! There are four sheets for the Maldives (nos 1011, 1012, 1013 and 1014) and more detailed charts of the areas around Male' (no 3323), Addu (no 2067) and Thuraakunu (no 2068). Marine chart specialists sell these for around US$50 per sheet.

Several tourist maps are available in Male' and in resort shops, but some of them are misleading because they show only the atolls in the tourism zone.

For divers and anyone else interested in the exact location of reefs, thilas (coral formations rising from the atoll floor up to 5m from the surface), channels etc, the best source is the sheet map *Maldives Travellers & Divers Map* and an atlas/directory called *Malways*, published by Atoll Editions and available at shops in Male' and most resorts, or from ⓦ www.atolleditions.com.au.

What to Bring

Light clothing is all you'll need, plus a shady hat, sunglasses and sun block. A waterproof cape or jacket may be useful, especially in the wetter months or if you'll be spending much time on boats. Plastic bags can help protect clothes, cameras and documents if you're out on the water in rough weather.

Even if you stay on a basic safari boat or a low-budget guesthouse you won't need a sleeping bag, but a sarong is a good idea. A torch/flashlight can be useful (take the old batteries home). Resorts don't always have condoms: bring your own supply.

Bring your own mask, snorkel and fins because most resorts charge to rent them. You'll save some money, you'll know the equipment suits you and you'll be able to go out at any time with a minimum of hassle.

INDEPENDENT TRAVEL

Fully independent travellers (FITs) are a rare species in the Maldives. If you arrive at Male' airport without a hotel reservation, the immigration authorities will ask you to go outside and make arrangements with one of the resort representatives or independent tour operators there. The official tourist information inside the airport arrivals area can assign an independent tour operator to help you, but it will be the next available one from their list, so there's no choice. Operators vary greatly in their helpfulness and integrity, so this can be pot luck. Small independent tour operators or travel agents (at the airport or elsewhere) may offer great deals and may also overcharge you. If an agent recommends a resort, try calling the resort or its Male' office, and ask what they'd charge if you booked directly with them.

It's best for arriving FITs to give the name of a hotel in Male', and allow a couple of days in town to shop around several tour operators and arrange onward travel. FITs who want to get on a safari boat will certainly have to make arrangements in Male' (see the Safari Cruises section later). Even the most resolutely independent traveller determined to see untouristed areas will benefit from the help of a good travel agent or operator.

TRAVEL AGENTS & TOUR OPERATORS

Male' travel agents are typically contracted to fill a certain number of rooms at a resort and usually do so in conjunction with a foreign tour company. They often have contacts at many resorts and up-to-the-minute information about availability and prices.

Tour operators don't usually have an allotment of rooms, but use their contacts to match travellers with available space in resorts or boats. Resort operators actually own and run resorts, and may sell some rooms direct to FITs. Especially outside high season, resorts may occasionally be desperate to fill some rooms, and will offer a special price through Male' tour operators and agents.

AAA Travel & Tours (☎ 324933, W www.aaatravel-maldives.com.mv) STO Trade Centre. Operator of several good mid-range resorts.

Capital Travel & Tours (☎ 315089, W www.capitaltravel.com) Iskandharu Magu. Inbound tour operator booking a number of mid-range resorts and safari boats.

Crown Tours (☎ 322432, W www.crowntoursmaldives.com) Boduthakurufaanu Magu. Big inbound tour operator representing many resorts and safari boats.

Inner Maldives (☎ 326309, W www.innermaldives.com) Ameer Amed Magu. Very well informed and helpful agency handling several resorts, inbound tour groups and FITs.

Picasso Travels (☎ 330626, fax 314103) Very small agency that might be able to help independent travellers.

Sun Travel & Tours (☎ 325975, W www.sunholidays.com) Meheli Goalhi. Big travel agent, tour and resort operator. It books resorts and safari boats.

Sunland Travels (☎ 324658, e sunland@dhivehinet.net.mv) STO Trade Centre. Inbound tour and resort operator.

Voyages Maldives (☎ 323617, W www.voyages.com.mv) Chandanee Magu. Well-established and efficient safari-tour operator that also offers quite low rates for many resorts.

TRAVEL OUTSIDE RESORTS

It's government policy to have tourists stay on island resorts or on boats within the 'tourism zone'. You need a permit to visit islands outside the tourism zone or to stay overnight on any nonresort island. To get a permit you need a sponsor to invite you to the island concerned (see Travel Permits under Visas & Documents later in this chapter). If you want to visit islands that are occupied by Maldivians rather than tourists, you still have a few options.

Firstly, you can stay in a resort and make day trips. Most resorts offer 'island hopping' trips that visit local fishing villages, though these villages often have conspicuous souvenir shops and persistent sellers. Some resorts are quite close to village islands; you can charter a dhoni (boat) to visit the village without a big group. Resorts won't allow you to use catamarans, windsurfers or canoes to visit nearby islands, but if you explain what you want and you find a sympathetic ear, you may get help. You won't be allowed to stay in any village after 6pm.

The best resort to choose if you want to visit local villages is the Equator Village Resort on Gan, in the far south of the country. Gan is linked by causeways to four other islands with quite large villages and towns, and you can cycle or walk through all of them. See the Southern Atolls chapter for more information.

The second option is to arrange a safari-boat trip to the areas you're interested in and make it clear to the operator that you want to visit fishing villages. The operator will arrange permits for all the people on the boat, and because you stay overnight on the boat, the accommodation problem is solved. You will have to charter the whole boat, so you'll need some other like-minded passengers to share the expense.

The third option is to spend a couple of weeks in Male'. It is, after all, a Maldivian island. It has over a quarter of the country's population, relatively few tourists and it's quite an interesting place in its own right. If you eat in local tea shops, spend time browsing in the craft and souvenir shops, go to the cinema and walk around in the evenings, you'll meet lots of locals. English is widely spoken and people will be more than willing to chat. There are a few inhabited nonresort islands which you could reach and return from in a day – Himmafushi, Huraa and perhaps Gulhi would be the main possibilities. You might get lucky and meet someone from an outer island who will sponsor you on a visit to their village, but you can't count on it.

SAFARI CRUISES

If you want to see more of the Maldives than a tourist resort, and particularly if you want to move around a number of different islands and have dive sites all to yourself, a safari cruise might be the best way to go. Safaris have been a growth industry in recent years, and the standard of boats and services has progressively improved. A typical, modern boat is air-conditioned,

spacious, and serves varied and appetising meals. It should have hot water, a sun deck, fishing and diving gear, mobile phone, wet bar, video player and cosy, comfortable cabins. A week on a boat with congenial companions is a wonderful getaway and gives a dazzling perspective on the atolls, islands and the underwater possibilities.

Costs start at around US$70 per person per day, including a US$6 per day bed tax and all meals, plus US$50 per day for diving trips. There's usually a minimum daily (or weekly) charge for the whole boat, and the cost per person is lower if there are enough passengers to fill the boat. You'll be charged extra for soft drinks and alcohol. Typical costs are US$2 for a can of soft drink, US$3 for a beer, and US$15–25 for a bottle of rum. You might splurge for the occasional meal at a resort, but generally there are few extras to spend money on.

The most basic boats are large dhonis with a small galley and communal dining area. They'll have two or three cramped cabins with two berths each, and a shared shower and toilet. Passengers often drag their mattresses out on deck for fresh air, and sleep under the stars. Food is prepared on board and varies from very ordinary to very good – it usually features lots of freshly caught fish. The bigger, better boats have air-conditioning, more spacious accommodation, and a toilet and shower for each cabin. The best boats have big cabins, a comfortable dining/lounge/bar area and complete on-board dive base.

Most safari trips are for diving (see the Snorkelling & Diving special section) or surfing (see the Surfing section under Activities, later in this chapter). A minority of safari trips are primarily for sightseeing, and usually offer a fair amount of fishing and snorkelling, stops at fishing villages and resorts, and picnics or a camp-out on an uninhabited island. Avoid trips where the passengers have divergent interests – a nondiver on a dive trip could feel pretty left out, while keen divers on a sightseeing trip may not get as much diving as they want.

On a scheduled trip, a single passenger may have to share a cabin with another, or pay a premium rate. Compatibility isn't usually a problem on diving or surf trips, where everyone has a common interest, but it can be an issue on longer sightseeing cruises. If you arrange your own group of six or so people, you can charter a whole boat and tailor a trip to suit your interests.

Choosing a Safari Boat

More than 80 safari boats are operating in the Maldives. Some specific suggestions are given here, but you'll need to do some research yourself. When you're considering a safari-boat trip, ask the operator about:

Boat Size Generally speaking, bigger boats will be more comfortable, and therefore more expensive, than small boats. Boats with more than 20 or so passengers may not have the camaraderie you'd get with a small group. Most boats have about 12 berths or less; few boats have more than 20.

Cabin Arrangements Can you get a two-berth cabin (if that's what you want)? How many cabins/people are sharing a bathroom?

Comforts Does the boat have air-con, hot water and desalinated water available 24 hours?

Companions Who else will be on the trip, what language do they speak, have they done a safari trip before? What are their interests – diving, sightseeing, fishing?

Food & Drink There's not much point asking if the food is good! Is there a bar serving alcohol, and if so, how much is a beer/wine/scotch etc?

Recreation Does the boat have a video player, CD player, fishing tackle or sun deck? Does the boat have sails or is it propelled by motor only?

Safari boats often change ownership, or get refitted or acquire a new name or both. The skipper, cook and divemaster can change too, so it's hard to make firm recommendations.

The following is a selected list of boats that have a good reputation, but there are many others offering good facilities and services. The boats listed here all have a bar on board, oxygen for emergencies, and some diving equipment for rent. The length of the boat and the number of cabins and berths will give an idea of its size. The two biggest boats are the most comfortable. Universal's *Atoll Explorer* is like a mini-cruise ship with a swimming pool on deck, and the Four Seasons *Island Explorer* is the most luxurious and the most expensive of all. The websites are those of the boat operators. Many of these operators have other boats as well, which may also be very good. If the website does not give booking information (or it's not in your language), most of these boats can be booked through the bigger tour

operators in Male' (see the section on Travel Agents & Tour Operators earlier in this chapter), or by overseas travel agents. The official tourism website (W www.visitmaldives.com) has reasonably up-to-date details on almost every safari and cruise boat.

Adventurer I (☎ 326734, 772518, W www .maldivesdiving.com) 22m; 6 cabins, 12 berths; air-con, hot water

Atoll Explorer (☎ 323080, W www.unisurf.com /atollexplorer) 48m; 20 cabins, 40 berths; air-con, hot water

Flying Fish (☎ 327066, W www.panorama-mal dives.com) 26m; 7 cabins, 14 berths; hot water

Haveyli (☎ 318354, W www.panorama-maldives .com) 30m; 11 cabins, 22 berths; hot water

Horizon (☎ 321169, W www.blue-horizon.com .mv) 20m; 8 cabins, 16 berths; air-con, hot water

Island Explorer (☎ 444888, W www.fourseasons .com/maldives/vacations/special_features .html) 39m; 11 cabins, 22 berths; hot water

Keema (☎ 313539, W www.interlinkmaldives.com) 27m; 6 cabins, 12 berths; air-con, hot water

Koimala (☎ 325336, W www.voyagesmaldives .com) 23m; 7 cabins, 14 berths; air-con

Maleesha Royal Cruiser (☎ 322265, W www .maleesha.com.mv) 33m; 11 cabins, 33 berths; air-con, hot water

Nautilus I (☎ 315253, 772381, W www.nautilus .at) 30m; 8 cabins, 16 berths; hot water

Nooraanee Queen (☎ 329338, W www.movin maldives.com) 43m; 19 cabins, 42 berths; air-con, hot water

Soleil (☎ 335060, 776569, W www.salongo.jp/ bluek/mletop.htm) 28m; 9 cabins, 17 berths; air-con, hot water

Sting Ray (☎ 314841, 772403, W www.maldives boatclub.com.mv) 31m; 9 cabins, 22 berths; air-con, hot water

Sultan of Maldives (☎ 310550, W www.sultans oftheseas.com) 30m; 8 cabins, 16 berths; air-con, hot water

Ummeedh 5 (☎ 318576, 771242, W www .guraabu.com.mv) 24m; 6 cabins, 12 berths; air-con, hot water

Itineraries & Permits

The usual safari trips loop through the tourist atolls. The shorter, seven-day trips will cover North and South Male' Atolls and Ari Atoll, and sometimes Rasdhoo. A 14-day trip may go south to Felidhoo Atoll, or north to Baa and Lhaviyani Atolls. To make a safari trip outside the tourism zone, the boat operator is required to get Inter-Atoll Travel Permits for all the passengers. These have to be arranged in advance and cost a little extra.

Most trips depart from Male' on a Sunday afternoon and return on a Saturday morning. This gives the crew time to clean up and restock. For trips to distant atolls, the boat might be able to go out ahead of time, and the passengers come out to meet it – by seaplane to a nearby resort, or by a scheduled flight to a domestic airfield. This could save days of cruising through the atolls. You may have to spend a night in Male' before or after your trip, which is a worthwhile experience.

RESPONSIBLE TOURISM
The Maldives' tourist industry is aimed at minimising social and environmental impact. People visiting Male' and/or local islands on resort excursions should be aware of Muslim sensibilities, dress modestly and behave appropriately (the tour guide will make this clear). Those who are fortunate enough to travel and stay outside the resort islands should be especially careful with their dress and demeanour. See Marine Environment Protection in Snorkelling & Diving special section.

TOURIST OFFICES
The official tourist office is the **Maldives Tourism Promotion Board** (☎ 323228; fax 323229; W www.visitmaldives.com; Boduthakurufaanu Magu, Male'). Its office on the 4th floor of the Bank of Maldives building has maps and other printed material, and can answer specific inquiries. The MTPB **airport information desk** is usually open when flights arrive, but be aware that if they introduce you to a tour operator, it will be the next on the list, not necessarily the best or most suitable for your needs.

The Maldives has only one official tourist office abroad: **Maldives Tourism Promotion Board** (☎ 69-2740-4420, fax 2740-4422; e maldivesinfo.ffm@t-online.de; Bethmannstrasse 58, Frankfurt am Main 60311, Germany). Most tourism promotion is done by private travel agents, tour operators and resorts.

VISAS & DOCUMENTS
Visas
Visas are not required. Most foreigners are given a free 30-day visitors' permit on arrival. Citizens of India, Pakistan, Bangladesh or Nepal are given a 90-day permit. Officially, a visitor must have at least US$25 for every day of their intended stay. In practice the authorities are unlikely to check, especially if you are booked into a resort and you look respectable.

Visa Extensions To apply for an extension, go to the **Immigration Office** (☎ 323913; open about 8am-1pm Sun-Thur) in the Huravee Building next to the police station in Male'. You must first buy an Extension of Tourist Visa form (Rf10) from the ground-floor desk. You'll need a local to sponsor you. The main requirement is evidence that you have accommodation, so it's best to have your resort, travel agent or guesthouse manager act as a sponsor and apply on your behalf. Have your sponsor sign the form, and bring it back to the office between 7.30am and 9.30am, along with your passport, a passport photo, the Rf750 fee and your air ticket out of the country. You have to have a confirmed booking for the new departure date *before* you can get the extension – fortunately, the airlines don't ask to see a visa extension before they'll change the date of your flight. Proof of sufficient funds (US$25 per day) or a credit card may also be required. You'll be asked to leave the documents at the office and return in a couple of days to pick up the passport with its extended visa (get a receipt for your passport).

Extensions are for a maximum of 30 days, but they give you only until the date on your ticket – the cost is the same, for one day or 30. Overstaying your visa (or extension), even by an hour, can be a major hassle as they may not let you board your flight, and you will have to go back to Male', book another flight, get a visa extension, and pay a fine before you can leave.

Travel Permits
Foreigners must have an Inter-Atoll Travel Permit to stay on any inhabited island other than Male' or a resort island, and permits are also required to visit uninhabited islands outside the tourism zone. You don't need a permit for a day trip organised by a resort.

Permits are issued by the **Ministry of Atolls Administration** (Boduthakurufaanu Magu) in Male' and cost Rf10. All foreigners must have a local sponsor who will guarantee their accommodation and be responsible for them. Note also that it is illegal for anyone to request payment for accommodation on an inhabited island.

Permit applications must be in writing, and include the applicant's name, passport number, nationality, the name of the island/atoll to be visited, dates of visit, name and address of sponsor, the name and registration number of the vessel to be used, and the purpose of the visit.

If you are going on a diving- or sight-seeing-safari trip through the atolls in a registered vessel with a registered safari company, the company will obtain the necessary permits before you start. In effect, the company is acting as your sponsor and supplying accommodation on the boat.

Your sponsor should be a resident of the island you wish to visit, and must be prepared to vouch for you, feed you and accommodate you. This support must be given in writing, preferably with an OK from the *kateeb* (island chief) and submitted with your application. It's best to have the sponsor submit the application on your behalf.

The most straightforward way to visit the outer atolls is with a registered safari boat, but a reputable tour company, travel agent or guesthouse proprietor may be able to help you make the necessary contacts to get a sponsor. Many Male' residents have friends or family in various outer atolls, but as they will be responsible for you when you visit the island, a great deal of trust is involved. Getting a letter of support-cum-invitation back from the island can take a couple of weeks if it's isolated from the capital.

The stated purpose of the visit can be something like visiting friends, sightseeing, photography or private research. A genuine purpose will help your application, but if it sounds like very serious research or professional filming, they may require additional permission from other government authorities. The permit will specify which atolls or islands you can visit. Permits are issued only between 8.30am and 11am on all days except government holidays.

As soon as you land on an island you must go to the island office to present the permit. A foreigner travelling in the outer atolls without a permit, or breaching its conditions, can be fined Rf100.

Travel Insurance
A travel insurance policy to cover theft, loss and medical problems is highly recommended. Some policies offer lower and higher medical-expense options; the higher ones are chiefly for countries which have high medical costs, and this would be a good idea for a Maldives trip. You may prefer to choose a policy that pays doctors or hospitals directly rather than your having to pay on the spot and claim later. If you have to claim later, make sure you keep all documentation. Some policies ask you to call back (reverse charge) to a centre in your home country where an immediate assessment of your problem is made.

Some policies specifically exclude 'dangerous activities', which can include scuba diving. You should ensure that your policy covers air ambulance (in a seaplane), evacuation by chartered speedboat, and an emergency flight home.

Even if the policy does not exclude diving accidents, it may not cover all the expenses associated with hyperbaric treatment in a recompression chamber. See Diving Health & Safety in the Snorkelling & Diving special section.

Vaccination Certificates
The only vaccination officially required by the Maldives is for yellow fever if you're coming from an infected area in Africa or South America.

Copies
All important documents (passport data page and visa page, credit cards, travel insurance policy, air tickets) should be photocopied before you leave home. Leave one copy with someone at home and keep another with you, separate from the originals.

It's also a good idea to store details of your vital travel documents in Lonely Planet's free online Travel Vault in case the photocopies are lost or you can't be bothered with them. Your password-protected Travel Vault is accessible online anywhere in the world – create it at w www.ekno.lonelyplanet.com.

EMBASSIES & CONSULATES
Maldives Embassies & Consulates
Maldivian diplomatic representatives overseas include:

Australia *Honorary Consul:* (☎ 03-9328 4133, e linton@eisa.net.au) 213 Flemington Rd, Box 135, North Melbourne, VIC 3051

Pergola by a pool deck, Kudahuraa island

Palm trees overhanging the shallows

Snorkelling over a reef

Popular beach resort

Aerial view of coral atolls

Sandy path through a grove of palm trees

Austria *Honorary Consul:* (☎ 01-369 6644) Weima Rer Strasse 104, A-1190 Vienna

Belgium *Honorary Consul:* (☎ 010-689212) Clos des Genets 17, 1325 Chaumont Gistoux

France *Honorary Consul:* (☎ 03-80-41-51-07) 24, rue Fontaine-Billenois, 2100 Dijon

Germany *Honorary Consul:* (☎ 06172-86293) Immanuel Kant Strasse 16, D-61350 Bad Homburg

India
Honorary Consul in Kolkata: (☎ 33-2485400) Hastings Chambers, Ground Floor, 7C Kiron Shankar Roy Rd, Kolkata
Honorary Consul in Chennai: (☎ 44-8594445) 855 Anna Salai, Chennai (Madras)
Honorary Consul in Mumbai: (☎ 22-2078041) 212-A Maker Bhavan 3, New Marine Lines, Mumbai (Bombay)
Honorary Consul in New Delhi: (☎ 11-5718590) 202 Sethi Bhavan, 7 Rajendra Place, New Delhi

Japan *Honorary Consul:* (☎ 03-3942 6222) 1-26-1 Otowa, Bunkyo-ku, Tokyo 112-865

Singapore *Trade Representative:* (☎ 2258955, e maldives@cyberway.com.sg) 10 Anson Rd, No 18-12 International Plaza

Sri Lanka *High Commission:* (☎ 01-586762, e maldhc@isplanka.lk) 23 Kavirathna Place, Colombo 6

South Africa *Honorary Consul:* (☎ 021-7979940) 69 Totnes Road, Plumstead 7800, Cape Town

UK *High Commission:* (☎ 020-7224 2135, e maldives.high.commission@virgin.net) 22 Nottingham Place, London WIU 5NJ

United Nations *Permanent Mission:* (☎ 212-599-6195, e mdvun@undp.org) 800 Second Avenue, Suite 400-E, New York, NY 10017

Embassies & Consulates in the Maldives

The foreign representatives in Male' are mostly honorary consuls with limited powers. There are no representatives for France or the USA. It may be necessary to contact your country's embassy or high commission in Colombo, Sri Lanka.

Sweden, Denmark, Finland & Norway *Honorary Consul:* (☎ 315174/5/6) Abdulla Saeed, Cyprea, 25 Boduthakurufaanu Magu

Germany & Austria *Honorary Consul:* (☎ 322971) Ibrahim Maniku, Universal Enterprises, 38 Orchid Magu

India *High Commission:* (☎ 323016) Ameer Ahmed Magu

Italy *Honorary Consul:* (☎ 322451) Bandhu Ibrahim Saleem, Cyprea, 25 Boduthakurufaanu Magu

Netherlands *Honorary Consul:* (☎ 323609) 1/1 Fareedhee Magu

New Zealand *Honorary Consul:* (☎ 322432) 30 Boduthakurufaanu Magu

Sri Lanka *High Commission:* (☎ 322845) Medhuziyaarai Magu

UK Honorary Consular Agent (☎ 311205) c/o Dhiraagu, Majeedi Magu. The honorary consular agent has very limited powers, and any serious matters are referred to the British High Commission in Colombo

CUSTOMS

No alcohol, pornography, pork, narcotics, dogs, firearms, spear guns or 'idols of worship' can be brought into the country. Baggage is X-rayed and may be searched carefully, and if you have any liquor it will be taken and held for you till you're about to leave the country. This service may not extend to other prohibited items. Magazines such as *Cleo* or *Cosmopolitan* may be regarded as pornographic if they have pictures of women in underwear. Prerecorded video cassettes are also prohibited – keep blank video cassettes sealed in the original packaging. Importing any sort of illicit drugs can land you in big trouble – in 1999, a man was

Idolatry

Most countries prohibit the importation of things like narcotics and firearms, and most travellers understand such restrictions, but when you're forbidden to bring 'idols of worship' into the Maldives, what exactly does that mean? The Maldives is an Islamic nation, and it is sensitive about objects which may offend Muslim sensibilities. A small crucifix, worn as jewellery, is unlikely to be a problem, and many tourists arrive wearing one. A large crucifix with an obvious Christ figure nailed to it may well be prohibited. The same is true of images of Buddha – a small decorative one is probably OK, but a large and ostentatious one may not be.

Maldivian authorities are concerned about evangelists and the things they might use to spread their beliefs. Inspectors would not really be looking for a Bible in someone's baggage, but if they found two or more Bibles they would almost certainly not allow them to be imported. It would be unwise to test the limits of idolatrous imports – like customs people everywhere, the Maldivian authorities take themselves very seriously. Even when the theme from *Jesus Christ Superstar* is being played as airport muzak.

busted at the airport with a tiny amount of hash oil and sentenced to 25 years.

Export of turtle shell, or any turtle shell products, is forbidden.

MONEY

For information about the costs of staying at a resort, see the Choosing a Resort chapter.

Currency

The unit of currency is the rufiya (Rf), which is divided into 100 larees. Notes come in denominations of 500, 100, 50, 20, 10, five and two rufiya, but the last two are uncommon. Coins are in denominations of two and one rufiya, and 50, 25 and 10 laree.

Exchange Rates

The exchange rate is displayed at banks, moneychangers and the cashier's office at a resort. For years the rate has been fixed relative to the US$, and all other currencies are traded relative to their current dollar value. It's possible that the country could change to a euro-based exchange rate.

country	unit		rufiya
USA	US$1	=	Rf12.75
Australia	A$1	=	Rf8.24
Euro zone	€1	=	Rf14.67
Japan	¥100	=	Rf10.85
NZ	NZ$1	=	Rf7.37
UK	UK£1	=	Rf20.44

Exchanging Money

Bring a credit card or US dollar travellers cheques or both. Most hotel and travel expenses will be billed in dollars. Some cash in small denomination US dollars is useful for tipping and to change into rufiya for use in local shops. If you're staying in a resort, all extras (including diving costs) will be billed to your room, and you pay the day before departure. Resorts accept cash or travellers cheques in euros, UK pounds, Swiss francs, Australian dollars and Japanese yen, but US dollar cheques are the best option.

Cash Outside resorts, cash US dollars are very common; British pounds and euros are also acceptable. You won't need Maldivian rufiya unless you're using local shops and services. Even these will usually take dollars, but not at full rate – if you pay US$1 for a Rf10 taxi trip, you won't get any change.

There are no restrictions on changing money into rufiya, but there's no need to change a lot. Rufiya are not readily negotiable outside the country. Reconvert excess rufiya at the bank counter in the airport when you leave – it's usually open, even when flights depart at night. In Male', change your excess rufiya at the Maldives Monetary Authority on Chandanee Magu. Officially, you may need receipts to prove that you bought the rufiya at the official rate, but you're rarely asked to show them.

Travellers Cheques Banks in Male' are near the harbour end of Chandanee Magu and east along Boduthakurufaanu Magu. They open Sunday to Thursday from about 8am to 1.30pm. They'll change travellers cheques and cash in US dollars, and possibly UK pounds, euros, Japanese yen and Swiss francs. Most will change US dollar travellers cheques into US dollars cash with a commission of US$5. Changing travellers cheques to Maldivian rufiya should not attract a commission.

Some shops and moneychangers in Male' will change US dollar (and possibly euro) travellers cheques, using the official exchange rates and charging a commission. The American Express representative is **Universal Enterprises** (☎ 322971; 39 Orchid Magu, Male').

ATMs There is only one ATM that allows you withdraw funds from international accounts – it's in front of the HSBC bank on Boduthakurufaanu Magu in Male'.

Credit Cards Every resort takes American Express and Visa, nearly all take MasterCard and some take Diners Club or JCB. A week of diving and drinking could easily run up a tab over US$2000, so make sure your credit limit can stand it. The cashier may want 48 hours' notice to check your credit. Many resorts apply a surcharge of 5% to credit-card payments, so it may be best to have enough travellers cheques to cover the bulk of your extras bill.

International Transfers Banks in the Maldives are not noted for their efficiency in international transactions. A transfer using the 'Swift' system seems to be the most efficient way to get money to the

Maldives. Villa Travel & Tours is the agent for **Western Union** (☎ 329990; e *money transfer@villatravels.com; Boduthakurufaanu Magu*), a reliable but expensive way to transfer funds. **HSBC Bank** (*Boduthakuru- faanu Magu*) might be the best bet. Try to have the money handed over to you in US dollars, not rufiya.

Tipping & Bargaining

If the service is good, and it usually is, it's quite customary to tip the room staff, wait- ers and bar staff in your resort at the end of your stay. US$10 to US$15 per couple per week is a suitable amount. US$10 per week is appropriate for the person who cleans your room. If the resort adds a 10% service charge to your bill, that's shared amongst all the staff (including the ones you don't see), but it's still customary to tip those that give you personal service. If you go on a boat trip for diving, it's usual to tip US$1 to the crew for handling the tanks and equipment. Give any tips to the staff personally, not to the hotel cashier – US dollars or local currency are equally acceptable.

In Male' the fancier restaurants usually add a 10% service charge, so you don't need to tip. Tipping is not customary in local tea shops. Taxi drivers are not tipped, but por- ters at the airport expect Rf10 or US$1.

Bargaining is limited to the tourist shops in Male' and island village souvenir shops where prices are not fixed.

POST & COMMUNICATIONS
Post

Postal services are quite efficient, with mail to overseas destinations delivered promptly; mail *from* overseas, especially packets and parcels, is subject to customs screening and can take considerably longer. The main Male' **post office** (☎ 344447; *Boduthaku- rufaanu Magu; open 7.30am-6pm*), is near the airport-boat landing. There is a poste restante service.

To send a postcard anywhere overseas costs Rf10 and a standard airmail letter costs Rf12 to most countries. A high-speed EMS service is available to many countries. Parcel rates can be quite expensive (up to Rf4800 for a 20kg parcel).

At the resorts you can buy stamps and postcards at the shop or the reception desk. Generally there is a mailbox near reception.

Telephone

Telephone services are provided by Dhiraagu, a joint venture of the government and the British Cable & Wireless company. A series of tall masts in the atolls provide microwave links over the length of the country, and also enable mobile phone services in most of the atolls. Every inhabited island now has a telephone connection, and very modern card-operated telephone boxes can be seen somewhat incongruously on the most tradi- tional island streets. Every business in Male' is on the phone, telephone cards are widely available and cardphones are numerous.

Calls within the capital cost 30 larees per 51 seconds. To other parts of the country, cost depends on distance – up to Rf3.25 per 51 seconds. International direct dial (IDD) calls can be made from all cardphones and are quite expensive, despite recent price reduc- tions. Costs depend on the destination and are lower from midnight to 8am.

zone	areas	normal (Rf/min)	off-peak (Rf/min)
1	SAARC & Singapore	16	12
2	Middle East, Asia Australia, NZ & UK	22	17
3	Europe, Caribbean N & S America	25	18
4	Africa, Pacific islands	28	20

All resorts have IDD phones, either in the rooms or available at reception. Charges vary from high to astronomical, starting around US$15 for three minutes. Some re- sorts have a cardphone in the staff quarters.

The international country code for the Mal- dives is 960. All Maldives numbers have six digits and there are no area codes. Operator and directory inquiry numbers are 110 for the Maldives and 190 for international inquiries. To make an international call, dial 00, then the country code, area code and number.

The mobile phone network covers most of the country and there are some 40,000 mobile phone accounts – everyone in Male' seems to have a mobile, and they're widely used on boats and on the remotest islands. Mobile numbers start with 77 or 78. Any GSM Global band mobile should work in the Maldives. Alternatively, you can subscribe to the Dhiraagu service and have them issue a SIM card for use in your hand- set, or get a prepaid mobile for about Rf500 (including Rf100 of talk time). Mobile calls on the local network cost Rf3.5 per minute.

Fax

Faxes are still used in business, especially the tourist industry, but have been largely superseded by email. Every resort will have a fax machine that you can use, for a price. The Dhiraagu office in Male' has a public fax service.

Email & Internet Access

Dhiraagu (W www.dhiraagu.com.mv) is the sole service provider, and runs public Internet cafés in Male' and in several of the more important and populous islands, charging Rf25 to Rf45 per hour. There are a couple of private Internet cafés too, with competitive prices. Some resorts offer Internet access, from US$5 to US$12 for half an hour.

If you bring your own PC with a 'global' modem, you can buy prepaid Internet access cards and plug into any phone.

A free ekno Web-based email account lets you use email anywhere in the world from any net-connected machine running a standard Web browser. Open your account at W www.ekno.lonelyplanet.com.

DIGITAL RESOURCES

The Lonely Planet website (W www .lonelyplanet.com) has succinct summaries on travelling to most places on earth and postcards from other travellers. On the Thorn Tree bulletin board you can ask questions before you go or dispense advice when you get back. The subwwway section links you to the most useful travel resources on other websites.

The Maldives is very Internet-savvy and hosts numerous websites, many in English or with English pages.

W **www.visitmaldives.com** The official Maldives Tourist Promotion Board site has background information and data about virtually every resort, safari boat and tour operator in the country.

W **www.themaldives.com** A very useful site with plenty of details about the Maldives and links to sites with information on official visits, sports events and development initiatives.

W **www.themaldives.net** Commercial site with links to resort information and other sources.

W **www.ourmaldives.com** Website of the *Hello Maldives* tourist information magazine, with information about nearly every resort.

W **www.presidencymaldives.gov.mv** President Gayoom's site will keep you informed of his official duties, speeches and other government information.

W **www.maldivesculture.com** Australian-based site with lots of background information, Maldives news archive and critical discussion of Maldivian issues.

W **www.maldivesstory.com.mv** Official site with Maldivian history and cultural information.

W **www.maldivesroyalfamily.com** Quirky New Zealand–based site hosted by a descendant of a Maldivian royal family – alternative takes on Maldives history.

W **www.haveeru.com.mv** Site of the daily Maldives *Haveeru* newspaper, updated daily with pictures and some material in English.

W **www.miadhu.com** Site of the daily *Miadhu* newspaper, with a few English stories, not so regularly updated.

BOOKS

If you plan to do a lot of reading, take a few paperbacks and swap them later with other guests. Most resorts have several shelves of dog-eared paperbacks, but 90% of them are in German (apparently any leftover English books are quickly snapped up by the staff).

Much has been written on the Maldives, but titles can be hard to find. Some interesting titles have been published locally by **Novelty Press** (☎ 322490, fax 327039). Many are available from the **Novelty Bookshop** (*Fareedhee Magu, Male'*), and some are sold in resort shops.

BIBLIOGRAPHY

Maldives Islands & Minicoy Bibliography, by Lars Vilgon, published by the National Centre for Linguistic & Historical Research, lists over 3000 manuscripts and books about the Maldives and neighbouring islands.

Diving

Diving & Snorkelling Maldives, by Casey Mahaney & Astrid Witte Mahaney, is a colourful dive guide published by Lonely Planet. It's one of the few dive books published since the 1998 coral bleaching changed so many of the Maldives' dive sites.

Travel

Give Me a Ship to Sail, by Alan Villiers, tells of the author's brigantine forays in and around the Indian Ocean.

Diversions of a Diplomat in Ceylon, by Philip K Crowe, sportsman, explorer and former US ambassador to Colombo, has an essay on Male'.

History & Politics

A Description of the Maldive Islands for the Journal of the Royal Asiatic Society, by HCP Bell, the most renowned historian of the Maldives and former British commissioner in the Ceylon Civil Service, draws from his archaeological expeditions in 1920 and 1922.

The Maldive Islands: Monograph on the History, Archaeology & Epigraphy, by HCP Bell, is his main work. The Ceylon Government Press published it in 1940, three years after his death. Original copies of the book are rare, but Novelty Press has reprinted it and it's available from several tourist shops and bookshops in Male'.

The Maldive Mystery, by Thor Heyerdahl, the Norwegian explorer of *Kon-Tiki* fame, describes a short expedition in 1982–83, looking for remains of pre-Muslim societies.

Travels in Asia & Africa 1325–54, by Ibn Battuta, has been reprinted in paperback by Routledge Kegan Paul. Ibn Battuta, a great Moorish globetrotter, was an early visitor to the Maldive islands and wrote this history of the early Muslim period.

The Story of Mohamed Thakurufaan, by Hussain Salahuddeen, tells the story of the Maldives' greatest hero who liberated the people from the Portuguese.

A Man for All Islands, by Royston Ellis, is an uncritical biography of President Maumoon Abdul Gayoom and gives some interesting insights into the development of the country over the last 60 years.

Natural History

Maldives, the Diver's Paradise, *Living Reefs of the Maldives* and *Diver's Guide to the Sharks of the Maldives*, by Dr Charles Anderson, are three great pictorials to whet your appetite before heading for the depths.

Common Reef Fishes of the Maldives (parts one, two and three), by Charles Anderson and Ahmed Hafiz, are identification guides published by Novelty Press.

Reef Fishes of the Indian Ocean, by Gerald R Allen & Roger C Steene, gives advice on fish identification and the marine environment.

A Guide to Common Reef Fish of the Western Indian Ocean, by KR Bock, is also reputable.

Photo Guide to Fishes of the Maldives, by Rudie Kuiter, an authoritative book covering many, many types of fish, has detailed descriptions and colour photographs. It's published by Atoll Editions (W www.atolleditions.com.au) and is widely available in the Maldives.

Indo Pacific Coral Reef Field Guide, by Gerald Allen & Roger Steene, is a useful source on corals, sponges, anemones and other underwater growths.

General

Maldives: A Nation of Islands, published by the Department of Tourism in 1983, has plenty of colour plates, though the text is somewhat jingoistic and dated.

Journey Through Maldives, by Mohamed Amin, Duncan Willets & Peter Marshall, has fine photos from even the remotest parts of the country.

Male' – Capital of the Maldives, by Adrian Neville, is a beautifully presented coffee-table book with great photos of Male' and its people.

The Maldives – Home of the Children of the Sea is another pretty picture book.

Maldive Impressions, by Ismail Abdullah, is also a fine photographic coffee-table book.

Mysticism in the Maldives, compiled by Ali Hussain, documents superstitions, encounters with jinnis, supernatural phenomena and weird stuff. Published by Novelty, it's out of print but still available in a few shops.

Classical Maldivian Cuisine, by Aishath Shakeela, is a fascinating and informative book with delicious recipes for fish soup, fish, coconut and curried fish – order from W www.maldivian cuisine.com.

NEWSPAPERS & MAGAZINES

The Maldives has three daily papers, printed in Thaana script with some text in English. They all cost Rf2.

Aufathis, which means 'new morning', comes out every morning and usually has two pages, plus the cinema ads, in English, except on Tuesday when there's an English special edition. *Miadhu*, which means 'today', comes out daily at noon, with four pages in English. Then there's *Haveeru* ('evening'), which appears daily except Friday and has one or two English pages.

Time and *Newsweek* are available from Novelty and Asrafee bookshops and on resorts.

RADIO & TV

The Voice of Maldives radio is broadcast to the whole country for 11 hours each day on medium wave, 1400kHz, and also at 104MHz. The news, in English, is read at 6pm for 10 minutes. TV Maldives broadcasts daily from 9am to midnight. It has two stations: TVM 1, with news, education and local drama, and TVM +, a pay station that broadcasts sport and news programming lifted from satellite broadcasts. Local news covers school sports, religious and cultural events, news from the islands and official appearances by the president. Local drama series, music videos and made-for-TV movies have also been produced on video over the last few years, mostly imitating Hindi productions.

Most resorts and Male' hotels have satellite TV, in the guest rooms or somewhere in a TV lounge. The most commonly available networks are BBC and CNN, with Italian, French and German news networks in many resorts, and the Indian version of MTV.

PHOTOGRAPHY & VIDEO
Travel Photography – A Guide to Taking Better Pictures by Richard I'Anson, published by Lonely Planet, has lots of good advice and suggestions.

Film & Equipment
A good selection of film is available in Male' at reasonable prices. Print film costs around Rf70 for a roll of 24, slide film about Rf90 to Rf130 for a roll of 36. Film is much more expensive in resort shops. Though the sunlight is very bright, you should still use reasonably fast film because many potential subjects will be in the shade (Maldivians never stay in the sun if they can avoid it). A polarising filter is highly desirable in the Maldives' bright, glary conditions. A lens hood can also be useful.

You can buy video cartridges in Male', but not at all the resorts, so bring some with you. Keep them in sealed packaging so customs won't want to subject them to censorship.

Restrictions
In Male', don't photograph the National Security Service (NSS) headquarters near the Grand Mosque, the Theemuge (president's residence) or any police or security establishment.

Photographing People
Most Maldivians don't seem to mind being photographed in a general scene – let them know you want a shot and they'll usually give you the nod. They can be more reticent about close-up portraits and you'll need to establish some rapport. Don't take pictures of people while they're praying.

Underwater Photography
The urge to photograph the underwater wonders is going to come upon many snorkellers and divers in the Maldives. Unfortunately,

underwater photography presents a number of technical problems which make it difficult to capture anything like the brilliance you see through your face mask.

Many resort dive centres rent underwater cameras so you can give it a try. You can also buy little, disposable cameras which are waterproof to about 5m. They cost about US$8 in a duty-free shop, but up to US$25 in resort shops. They're easy and fun to use, but not likely to produce very good photos.

As you go deeper under water, natural colours are quickly absorbed, starting with the red end of the spectrum. The deeper you go, the more blue things look – there's no red at all more than 10m down. You can capture some colours snorkelling in a metre of water, but photos taken more than 2m or 3m down will be monochrome blue-grey. To put the colour back in you need artificial lighting, and to work effectively under water it has to be more powerful than a flash above water. Underwater lighting equipment might cost as much as the underwater camera, but it can reveal colours which simply can't be seen 10m under water.

Although objects appear closer under water, you have to get close to achieve good results. Lenses longer than 28mm or 35mm do not work well under water.

Dive centres and conservationists stress the importance of underwater photographers exercising care and skill to avoid environmental damage. To get close to a subject, frame the photo, operate the lights and work the camera without fins, tanks or equipment hitting anything requires perfect buoyancy and control, especially in a confined space or a strong current.

TIME
The Maldives is five hours ahead of GMT/UTC, in the same time zone as Pakistan. When it's noon in the Maldives, it's 7am in London, 8am in Berlin and Rome, 12.30pm in India and Sri Lanka, 2.30pm in Singapore and 4pm in Tokyo.

A number of resorts operate one hour ahead of Male' time to give their guests the illusion of extra daylight in the evening and a longer sleep in the morning.

ELECTRICITY
With no national electricity grid, all resorts rely on diesel-powered generators which usually

operate 24 hours a day (fuel is one of a resort's major expenses). Male' has a reliable electricity supply. Most inhabited islands have generators, but in some cases they only run in the evening between 6pm and 11pm.

Electricity supply is 220V to 240V, 50Hz AC. Most resorts have a multiuse socket in the bathroom which can accept razors using 110V with a variety of pin configurations. For other 110V appliances, you'll need a transformer.

The most common type of socket accepts a plug with three square pins, but various other types are also in use, so bring a multisocket adaptor.

WEIGHTS & MEASURES

Although officially converting to the metric system, imperial measures are widely used. Metric measurements are used in this book, but there is a metric/imperial conversion chart at the end of the book if you need it.

LAUNDRY

Resorts will do laundry for as much as US$3.50 for a shirt, US$4.50 for pants. You can wash cloths by hand, but some of the stuffier resorts don't like laundry hanging in front of rooms. Laundries in Male' charge between Rf5 and Rf15 per item – ask at your guesthouse.

TOILETS

Male's public toilets charge Rf2. On local islands, you may have to ask where the *fahana* is.

HEALTH

The Maldives is remarkably free of health problems, especially the resorts, which have a vested interest in ensuring that their guests stay healthy.

Predeparture Planning

Immunisations The only vaccination officially required by the Maldives is for yellow fever if you're coming from an area where yellow fever is endemic. Malaria prophylaxis is not recommended.

Divers' Medical Check If you plan to do a diving course in the Maldives, you should get a diving medical checkup before you leave. There's a special form for this – a local diving club or dive shop will have the form and a list of doctors who can do a diving medical check. In the Maldives, you can have it done at the ADK Hospital in Male'.

Health Insurance Make sure that you have adequate health insurance and it covers you for expensive evacuations by seaplane or speedboat, and for any diving risks.

Travel Health Guides If you are planning an extended stay in the outer atolls, you may consider taking a more detailed health guide like Lonely Planet's *Healthy Travel Asia & India*. On the Internet, Lonely Planet's home page has links to the World Health Organization and the US Centers for Disease Control & Prevention (ⓦ www.lonelyplanet.com/subwwway).

Basic Rules

Food Eating in a resort is as safe as in any modern restaurant in Western Europe. In local eateries food is prepared in advance and laid out on a counter, and may carry some risk. Overwhelmingly, however, these places are very clean, as are the staff and the other patrons. The experience of eating Maldivian food is worth the minimal danger of an upset stomach.

Water Bottled water is available at resorts and in Male'. The tap water in most resorts is desalinated sea water and quite OK to drink (see the boxed text 'Water, Water, Everywhere', following). It may be very slightly salty, but is most unlikely to contain harmful bacteria. Male' guesthouses provide drinking water from the public supply, which is desalinated. Make sure you drink enough – don't rely on feeling thirsty to indicate when you should drink. Not needing to urinate or very dark yellow urine is a danger sign. Carry a water bottle on long boat trips.

Medical Problems & Treatment

Self-diagnosis and treatment can be risky, so seek qualified help if you need it. Some large resorts have a resident doctor, but otherwise it may be necessary to go into Male', to the nearest atoll capital, or have a doctor come to you.

Medical Care in the Maldives

The Maldivian health service relies heavily on doctors, nurses and dentists from

Water, Water, Everywhere

Ensuring a supply of fresh water has always been imperative for small island communities. Rainwater quickly soaks into the sandy island soil and usually forms an underground reservoir of fresh water, held in place by a circle of salt water from the surrounding sea. Wells can be dug to extract the fresh ground water, but if water is pumped out faster than rainfall replenishes the supply, then salty water infiltrates from around the island and the well water becomes brackish. Decaying organic matter and septic tanks can also contaminate the ground water, giving it an unpleasant sulphurous smell.

One way to increase the fresh-water supply is to catch and store rainwater from rooftops. This wasn't feasible on islands that had only small buildings with roofs of palm thatch, but economic development and the use of corrugated iron has changed all that. Nearly every inhabited island now has a government-supported primary school, which is often the biggest, newest building on the island. The other sizeable building is likely to be the mosque, which is a focus of community pride. Along with education and spiritual sustenance, many Maldivians now also get their drinking water from the local school or the mosque.

Expanding tourist resorts required more water than was available from wells or rooftops and, as resorts grew larger, the tourists' showers became saltier. Also, the ground water became too salty to irrigate the exotic gardens that every tourist expects on a tropical island. The solution was the desalination of sea water using 'reverse osmosis' – a combination of membrane technology and brute force.

Now every resort has a desalination plant, with racks of metal cylinders, each containing an inner cylinder made of a polymer membrane. Sea water is pumped into the inner cylinder at high pressure and the membrane allows pure water to pass through into the outer cylinder from which it is piped away. Normally, when a membrane separates fresh water from salt water, both salt and water will pass through the membrane in opposite directions to equalise the saltiness on either side – this process is called osmosis. Under pressure, the special polymer membrane allows the natural process of osmosis to be reversed.

Small, reliable desalination plants have been a boon for the resorts, providing abundant fresh water for bathrooms, kitchens, gardens and, increasingly, for swimming pools. Of course it's expensive, as the plants use lots of diesel fuel for their powerful pumps and the polymer membranes need to be replaced regularly. Many resorts ask their guests to be moderate in their water use, while a few are finding ways to recycle bath and laundry water onto garden beds. Most have dual water supplies, so that brackish ground water is used to flush the toilet while desalinated sea water is provided in the shower and the hand basin.

Is desalinated water good enough to drink? If a desalination plant is working properly, it should produce, in effect, 100% pure distilled water. The island of Thulusdhoo, in North Male' Atoll, has the only factory in the world where Coca-Cola is made out of sea water. In most resorts, the water from the bathroom tap tastes just fine, but management advises guests not to drink it. One story is that the water is too pure and lacks the trace minerals essential for good health. Another is that the water is purified in the plant, but in the pipes it can pick up bacteria, which may cause diarrhoea. Usually, the resort and hotel management will suggest that guests buy mineral water from the bar, shop or restaurant, where it will cost between US$2 and US$4 for 1.5 litres. This water is bottled in the Maldives using purified, desalinated water.

overseas, and facilities outside the capital are limited. The country's main hospital is the **Indira Gandhi Memorial Hospital** (☎ 316647; *Boduthakurufaanu Magu*) in Male'. Male' also has the **ADK Private Hospital** (☎ 313553; *Sosun Magu*), which offers high-quality care at high prices. The capital island of each atoll has a government hospital or at least a health centre – these are being improved, but for any

serious problem you'll have to go to Male'. Patients requiring specialist operations may have to be evacuated to Colombo or Singapore, or taken home.

Emergency evacuations from resorts are coordinated by the Coast Guard and the two seaplane companies. Seaplanes can only do evacuations during daylight hours from a limited number of landing/takeoff sites.

Environmental Hazards

Heat Exhaustion Dehydration and salt deficiency can cause heat exhaustion. Take time to acclimatise to high temperatures, drink sufficient liquids and do not do anything too physically demanding.

Salt deficiency is characterised by fatigue, lethargy, headaches, giddiness and muscle cramps; salt tablets may help, but adding extra salt to your food is better.

Heatstroke This serious condition can occur if the body's heat-regulating mechanism breaks down and the body temperature rises to dangerous levels. Long, continuous periods of exposure to high temperatures and insufficient fluids can leave you vulnerable to heatstroke.

The symptoms are feeling unwell, not sweating very much (or at all) and a high body temperature (39° to 41°C or 102° to 106°F). Where sweating has ceased, the skin becomes flushed and red. Severe, throbbing headaches and lack of coordination will also occur, and the sufferer may be confused or aggressive. Hospitalisation is essential, but in the interim get the victim out of the sun, remove their clothing, cover them with a wet sheet or towel and then fan continuously. Give fluids if they are conscious.

Prickly Heat This itchy rash is caused by excessive perspiration trapped under the skin. It usually strikes people who have just arrived in a hot climate. Keeping cool, bathing often, drying the skin and using a mild talcum or prickly heat powder or resorting to air-conditioning may help.

Sunburn In the tropics you can get sunburnt surprisingly quickly, even through cloud. Use a sunscreen, a hat, and a barrier cream for your nose and lips. Calamine lotion, aloe vera, or a commercial after-sun preparation are good for mild sunburn. Protect your eyes with good-quality sunglasses, particularly when you're near water and sand which reflect UV radiation. It's easy to burn while snorkelling – wear a Lycra vest, light wetsuit or a T-shirt.

Motion Sickness If you are prone to motion sickness on boats, try to find a place that minimises movement. On a large boat or a traditional Maldivian dhoni, sit close to the middle. On a small speedboat, there is usually less movement at the stern. If you start to feel queasy, try standing up, watching the horizon, and using your legs to absorb the movement of the boat. Fresh air usually helps; reading and cigarette smoke don't. Commercial motion-sickness preparations have to be taken before the trip commences. Eating lightly before and during a trip will reduce the chances of motion sickness, and sucking a mint or a sweet can help.

Infectious Diseases

Diarrhoea A change of water, food or climate can all cause a mild bout of diarrhoea, but a few rushed toilet trips with no other symptoms is not indicative of a serious problem. Dehydration is the main danger with any diarrhoea. Fluid replacement remains the mainstay of management.

Fungal Infections These infections occur more commonly in hot weather and are usually found on the scalp, between the toes (athlete's foot) or fingers, in the groin and on the body (ringworm). Moisture encourages these infections.

To prevent fungal infections wear loose, comfortable clothes, avoid artificial fibres, wash frequently and dry yourself carefully. If you do get an infection, wash the infected area at least daily with a disinfectant or medicated soap and water, and rinse and dry well. Apply an antifungal cream or powder like tolnaftate. Try to expose the infected area to air or sunlight as much as possible and wash all towels and underwear in hot water, change them often and let them dry in the sun.

Insect-Borne Diseases

Mosquitoes aren't troublesome in Maldivian resorts because there are few areas of open fresh water where they can breed. If mosquitoes do annoy you, use repellent or burn mosquito coils, available from resort shops.

Dengue Fever, a viral disease transmitted by mosquitoes, occurs in Maldivian villages but is not a significant risk on resort islands or in the capital.

Cuts, Bites & Stings

Skin punctures can easily become infected in hot climates and may be difficult to heal. Treat any cut with an antiseptic such as povidone-iodine. Where possible avoid bandages and Band-aids, which can keep wounds wet. To avoid injury, don't walk on reefs or in shallow water between reefs.

Coral Cuts & Stings Coral is sharp stuff and brushing up against it is likely to cause a cut or abrasion. Most corals contain poisons and you're likely to get some in any wound, along with tiny grains of broken coral. The result is that a small cut can take a long time to heal. Wash any coral cuts very thoroughly with fresh water and then treat them liberally with antiseptic. Brushing against fire coral or the feathery hydroid can give you a painful sting and a persistent itchy rash.

Stonefish These fish lie on reefs and the sea bed, and are well camouflaged. When stepped on, their sharp dorsal spines pop up and inject a venom that causes intense pain and sometimes death. Stonefish are usually found in shallow, muddy water, but also on rock and coral sea beds. They are another good reason not to walk on coral reefs.

Bathing the wound in very hot water reduces the pain and effects of the venom. An antivenene is available and medical attention should be sought as the after-effects can be very long lasting.

Butterfly Cod These fish are closely related to the stonefish and have a series of poisonous spines down their back. Even brushing against the spines can be painful, but a stab from them could be fatal.

Sea Urchins Don't step on sea urchins as the spines are long and sharp, break off easily and once embedded in your flesh are very difficult to remove.

Sea Lice You may encounter these tiny creatures when swimming or snorkelling. They are too small to see, but they cause annoying little stings on exposed skin – they feel like mosquitoes but you can't swat them. They don't cause any lasting discomfort.

Anemones These colourful creatures are also poisonous and putting your arm into one can give you a painful sting.

Stingrays These rays lie on sandy sea beds, and if you step on one its barbed tail can whip up into your leg and cause a nasty, poisoned wound. Sand can drift over stingrays so they can become all but invisible while basking on the bottom. Fortunately, stingrays will usually glide away as you approach. If you're wading in the sandy shallows, try to shuffle along and make some noise. If stung, bathing the affected area in hot water is the best treatment; medical attention should be sought to ensure the wound is properly cleaned.

Cone Shells The white-banded cone shell (*Conus omaria*) is found in Maldivian waters and can sting dangerously or even fatally.

Sharks There is a negligible danger from sharks if they are not provoked. Many types of shark inhabit the Maldives, but they all have plentiful supplies of their natural food, which they find far tastier and more conveniently bite-sized than humans. Some people have been injured when feeding sharks by hand, and this practice is now banned.

Fish Bites Lots of fish will bite if you put your fingers in their mouths. You are unlikely to be bitten if you follow the rules of not feeding or touching any fish. A bite from most small fish is nothing more than a playful nip, but stingrays, moray eels and many other large fish can give painful bites and cause injuries.

Diving Health
See the Snorkelling & Diving special section for diving related problems.

SOCIAL GRACES
Maldivian resorts make it quite clear what guests should and shouldn't do. Guests must respect the environment (no damage to fish or coral) and they must respect Muslim sensibilities. Nudity is strictly forbidden and women must not go topless; bikinis and brief bathers are quite acceptable in resorts, though most prefer that you cover up in the bar, dining and reception areas. In Male' and on other inhabited islands, travellers should make an effort not to offend local standards. Men should never go barechested and women should avoid low-cut tops and tank tops. Long pants or long skirts are preferable, but shorts are OK if they cover the thighs.

It's best to dress neatly and conservatively when dealing with officials and businesspeople. Maldivian professional men always wear long trousers, clean shoes (often slip-ons), a shirt and usually a tie. Women usually wear dresses below the knee and covering the shoulders and arms.

Those who spend time outside the resorts should be aware of a few more points:

Lose the Shoes People take their shoes off before going inside a house or mosque. Maldivians can slip off their footwear without breaking step, but visitors may find it inconvenient. Slip-on shoes are easier than lace-ups, and thongs (flip-flops) are easier than sandals.

Keep Your Cool Be patient and polite, especially in government offices that can be painfully slow and frustrating.

Payment Etiquette If you ask someone to lunch, that means you'll pay for it; and if someone else asks you, don't reach for the bill.

Religion Rules Islam is the state religion, so be aware that prayer times take precedence over business and pleasure, and that Ramazan, a month of fasting, places great demands on local people. Visiting a mosque requires long pants or a long skirt and no shoes. No-one should have alcohol or pork outside resorts.

WOMEN TRAVELLERS

Culturally, resorts are European enclaves and visiting women will not have to make too many adjustments. Topless bathing and nudity are strictly forbidden, but brief bikinis are perfectly acceptable on resort beaches.

Reasonably modest dress is appropriate in Male' – shorts should cover the thighs and shirts should not be very low cut. Women may be verbally harassed on the street in Male', especially if their dress or demeanour is seen as provocative. Local women don't go into tea shops in Male', but a foreign woman with a male companion would not cause too much excitement.

In more out-of-the-way parts of the country, quite conservative dress is in order. It is very unlikely that a foreign woman would be harassed or feel threatened on a local island. They are very closed, small communities and the fact that a woman would be associated with a local sponsor should give a high level of security.

GAY & LESBIAN TRAVELLERS

There doesn't seem to be any restriction on what tourists do in resorts in private, but it's unlawful for Maldivians to engage in just about any form of extramarital sex. A gay couple should have no problem booking a resort room with a double bed but public displays of affection may be frowned upon. Use your own discretion. None of the resorts makes any appeal to the gay market or has any noticeable gay scene.

DISABLED TRAVELLERS

At Male' International Airport, passengers must use steps to get on and off planes, so contact your airline to find out what arrangements can be made. The arrivals area is all at ground level, but departure usually involves going up and down stairs.

Transfers to nearby resorts are by dhoni or speedboat and a person in a wheelchair or with limited mobility will need assistance. Transfer to more distant resorts is often by seaplanes, which can be more difficult to access, but staff are quite experienced in assisting passengers in wheelchairs or with limited mobility.

Most resorts have few steps, ground-level rooms and reasonably smooth paths to beaches, boat jetties and all public areas. Staff will be on hand to assist disabled guests. When you decide on a resort, call them directly and ask about the layout. It's usually a good idea for guests to advise the tour agency of any special needs, but if you want to find out about specific facilities, it's best to contact the resort itself.

Quite a few resort activities are potentially suitable for disabled guests, apart from the very popular sitting-on-a-beach-doing-nothing. Fishing trips and excursions to inhabited islands should be easy, but uninhabited islands may be more difficult to disembark on. Catamaran sailing and canoeing are possibilities, especially if you've had experience in these activities. Anyone who can swim will be able to enjoy snorkelling. The International Association for Handicapped Divers (**w** www.iahd.org) provides advice and assistance for anyone with a physical disability who wishes to scuba dive. Resort dive schools should be able to arrange a special course or program for any group of four or more people with a similar disability.

No dogs are permitted in the Maldives, so it's not a destination for anyone dependent on a guide dog.

SENIOR TRAVELLERS

Most resorts have a good mix of age groups and some guests are well over retirement age. Once you arrive, there are no special deals or discounts for senior citizens, but when you book your holiday be on the lookout for any tour company promotions aimed at the older market.

TRAVEL WITH CHILDREN

Younger children will enjoy a couple of weeks on a Maldivian resort island, particularly if they like playing in the water and on the beach. Though exotic cuisine is sometimes on the menu, there are always some pretty standard Western-style dishes that kids will find OK.

Older children and teenagers could find a resort a little confining after a few days and they may get bored. Canoeing and fishing trips may provide some diversion, while a course in sailing or windsurfing could be a great way to spend a holiday. Table tennis, tennis, volleyball or badminton might also appeal. Parents should allow an extra few hundred dollars for these activities. The minimum age for scuba diving is 16 years, but some resorts offer a 'bubble blowers' introduction for younger kids.

The main danger is sunburn, so bring sun hats and sun block. Lycra swim shirts are an excellent idea – they can be worn on the beach and in the water and block out most UV radiation. Bring a kid-sized mask, snorkel and fins and some children's games, books and beach toys.

For more advice on travelling with children, pick up Lonely Planet's *Travel with Children*, by Cathy Lanigan. See the Choosing a Resort chapter for tips on finding a family-friendly resort.

USEFUL ORGANISATIONS

For serious students of Maldivian history and culture, the National Centre for Linguistic & Historical Research (☎ 323206; *Sosun Magu*) might be useful.

The office of the British **Voluntary Service Overseas** (VSO; ☎ 323167; *Rahdeebai Magu*) is in the centre of Male' near Majeedi Magu. Volunteers, based in Male' and in the outer atolls, include teachers, health professionals, agricultural advisers and so on. VSO staff have a very good knowledge of the country, though it's not their job to help foreign visitors. If you need some information, telephone first.

DANGERS & ANNOYANCES

Apart from a few marine dangers and any risks associated with diving, surfing or other activities, the Maldives is a particularly safe destination.

Don't touch coral, shells or fish. Beware of the possibility of strong currents and don't swim too far out from an island's fringing reef, or too far from a boat on a snorkelling trip. Don't try surfing unless you know where you are and what you're doing – the surf breaks over coral reefs and you could be badly grazed, or knocked unconscious.

It would be unlucky to be hit by a falling coconut, but it does happen, more so in windy weather. Imagine a 2kg coconut falling 15m onto your head. Check if a coconut tree is laden with big coconuts before lying underneath it.

Crimes of violence are very unusual, but there are burglaries and theft in the capital. There are very few cases of theft from resort rooms. Nevertheless, it's wise to deposit your valuables with the resort office, to keep your room locked and not leave cash lying around.

EMERGENCIES

If there's an emergency in a resort, call the duty manager or go to the front desk. See the Male' chapter for emergency phone numbers there, and the Snorkelling & Diving special section for information about diving emergencies.

LEGAL MATTERS

Alcohol is illegal outside resorts – you're not even allowed to take a can of beer out on a boat trip. Some foreign residents in the capital have a liquor permit, which entitles them to a limited amount per month, strictly for personal consumption at home.

Illicit drugs are around, but are not widespread. Penalties are heavy. 'Brown sugar', a semirefined form of heroin, has become a problem amongst some young people in the capital and even in some outer islands. This has been blamed for an increase in thefts and burglaries.

The baggage of arriving passengers is X-rayed and searched – mainly for alcohol, but drugs will not be overlooked. Visitors are unlikely to encounter drugs in any resort, and the resort management would be obliged to report any instance of drug use to the authorities. Anyone offering to sell drugs is likely to be an informant or an undercover cop.

With a scattered island population and limited resources, the Maldivian authorities rely heavily on delegation. Apart from the police and the military, there is a chief on every atoll and island who must keep an eye on what is happening, report to the central government and be responsible for the actions of local people.

Every foreigner in the country has, in effect, a Maldivian minder who is responsible for him or her. Resorts are responsible for their guests and for what happens on their island. If a guest goes swimming in the nude, the resort can be fined as well as the visitor. If a foreigner lands illegally on an island, the skipper or owner of the boat will be held responsible. If a diver in the outer atolls damages a reef or spears a fish, the operator of the safari boat is liable.

BUSINESS HOURS

Most tourist resort services are available when guests need them, whether it's an early morning airport transfer or a late night snack. Friday and Saturday are the usual Maldivian days off, and may not be the best times to visit Male' or local islands for shopping or business. Government offices are open Sunday to Thursday from 7.30am to 2pm. During Ramazan, hours are from 9am to 1.30pm.

In Male' the shops open between 7.30am and 9am and close between 9pm and 11pm, except on Friday when they open at 1.30pm. When prayer is called doors close for about 15 minutes. The streets are pretty quiet in the middle of the day, from about 1pm to 3pm, and also around the time of the last two prayer calls, between 6pm and 8pm.

Tea shops can open very early or close very late. During Ramazan the places where locals go to eat will probably be closed during daylight hours, but will bustle after dark.

PUBLIC HOLIDAYS & SPECIAL EVENTS

If you're in a resort, Maldivian holidays won't affect you – service will be as normal. If you visit Male' or a local island on a holiday, you might see some parade or public celebration, shops may not open or may open late in the day, and government offices and most businesses will be closed. Christmas, New Year, Easter and European school holidays will affect you more – they're the busiest times with the highest resort prices.

If a holiday falls on a Friday or Saturday, the next working day will be declared a holiday 'on the occasion of' whatever it was. Most Maldivian holidays are based on the Islamic lunar calendar and the dates vary from year to year.

Ramazan Known as Ramazan or *roarda mas* in the Maldives, the Islamic month of fasting is an important religious occasion which starts on a new moon and continues for 28 days. Expected starting dates for the next few years are 27 October 2003, 16 October 2004, 5 October 2005, 24 September 2006. The exact date depends on the sighting of the new moon in Mecca and can vary by a day or so either way.

Kuda Eid Also called Id-ul-Fitr or Fith'r Eid, this occurs at the end of Ramazan, with the sighting of the new moon, and is celebrated with a feast.

Bodu Eid Also called Eid-ul Al'h'aa, the Festival of the sacrifice, 66 days after the end of Ramazan, is the time when many Muslims begin the pilgrimage *(haj)* to Mecca. It's the longest holiday of the year, from five to seven days, and many people visit family on their home island. Celebrations involve sports, music and dance.

Islamic New Year

National Day A commemoration of the day Mohammed Thakurufaanu and his men overthrew the Portuguese on Male' in 1578. It's on the first day of the third month of the lunar calendar.

Prophet's Birthday The birthday of the Prophet Mohammed is celebrated with three days of eating and merriment. The dates are: 14 May 2003, 3 May 2004, 23 April 2005, 12 April 2006.

Day the Maldives Embraced Islam

Huravee Day The day the Malabars of India were kicked out by Sultan Hassan Izzuddeen after their brief occupation in 1752.

Martyr's Day Commemorates the death of Sultan Ali VI at the hands of the Portuguese in 1558.

Fixed holiday dates are:

New Year's Day 1 January

Independence Day 26 July – the day the British protectorate ended.

Victory Day 3 November – celebrates the victory over the Sri Lankan mercenaries who tried to overthrow the Maldivian government in 1988. A military march is followed by lots of schoolchildren doing drills and traditional dances, and more entertaining floats and costumed processions.

Republic Day 11 November – commemorates the second (current) republic, founded in 1968. Celebrated in Male' with lots of pomp, brass bands and parades. Sometimes the following day is also a holiday.

ACTIVITIES

Water sports are the most common activities, except for spearfishing, which is prohibited. Some resorts have tennis, badminton or squash courts, and most will have beach volleyball. The bigger islands have football (soccer) fields where enthusiastic staff teams regularly trounce the guests. See the Choosing a Resort chapter for advice on which resorts are best for which activities.

Surfing

There's some great surf in the Maldives, though only a few breaks are in the tourism zone, and they only work from March to November. Surfers have a choice of basing themselves at a resort and taking a boat to nearby breaks, or arranging a live-aboard safari cruise. In either case, make arrangements in advance with a reputable surf travel operator who knows the area well. The Maldives is definitely not the sort of place where a surfer can just turn up and head for the waves.

The period of the southwest monsoon (May to November) generates the best waves, but March and April are also good and have the best weather. June can have bad weather and storms, and is not great for boat trips, but it is also a time for big swells. The best breaks occur on the outer reefs on the southeast sides of the atolls, but only where a gap in the reef allows the waves to wrap around.

Surfing in the Maldives was pioneered by Tony Hussein (aka Tony Hinde), a Sydney surfer who was shipwrecked in the Maldives in the early 1970s. Before the first tourist resorts were opened, he discovered, surfed and named all the main breaks, and had them all to himself for many years. Surfing has caught on with many young Maldivians – check the local surf scene on **w** www.maldivesurf.org.mv.

North Male' Atoll
This is where the best-known breaks are, and they can get a bit crowded, especially if there are several safari boats in the vicinity. The following breaks are listed from north to south.

Chickens A left-hander which sections when small, but on a bigger swell and a higher tide it all comes together to make a long and satisfying wave. It's named for the old poultry farm onshore, not because of any reaction to the conditions here.

Cola's A heavy, hollow, shallow right-hander; when it's big, it's one of the best breaks in the area. This is a very thick wave breaking hard over a shallow reef, so it's definitely for experienced, gutsy surfers only. Named for the Coca-Cola factory nearby on the island of Thulusdhoo, it's also called Cokes.

Lohi's A solid left-hander which usually breaks in two sections, but with a big enough swell and a high enough tide the sections link up. You can

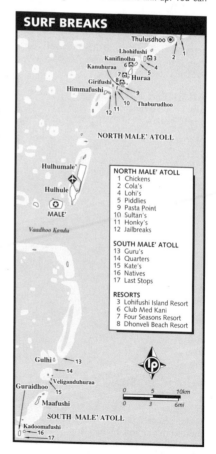

SURF BREAKS

Thulusdhoo
Lhohifushi
Kanifinolhu
Kanuhuraa
Girifushi
Himmafushi
Huraa
Thaburudhoo

NORTH MALE' ATOLL

Hulhumale'
Hulhule
MALE'
Vaadhoo Kandu

NORTH MALE' ATOLL
1 Chickens
2 Cola's
4 Lohi's
5 Piddlies
9 Pasta Point
10 Sultan's
11 Honky's
12 Jailbreaks

SOUTH MALE' ATOLL
13 Guru's
14 Quarters
15 Kate's
16 Natives
17 Last Stops

RESORTS
3 Lohifushi Island Resort
6 Club Med Kani
7 Four Seasons Resort
8 Dhonveli Beach Resort

Gulhi
Veliganduhuraa
Guraidhoo
Maafushi
SOUTH MALE' ATOLL
Kadoomafushi

0   5   10km
0   3   6mi

paddle out there from the resort island of Lohifushi, and guests of that resort have exclusive access to the break.

Piddlies A slow, mellow, mushy right-hander, a good Malibu wave. It's also called Ninja's because of its appeal to Japanese surfers. It's off the island of Kanifinolhu, home of the Club Med Kani resort, but it's very difficult to reach from the shore, and the wave is available to any boat-based surfer, not just Club Med guests.

Pasta Point A perfect left which works like clockwork on all tides. There's a long outside wall at the take-off point, jacking into a bowling section called the 'macaroni bowl'. On big days the break continues to another section called 'lock jaws' which grinds into very shallow water over the reef. It's easily reached from the shore at Dhonveli Beach resort, whose guests have exclusive use of this break. This used to be an all-Italian resort (hence the name of the break), but now it also attracts surfers from all over.

Sultan's This is a classic right-hand break, and the bigger the swell, the better it works. A steep outside peak leads to a super-fast wall and then an inside section which throws right out, and tubes on every wave.

Honky's During its season, this is the best wave in the Maldives. It's a super long, wally left-hander that wraps nearly 90 degrees and can nearly double in size by the end section.

Jailbreaks A right-hander that works best with a big swell, when the three sections combine to make a single, long, perfect wave. There used to be a prison on the island and the surrounding waters were off-limits, but now it's open to surfers.

South Male' Atoll The breaks in South Male' Atoll are smaller than those in North Male' Atoll and generally more fickle. It will be harder here to find a boatman who really knows the surf scene.

Guru's A nice little left off the island of Gulhi; it can get good sometimes.

Quarters Another small right-hander, rarely more than a metre.

Kate's A small left-hander, rarely more than a metre.

Natives A small right-hander, rarely more than a metre.

Last Stops This is a bowly right-hander breaking over a channel reef. It's a Protected Marine Area, and can get very strong currents when the tides are running.

Outer Atolls Only a few areas have the right combination of reef topography and orientation to swell and wind direction.

Laamu (Hadhdhunmathee Atoll) and Addu both have surfable waves on occasions, but they're not reliable enough to be worth a special trip.

Gaaf Dhaal (South Huvadhoo Atoll) has a series of reliable breaks which are accessed by safari boats in the season. From west to east, the named breaks are Beacons (right), Castaways (right), Blue Bowls (right), Five Islands (right), Two Ways (also called Twin Peaks; left and right), Love Charms (left), Antiques (right) and Tigers (left). They're all outside the tourism zone and can only be visited with permits from Atolls Administration.

Resort-Based Surfing The most accessible surf breaks are in the southeastern part of North Male' Atoll. Half a dozen resorts are within a short boat ride, but only a couple of them cater for surfers by providing regular boat service to the waves.

Dhonveli Beach is the resort that's best set up for surfers – the reliable waves of the 'house break', Pasta Point, are just out the back door, while Sultan's and Honky's are close by. A surfside bar provides a great view of the action. Surfing packages at Dhonveli Beach include unlimited boat trips to the other local breaks with surf guides who know the conditions well, leaving and returning on demand. The surf programme is run by Atoll Adventures under the direction of Maldives surf pioneer Tony Hussein/Hinde and can be booked only through a limited number of surf travel agents.

Lohifushi, a few kilometres northeast of Dhonveli, is a bigger, more expensive resort with more facilities and it also has its own, exclusive surf break at the southern tip of the island. A bar and a viewing terrace overlook the wave, which has hosted international surfing competitions. Most of the rooms are quite a long walk from the surf. Boats to other surf breaks go for three-hour sessions, one leaving at about 9am, the other at about 2pm (US$7.70 per person for three hours, extra hours US$2 per person). Boat trips must be booked by 8pm the day before. Many agents and tour companies sell rooms in Lohifushi.

Club Med Kani is the other resort island with an adjacent surf break, but you need a boat to reach it from the resort. There's no surfing program, no surf guides and no boats available for surfers.

Surfing Safaris Most of the safari boats in the Maldives claim to do surfing trips, but very few of them have a specialised knowledge of surfing or any experience cruising to the outer atolls. Ideally, a surfing safari boat should have an experienced surf guide, and a second, smaller boat to accompany it, for accessing breaks in shallower water and getting in close to the waves. A surfing safari ('surfari') boat should also be equipped with fishing and snorkelling gear, for when the surf isn't working or you need a rest.

An **Inner-Atolls Surfari** will just cruise around North Male' Atoll, visiting breaks that are also accessible from resorts in the area. If the swell is big and the surf guide is knowledgable, the boat may venture down to South Male' Atoll to take advantage of the conditions. A one-week inner-atoll surf trip will cost from around US$850 per person. This might be cheaper than resort-based surfing, but it won't be as comfortable, and it won't give access to a handy and uncrowded house break.

An **Outer-Atolls Surfari** is the only feasible way to surf the remote waves of Gaaf Dhaal – an experienced outer atoll guide is essential. Ideally, the safari boat should be based in Gaaf Dhaal, and the surfers take an Island Aviation flight to the domestic airport on the island of Kaadedhoo where the boat crew meets them. This requires good coordination and management, but the experienced surfing tour operators have the procedure well organised. They should also have a good relationship with Atolls Administration, so that they can get the necessary permits before you arrive.

You need at least six people to make a safari boat affordable; the surfing specialists should be able to put together the necessary numbers. Don't book on to a safari trip that is primarily for diving or cruising. Allow at least two weeks for the trip or you'll spend too much of your time getting to the waves and back. A 10-night surfari will cost from about US$2000 per person, including domestic airfares.

Surf Travel Operators The following agents specialise in surf travel and book tours and safaris to the Maldives.

Atoll Travel (☎ 1800-622310, 03-5682 1088, **w** www.atolltravel.com) Box 205, Foster, VIC 3960, Australia. Australian and international agent for Atoll Adventures. It offers surfing packages to Dhonveli Beach resort (US$1350 per surfer for seven nights, full board, unlimited surf transfers), premium surfing safari tours in Male' Atoll (from US$830 for a seven-day trip, including all meals; airfares extra) and to the outer atolls (US$1285 for a 10-day trip, including all meals, internal airfares, boat transport and accommodation).

Maldives Scuba Tours (☎ 014-4978 0220, **e** info@scubascuba.com) Walsham Road, Finningham, Suffolk, IP14 4JGPH, UK. Maldives dive travel agency and UK agent for Atoll Adventures.

Surf Travel Company (☎ 02-9527 4722, **w** www.surftravel.com.au) Box 446, Cronulla, NSW 2230, Australia. Venerable surf travel operator under new management; it books surfers into Lohifushi resort (from US$80 per person day, twin share in low season) and does boat-based tours in North and South Male' Atolls (from US$680 per person for a seven night trip).

Turquoise Surf Travel (☎ 9113 9491, **w** www.turquoise-voyages.fr) 8 rue Neuve St Martin, Marseille, France. This agent offers surfing holidays at Lohifushi Island Resort and boat-based surfari trips in Male' Atoll.

VB Travel (☎ 928-270577, **e** vbtravellp@grupo boluda.com) RAVEL, Presidente Alvear 28, Las Palmas 35007, Canary Islands, Spain. Spanish agent for Atoll Adventures.

Waterways Travel (☎ 1800-928-3757, 818-376-0341, fax 818-376-0353, **w** www.water ways.com) 15145 Califa St, Van Nuys, CA 91411, USA. A well-run agency that does surfing tours to many destinations; US agent for Atoll Adventures.

World Surfaris (☎ 1800-611163, 07-5444 4011, **w** www.worldsurfaris.com) Box 180, Suite 8, 47 Brisbane Rd, Mooloolaba, QLD 4557, Australia. Offering tours to various surfing destinations, it books surfers into Lohifushi Island Resort (from A$850 for seven nights, half board, two boat trips per day) and also does boat-based trips in the inner atolls (A$1025 for seven nights, full board).

Whale & Dolphin Watching

Whales are most common in the open sea (not inside the atolls) from February to May. During those months, UK-based **Out of the Blue Holidays** (☎ 012-4944-9500; **e** bluetravel@wdcs.org) offers an 11-night whale-watching cruise in conjunction with the Whale & Dolphin Conservation Society (**w** www.wdcs.org) for £1690. The boat is a 25m, seven-cabin, ocean-going catamaran. Trips have expert guides, and would expect to have 70 to 100 sightings, including beaked, blue, Bryde's, dwarf, false killer, melon-headed, sperm and pilot whales, and bottlenose, Fraser's, Risso's, spotted, striped and spinner dolphins.

Sailing

Most resorts have catamarans for rent and will give lessons for beginners. Prices vary but, generally, it's US$35 per hour for rental, US$50 with lessons. It's cheaper by the day or week, but for a lot of sailing you should budget US$275 per week. A 10-hour course will cost about US$220. You may have to do at least one lesson to convince the staff you're a safe sailor. The boats are usually Hobie Cats or Top Cats, with fibreglass hulls and two sails – no spinnakers.

Windsurfing

The lagoons around most resort islands are shallow and sheltered. This makes for a good beginners area, but falling off a windsurfer in shallow water over a coral reef can be painful. Some of the lagoons are large enough for experienced windsurfers to enjoy, but winds are usually well under 15 knots so it's not super challenging.

Most resorts offer windsurfer rental, for US$10 to US$18 per hour, depending on the standard of the resort. It's much cheaper if you take it for a longer period – maybe US$180 for unlimited use for a week. Private lessons can be as much as US$45 per hour, but a six-hour course, at around US$190, is better value.

Kitesurfing

This new and exciting wind and water sport is available at a few resorts, though winds aren't usually strong enough to make it really challenging for experts. Equipment rental is around US$35 per hour, and an eight-hour course will be about US$350.

Island Hopping

Every resort offers guests the opportunity to visit some of the nearby islands, usually on a half- or full-day 'island-hopping' trip. In general, a full-day trip will include a visit to a fishing village on an inhabited island, a stop at an uninhabited island for snorkelling and a barbecue lunch, and then at another resort island where you can have a drink and enjoy the facilities. Costs are generally between US$35 and US$50 (including lunch). Half-day trips usually just go to a

fishing village and an uninhabited island for snorkelling, and cost around US$25.

Visiting a village on an inhabited island allows you to see the local way of life, but many of the islands visited by tourists have many souvenir shops, which are hard to avoid on a short visit. Tours go to islands in the middle of the day, when most Maldivians are resting inside or in the shade, so the 'inhabited' island may seem deserted.

Try to get a trip that will stop longer at the village, and get yourself well away from the souvenir shops. Look along the waterside for a dhoni under construction and try to find the village office, the school and the mosque. If your resort is close to an inhabited island, you can usually charter a dhoni to take you on a special trip – this is much better than arriving with a group, and you have more time to look around and meet people. Villagers can be reserved at first, but are friendly if you have a little time and a good disposition. Note that some inhabited islands do not allow tourists to visit at all, and in all cases the visitors must leave the island before 6pm.

Fishing

Most resorts organise regular night-fishing trips. About a dozen people go out in a dhoni for two or three hours with a handline each and a bucket full of bait. On a typical evening over 80% of them catch something, and everyone gets a few nibbles. They generally cost around US$15 per person, and you can usually arrange to have your catch prepared by the resort's chef.

Some resorts arrange traditional Maldivian fishing trips, which start early in the morning and return in the afternoon. Traditional fishing is for tuna, with a pole, line and unbaited hook. This is a much more authentic experience, but is only offered by a few resorts, including Kuredu and Asdu.

For the high rollers there's game fishing on the open sea between the atolls with a fast, modern boat and some specialised equipment. The boat costs at least US$300 for four hours or US$500 for six hours, with a maximum of four to six fishing passengers to share the cost. The main species of game fish are yellowfin tuna, sailfish, blue and black marlin, barracuda, wahoo, jackfish, shark and dorado. The policy of the Maldives game fishing industry is 'tag and release', especially for bill-fish such as marlin and sailfish. If you plan to make any record-breaking catches, bring a camera along.

Canoeing

Most resorts hire canoes, usually fibreglass touring kayaks from US$8 per hour. They're ideal for exploring the lagoon, but you're not usually permitted to take them on a long trip, or to another island.

Tennis

Quite a few resorts have tennis courts, sometimes included in a package, but usually subject to an extra charge of US$5 to US$10 per hour, often more at night. Sometimes racquets and balls are rented separately, for an extra dollar or two per hour. If you're a keen player, bring your own balls and racquets.

Motorised Water Sports

Only a few resorts offer activities involving power boats, and they're pretty pricey. For example, there's the 'banana ride', where eight or so guests climb onto a giant, inflatable banana and scream as they are dragged around the lagoon by a speedboat. At US$10 to US$15 per round, it's not exactly a cheap thrill, but youngsters love it.

Water-skiing is available on some islands at around US$15 per quarter hour. Parasailing is about US$35 a go, and jetskis cost around US$25 for 15 minutes. Even at big, busy resorts, the power-boat activities only happen for a short time each day, and they're usually confined to one part of the lagoon, so they don't really disturb those who want to sit quietly on a beach.

COURSES

Diving courses are a particular attraction in the Maldives. The standard learn-to-dive course is an open-water certificate, but the bigger dive centres offer a host of advanced and speciality courses, including advanced open water, divemaster, night diving and so on (see the Snorkelling & Diving special section for more information).

WORK

Many foreigners work in the Maldives, most of them from the South Asian Association for Regional Cooperation (SAARC) countries employed in construction, education, health care, maintenance and resort work. Foreigners from non-SAARC countries, mostly Europeans, get work permits for tourism-related employment – diving and water-sport instructors, tour company representatives, chefs and airline crews. It is the employer's responsibility to obtain the work permit. Find a job first, then let the employer sort out the permits and visas. A number of volunteer aid workers are based in Male' and outer islands. Contact the aid organisations in your home country if you have skills which may be needed and you want to contribute.

If you are intending to work in the Maldives, you must advise the immigration authorities of this when you enter the country. If you organise work while in the Maldives, you will have to leave the country while the employer gets the permit, then re-enter.

ACCOMMODATION

Most visitors stay in tourist resort – see the Choosing a Resort chapter for detailed information. For information about hotels and guesthouses in Male' and at the airport, see the Male' chapter.

There's no commercial accommodation in the island villages and visitors are not legally permitted to pay for a place to stay. Official visitors are usually put up in the house of the *kateeb*, or a house maintained for the purpose. Accommodation for other visitors is arranged by the host who sponsored the Inter-Atoll Travel Permit application (see Travel Permits earlier in this chapter), but not necessarily in their own house. All meals will be arranged by the host, but visitors may be expected to dine separately from the host family.

Most island villages now have houses with running water, septic tank toilets and reliable electricity. In some less developed islands, houses may have a traditional *gifili* (bathroom) out the back, consisting of a well surrounded by a thatched fence. The well out the front functions as the kitchen sink. Water is drawn up by a tin can on the end of a pole. Rainwater is used for drinking, never well water. Electricity may be available only from about 6pm to 11pm. Traditional houses have coral-stone walls or woven palm-leaf walls, a palm-thatched roof and few windows. Old houses tend to get modified, extended, renovated and rebuilt, and new construction is with concrete blocks, corrugated iron roofs and bigger windows.

As a matter of protocol, guests should introduce themselves to the *kateeb* upon arrival or shortly after. If the island is the atoll capital, guests should also introduce themselves to the atoll chief. The other person to introduce yourself to is the *gazi* (champion of the faith), the island's religious leader and judge.

It is always best to dress as smartly as possible when meeting officials. Wear a shirt rather than a T-shirt, shoes not thongs, and long trousers or a skirt instead of shorts.

FOOD

The coconut thrives in the Maldives, mangoes, papayas and pineapples are grown, fish are plentiful, but almost everything else is imported. Most visitors will eat only in resorts, where the food is international style and the quality varies from cafeteria cooking to *haute cuisine* – see the Choosing a Resort chapter for information about the style and quality of resort meals. See the Male' chapter for information about the town's many eateries.

For the Maldivian people, fish and rice are the staple foods; meat and chicken are saved for special occasions. Maldivian food is similar to some Indian styles, and is often hot and spicy. If you're going to eat local food, prepare your palate for fish curry, fish soup, fish patties and variations thereof. Many resorts now have an occasional Maldivian dish in their buffet selection, and sometimes a Maldivian barbecue dinner. These can be quite authentic versions of the food that's served on special occasions, and are definitely worth trying. Everyday Maldivian food is a little simpler, and can be very spicy.

A favourite Maldivian breakfast is *mas huni*, a healthy mixture of tuna, onion, coconut and chilli, eaten cold with *roshi* (unleavened bread, like an Indian chapati) and *sai* (tea).

For snacks and light meals, Maldivians like *hedhikaa*, a selection of little finger foods. In homes the *hedhikaa* are placed on the table, and everyone helps themselves. In tea shops this is called short eats – a choice of things like *fihunu mas* (fish pieces with chilli coating), *gulha* (fried dough balls filled with fish and spices), *keemia* (fried fish rolls in batter) and *kuli boakiba* (spicy fish cakes). There are also samosa-like triangles of curried vegetables, and even small pizza squares are appearing in tea shops now. Sweets include little bowls of *bondi bai* (rice pudding), tiny bananas and *zileybee* (coloured coils of sugared, fried batter). They're all displayed on the counter and you select the ones that look good, and take them to your table with a cup of tea and a glass of water. Generally, anything small and brown will be savoury and contain fish, and anything light or brightly coloured will be sweet. The only rude shock is the pale yellow block with a brown top – custard with fried-onion icing!

A main meal will include rice or *roshi* (unleavened bread) or both, plus soups, curries, vegetables, pickles and spicy sauces. In a tea shop, a substantial meal with rice and *roshi* is called long eats. The most typical dish is *garudia*, a soup made from dried and smoked fish, often eaten with rice, lime and chilli. The soup is poured over rice, mixed up by hand and eaten with the fingers. Another common meal is *mas riha*, a fish curry eaten with rice or *roshi* – the *roshi* is torn into strips, mixed on the plate with the curry and condiments, and eaten with the fingers. A cup of tea accompanies the meal, and is usually drunk black and sweet.

The Maldivian equivalent of the after-dinner mint is the *areca* nut, chewed after a meal or snack. The little oval nuts are sliced into thin sections, some cloves and lime paste are added, the whole lot is wrapped in an areca leaf, and the wad is chewed whole. It's definitely an acquired taste.

DRINKS

Soft drinks and bottled water are available in Male' and in villages, at prices much lower than in resorts. Alcohol is prohibited for Maldivians. Foreigners can drink in resorts and in the airport hotel. Safari boats can serve alcohol, but the bar must be locked when the boat is in port.

Raa is the name for toddy tapped from the crown of the palm trunk at the point where the coconuts grow. Every village has its toddy man or *raa veri*. The *raa* is sweet and delicious if you can get over the pungent smell. It can be drunk immediately after it is tapped from the tree, or left to become a little alcoholic as the sugar ferments.

SPECTATOR SPORTS

Soccer is the most popular sport and is played all year round. On most islands, the late-afternoon match among the young men is a daily ritual. There's a league competition in Male', played between club teams with names such as 'Valencia' and 'Victory', and annual tournaments against teams from neighbouring countries.

Cricket is played in Male' for a few months, beginning in March. The president is a keen cricket fan and played for his school in Sri Lanka. Volleyball is played indoors and in the waterfront parks. The two venues for indoor sport are the Centre for Social Education, on the west side of Male', and a new facility just east of the New Harbour, used for basketball (men and women), netball, volleyball and badminton.

Traditional games include *bai bala*, where one team tries to tag members of the other team inside a circle, and *wadhemun*, a tug-of-war. *Bashi* is a girls game, played on something like a tennis court, where a girl stands facing away from the net and serves a tennis ball backwards, over her head, to a team of girls on the other side who try to catch it.

Thin mugoali ('three circles') is a game similar to baseball that has been played in the atolls for more than 400 years. The *mugoali* or 'bases' are made by rotating on one foot in the sand through 360 degrees leaving a circle behind. You'll sometimes see *bashi* in Male' parks or on village islands in the late afternoon, but traditional games are becoming less popular as young people opt for international sports.

SHOPPING

A good selection of souvenirs is available in resort shops, in Male' and in local villages, though many are imported from India, Sri Lanka or Southeast Asia. Souvenirs made in the Maldives include T-shirts, colourful, carved coral fish and carved rosewood manta rays. These can be attractive and well made, but are not as distinctive as the traditional crafts.

There are many skilled artists and craftspeople in the Maldives, but it's difficult to make a living producing traditional crafts. There is a real concern that some traditional arts and techniques may disappear altogether within the next few decades. Some organisations are working to revive and promote traditional skills, and to make crafts more commercial. For information about traditional crafts, check

w www.amu.com.mvfeatures/maldivian_handicrafts/handicrafts_article.htm. Tourists can make an important contribution to the preservation and promotion of traditional crafts By appreciating and purchasing quality local products, .

Male' is the best place for shopping, with lots of tourist shops and some fascinating places selling items that local people use every day in their homes or on their boats. A few shops have antiques and ephemera acquired from villages in the outer atolls, though articles made from traditional materials like wood, leaves and cotton don't last very long in the tropical climate. Resorts' island-hopping excursions will visit island villages where the souvenir shops may be cheaper than in town, but the range of crafts and souvenirs is more limited.

Every second year (in even-numbered years), usually in September, the Maldivian Trade and Craft Fair exhibits some of the best work from each atoll and there are awards in many categories. Many of the best pieces are sold to dignitaries in advance of the public opening, but remain on display until the end of the exhibition. The event is well publicised locally – for information contact the tourist board (**e** mtpb@visitmaldives.com).

Mats

The fine woven mats known as *kunaa* are one of the most attractive and uniquely Maldivian crafts, with their geometrical patterns and subdued natural colouring. They are made only in Gaaf Dhaal (South Huvadhoo Atoll), but a small selection is available in the souvenir shops in Male'. Prices vary from Rf250 for a small piece (35 sq cm), up to Rf3000 and more for a full-sized prayer mat. The best ones are tightly woven, finely patterned and have a soft feel. They can be rolled, but not folded, and are easy to carry. It's likely that quality examples of this craft will become increasingly rare.

Lacquer Work

Turned wooden boxes, lacquered in black with incised red, yellow and green floral patterns, are another attractive and distinctive Maldivian craft product called *liyelaa jehung* or *laajehun*. Traditionally, lacquer

Turtles, Coral & Conservation

In the interests of conservation, the Maldivian government has banned the capture of turtles and the import, export and sale of all turtle-shell products. You're unlikely to see turtle-shell products in shops. If you're tempted, remember that the import of any turtle products is strictly forbidden to countries that are party to the Convention on International Trade in Endangered Species (CITES) – that includes all EU countries.

It's also forbidden to sell or export any 'unfinished' coral and shell products. This means that shells and mother-of-pearl can be used for crafts, and carvings can be sold and exported, but it's illegal to sell coral branches or shells in their natural state. Most coral carvings and souvenirs are made from dead coral that has been washed ashore. Many of the painted model fish on sale are not carved coral, but a mixture of ground coral and plastic resin set in a mould. It's illegal for visitors to remove any shells or coral from beaches or during dives.

Black coral is a special case. There is some concern that natural growths of black coral are in decline due to over-exploitation, and in more accessible areas this is true. There is some talk of banning trade in black-coral products, but it is a superb material for carving and has been used for a long time.

work was for containers, bowls and trays used to present gifts and serve food. Vases and small boxes are the most common lacquer work items in tourist shops. They are very colourful and beautifully finished, and range in price from Rf250 for a small box to Rf4500 for a top-quality 40cm vase.

Jewellery
Though gold and silver work is a traditional craft *(thileyrukan)* on some islands, it is difficult to find good examples of local work. Antique bracelets, rings, necklaces and decorated boxes are now very rare, as is the traditional silver belly chain or *fattaru*. Most of the quality jewellery in shops comes from Sri Lanka, which is also a source of fine gem stones, especially sapphires. There are some stunning pieces available at good prices (look at shops on Chandanee Magu), but they are not Maldivian.

Most of the local artisans are now working in local materials like mother-of-pearl and black coral. They make beautiful 'sea jewellery' and decorative items, including rings, bracelets, necklaces and carved model dhonis.

Woodcarving
Traditionally, wood and stone carvings decorated mosques and gravestones, and wonderfully intricate and flowing designs can still be seen on several old mosques. The most interesting wooden souvenirs are beautifully made model dhonis and carved Quran rests.

Dresses
The traditional woman's *libaas*, a silk dress with the collar richly embroidered with concentric patterns of silver and gold thread *(kasabu)*, can be bought in some souvenir shops. You'll probably only find them in small sizes.

Music
Quite a few shops in Male' sell cassettes and CDs with Maldivian music, both traditional and contemporary. You can buy the Maldives' national instrument, the *bodu beru* (big drum) made from a hollowed coconut-tree trunk and covered with stingray skin – the best ones come from Felidhoo Atoll.

Maldiviana
General household items that can make good souvenirs or gifts are anything made from a coconut shell, such as toddy holders *(raabadhi)* and cups, woven palm-leaf baskets and mats *(sataa)*, and folding, carved Quran rests. Hardware and general stores in Male' sell some interesting everyday items, like wooden scoops for bailing boats, fittings for hookahs, woven trays for winnowing rice and an amazing assortment of medicinal herbs and potions.

Duty Free
The airport duty-free shops have a good range of liquor, perfume, cameras and electrical goods. Sifani Jewellers has some beautiful work with sapphires, rubies and other gems from Sri Lanka.

Choosing a Resort

You're dreaming about a Maldives holiday, looking at brochures or seeing some lovely photos as you surf the net. All the resorts look stunning, with sunny skies, swaying palm trees, white sand and blue sea, and they all promise comfortable accommodation, fine food, fun activities and great diving. How do you decide which resort is right for you?

Most visitors book into a single resort for their entire stay, and their choice is often determined by the packages and prices presented by their travel agent, rather than by any real knowledge of what the various resorts have to offer. The resorts differ considerably in their cost, comfort, cuisine, character, clientele and in their suitability for various activities.

The later chapters of this book cover all the atolls of the Maldives and include a review of every resort. This chapter gives a general overview of what resorts are like, what to look for, and what resorts are best in various categories. If diving, food, family fun or water sports appeals to you, look for the resorts suggested in that category, then check the resort review in the appropriate atoll chapter (to find the resort easily, look in the index under 'resorts'). Look at the information about that atoll too, and find the resort on the atoll map. When you find some resorts that seem just right, look for a good package tour to those places, or contact the resort directly.

If you see some great package deal advertised for Maldives holidays, find the name of the resort that the package is for, read the resort review in the text and check the location. Then look at the general resort information in this chapter, and decide if the advertised resort has the features that are important to you.

Almost every resort has its own website, and you'll find the address in the resort review. Resort websites can be great if you want to find the difference between a 'superior' and a 'deluxe' room, see a picture of the swimming pool, or get the price of weekly windsurfer rental. You may also be able to ask for room rates (you'll have to specify your exact travel dates and other details).

Every resort has a scuba-diving centre, and many of these now have their own web-sites. The best ones have dive-site maps, dive descriptions, excellent underwater photographs and information about the cost of dives, courses and equipment rental.

The quality of a resort is related to price, but the more budget resorts are of a reasonable quality and even the best resorts have less expensive rooms and cheaper low-season rates. Just about every guest in every resort seems to enjoy their holiday, so it's hard to go wrong. This book should help you find a resort that's just right.

Resort Reviews

In the later chapters of this book, covering all the atolls of the Maldives, there's a review of every resort. In some chapters, they are categorised as 'Budget Resorts', 'Mid-Range Resorts' and 'Top-End Resorts', and within each category resorts are listed from north to south, in the same order as they appear on the atoll map.

Each review gives the name of the resort and the name of the island it's on – sometimes these are the same, or similar names with different spelling. There's the resort phone number (no area codes are needed in the Maldives) and usually the resort's website address.

Then there's an indicative price for a single/double room. Prices of Maldivian resorts are a complex issue (see Price Structures under Resort Packages later in this chapter), but to form a consistent basis for comparison, the price given here is for a standard room (ie, the least expensive), with full board (including breakfast, lunch and dinner), in high season (usually March; but not the Christmas–New Year peak season). The price is based on the 'published rates' (which are often not published at all), or the 'FIT rates' (the rates payable by 'fully independent travellers'). In this book, a budget resort is under US$160 a night for a double room, a mid-range resort is US$160 to US$500, and a top-end resort is over US$500.

The price that you actually pay for a room as part of a package tour will probably be lower than the price in the resort review. Most prices are in US dollars, but a few are published in euros.

Transfers from the airport to/from the resort can involve quite long boat trips (the average time is given in the review). A few resorts do transfers by dhonis (traditional Maldivian boats), but most boat transfers are by speedboat or fast launch. The time given for seaplane transfer is the flight time, but you may also spend an hour or more at the airport waiting, and some more time getting from the seaplane pontoon to the resort. Transfer costs are usually included in package holidays, but they can be a significant hidden expense – the figure in the review is for an adult return fare.

The number of rooms is an indication of the size of the resort. Anything under 60 rooms is pretty small. Larger resorts usually offer a wider choice of activities, more dive courses, more varied dive groups, bigger buffets and livelier nightlife.

The rest of the review concentrates on the things that make the resort distinctive, whether it's the natural beauty of the island, rooms, architecture, water sports on offer, mix of guests, food, nightlife, spa or snorkelling. Because diving is a major attraction and a significant expense, most reviews have information about the dive centre and dive costs.

MALDIVES RESORTS
The Resort Experience

As soon as you step out of the arrivals hall, a representative from your resort or tour company will be there to meet you. You might have to wait a while for your resort transfer (other guests may be on later flights), but most visitors start relaxing and shedding excess clothing about now. Night arrivals spend a night at the airport hotel or in Male'. Most guests have a short walk to a waiting boat and are soon speeding across the blue water to their resort. Others are bussed to the other side of the airport island where the seaplanes take off for more distant islands, flying over the surrealistic panorama of reefs, lagoons and islands.

Seaplanes usually 'land' on a lagoon and tie up at a pontoon, and a boat takes guests to the resort's main jetty. All new arrivals are greeted on the jetty (some resorts make a song and dance of this, literally) and proceed to reception where a 'welcome drink'

Quality Tourism Strategy

The first Maldivian resorts were basic beach huts made of local materials. Early visitors loved them, but the local economy didn't benefit much, environmental problems loomed, and the cultural impact was seen as a real threat. In 1978 President Gayoom came to power and the country adopted a strategy based on 'quality tourism', which is administered by tourism laws.

Resorts can be established only on uninhabited islands when the government makes them available for commercial leases. Corporations bid for the lease with a development plan that must conform to strict standards. Resort buildings cannot cover more than 20% of an island's area or be higher than the surrounding vegetation. The maximum number of rooms is limited according to the size of the island, and the resort developer must provide all the necessary infrastructure, from electricity and water supply to sewage treatment and garbage disposal.

When the lease on an island expires, the government can require a major renovation and upgrade as a condition of renewal, or it can make the island available for a new lease and call for bids and a redevelopment proposal. The bidding process is very competitive. Environmental impact and staff welfare are considerations in selecting the successful bid, but the main criterion is money – how much rent will the developer pay the government? This means that successful developers must earn the maximum return on each room, so new resorts are pushed towards the quality end of the market and old resorts are progressively upgraded. It also means that resorts need to fill their rooms, so prices are also competitive, especially during off-peak periods.

Because every resort is on its own island, a Maldives resort is an isolated and totally managed environment. Resorts can offer every modern convenience but still preserve that perfect tropical island ambience – the 'Robinson Crusoe' factor. There is minimal contact with the local people, and therefore little of the 'cultural pollution' that Maldivians saw as so undesirable in tourist destinations like Goa, Bali and the Thai coast. And resorts have a vested interest in preserving their immediate environment, so there's no litter, no noise and no pollution.

awaits (usually fancy, never alcoholic), along with a registration card to fill out. The reception area will have information from tour companies about the Maldives in general and the resort in particular. Tour company 'reps' can be contacted by phone if their clients have any problems.

Then it's off to your room, where you'll turn on the ceiling fan, take off your shoes and most of your clothes, and put them away for the rest of your stay. If the resort staff think you're on a honeymoon or romantic getaway, your bed will be decorated with flower petals.

When you go to the main restaurant for your first meal, you'll be assigned a table. You're expected to sit at the same table for the rest of your stay, so your waiter can get to know what you like. Most meals are buffet style, but the waiters get your drinks. If you don't finish your bottle of water or wine, it will be on your table for the next meal. If you don't like your table, or the people you may be seated with, you can ask for another place.

Scuba divers should head for the dive centre as soon as they can, and talk to the staff. If you have a certificate, log book and some recent dives, they'll put you with a group for your first dive. If your credentials aren't so good, they'll ask you to do a check dive first. If you're a beginner, you can book into a diving course. If you're not sure, you can try a free introductory dive at some resorts. If you just want to snorkel, rent an ABC (mask, snorkel, fins, don't ask why), and find out about the house reef or the next snorkelling boat trip.

For windsurfing, sailing, canoes, kite-surfing, water skiing or banana rides, find the water-sports centre. For island-hopping excursions, shopping trips, submarine rides, seaplane photo flights, fishing trips and romantic dinners on deserted islands, ask at the reception desk.

After a big buffet lunch, you might opt for a siesta in the hottest part of the day. Later in the afternoon you can dive or snorkel again, or have a massage or manicure. Towards the end of the day, get together for an impromptu game of beach volleyball or a football match with staff and guests from eight or more countries. Then it's off to the bar for a 'sun-downer' – a cool beer or a long cocktail as you watch the sun slip into the tropical sea.

There might be dancing at a disco, a video movie, cultural show or crab race. The romantically inclined can enjoy a drink under the stars, a stroll on the beach, a midnight swim or an early night in the flower strewn sheets.

When it comes to paying the bill, keep in mind that there is a 10% service charge on what you consume, whether it be food and drinks, aromatic massages or diving. When you leave the resort, you'll find the resort staff on the jetty, wishing you farewell from the island which is now so familiar to you.

Eating

The quality of food in Maldivian resorts has improved greatly over the years, partly due to better resort standards, and partly because the importation and distribution of ingredients has become more diversified and more reliable. Resorts can order supplies directly from overseas sources, and much of it comes in refrigerated shipping containers, or even by air freight, to Male'. Staff or contractors in Male' arrange customs clearance and trans-shipment to the resort. A few of the bigger resort islands grow vegetables and herbs which provide some fresh flavours, but not self-sufficiency.

The majority of resorts serve all meals in buffet style, so you can choose what you want and eat as much as you like. The quality and variety of the food is generally in proportion to the price and size of the resort – most buffets offer consistently tasty though not-so-original meals. The resort kitchen has to please a diverse group of nationalities and ages and still keep to an economical budget.

All-Italian resorts, however inexpensive, tend to have excellent food, and any resort with a substantial number of Italian guests will serve pasta at every meal. Those that attract lots of Brits will do bangers and mash, porridge, roast beef and even beef stew, or steak and kidney pie. A few resorts cater well to their Asian guests with Japanese-, Chinese- and Malay-style dishes.

Typically, breakfast will include a choice of cereals, canned and fresh fruit, fruit juice from cans or concentrate, instant coffee, tea, bread rolls, toast, omelettes or fried eggs done as you like, sausages, bacon, baked beans, and often a curry and rice. At more upmarket resorts you could also have muesli, yoghurt, more fresh fruits, fresh-squeezed fruit juice, brewed coffee, better bread, croissants and real ham.

For lunch, most resorts manage soup and a simple salad, pasta, rice, instant noodles, and at least one each of fish, beef and chicken dishes, often prepared as curry, casserole or stew, with fruit and desert to finish. Better resorts offer more varied salad vegetables, pasta freshly tossed with a choice of sauces, Hokkien noodles, freshly fried fish fillets and more creative chicken and beef dishes.

Dinner will usually have the biggest selection, and may be a 'theme night' specialising in some regional cuisine like Italian, Asian, Indian or Maldivian. Most resorts will have soup, salad and a dozen or so hot dishes, with at least two each of fish, beef and chicken. A few dishes will be vegetarian – ratatouille, vegetable curry, pasta *alla fungi* or potatoes Provençale. There'll be a pasta dish or three, possibly a lasagne, and stirfried noodles, as well as plain rice, saffron rice, fried rice, and maybe risotto. There's a trend for 'live cooking stations' at one or more places along the buffet tables where food is fried or barbecued to taste while you watch – great for fresh fish, prawns, pasta, steak and shish kebab. Whole fish and roast meats are carved and served as you like. Fancier resorts feature more and fresher seafood and it's less likely to be overcooked – the best places serve sashimi. Salad is another class marker – a budget resort will serve iceberg lettuce, coleslaw and cucumber with a basic bottled mayo, French or Thousand Island dressing. A better resort will have cos lettuce, rocket, radicchio, spinach leaves and three kinds of cabbage, with freshly made mayonnaise and your choice of vinegars and olive oils. Only the very best resorts have ripe, red, tasty tomatoes.

Desserts can be delicious, with pastries, fruit pies, tarts, tiramisu, mousse, blancmange, custard and cheesecake all on offer at the far end of the buffet. The best resorts might have crepes prepared at a live cooking station, and a choice of cheeses too.

Buffet meals seem to taste better if the food is well presented, and some resorts have made an art of laying out the tables, decorating them with flowers and palm

---

A Taste of the Maldives

It used to be rare to find Maldivian food in tourist resorts – the opinion was that Western stomachs couldn't cope with the spices. Now many resorts do a Maldivian barbecue once a week, which is very enjoyable if not totally authentic. These barbecues can be on the beach, by the pool or held in the restaurant. The main dishes are fresh reef fish, baked tuna, fish curries, rice and *roshi* (unleavened bread). The regular dinner buffet might also feature Maldivian fish curry. Less common is the Maldivian breakfast favourite *mas huni*, a healthy mixture of tuna, onion, coconut and chilli, eaten with *roshi*. If there's nothing Maldivian on the menu, you could ask the kitchen staff to make a fish curry or a tray of short eats – they may be making some for the staff anyway. Small resorts are usually amenable to special requests. Otherwise, do a trip to Male' or an island-hopping excursion to a fishing village, and try out a local tea shop.

---

leaves, and lighting the selection so it really looks appealing. Even inexpensive resorts can do this delightfully, while a few more pricey places feature a tacky butter sculpture and dribbling bains-marie with misspelled labels. Some resorts try to offer a vast range of dishes but don't make any of them especially well, while other, smaller resorts do a much more limited selection that's simple, well prepared and satisfying.

Budget resorts might offer a set menu only for some meals – perhaps for lunch, or on alternate days for dinner. These are OK, and will give your waistline some respite. At the other end of the market, the best resorts serve some meals à-la-carte – the chef has a chance to do something special and creative, and the waiters enjoy giving full table service.

As well as the main buffet restaurant, big resorts usually have 'speciality restaurants' serving regional cuisine (Thai, Japanese, Italian, Indian etc) or grills and seafood. These can be expensive (main courses US$15–25) and often seem poorly patronised. Speciality restaurants at the best resorts are generally excellent, like a quality restaurant in a big city (main courses around US$25–40). If full-board guests eat in speciality restaurants they should get a discount (from 10% to 25%) to offset the fact that they've already paid for all their meals. If you choose a big resort because you want the choice of several restaurants, a half-board or breakfast-only package may suit you better.

Most resorts have a 'coffee shop' serving light meals, coffee and drinks, often 24 hours a day. They're good for people on half board who want a snack in the middle of the day. A sandwich will cost about US$4–6, and a small pizza US$6–10, so this is no bargain, but it's less expensive than paying full-board rates when you don't really want a big buffet lunch.

Another alternative to the usual buffet is a 'speciality meal'. This might be a barbecue or a curry night, served on the beach, open to anyone who pays the extra charge, perhaps US$25 (unlike a theme night in the main restaurant which is not charged as an extra). Or it can be a private dinner for two in romantic surroundings – on an inhabited island, on the beach, or on a sandbar in ankle deep water. Most resorts will do special meals on request.

Drinking

Alcoholic drinks at resorts are available to non-Muslim guests and are a big earner. Expect to pay US$2.50 to US$5 for a can of beer, at least US$4 for spirits and US$6 for cocktails, and much more in some resorts. Soft drinks are usually US$2 a can.

The Lobster Dilemma

You might see lobsters when you're snorkelling on the house reef, but don't expect to find them on the buffet selection for dinner. The 'lobster dinner for two' is a special event and it can cost US$60 per person with wine and all the trimmings. Lobster lovers are willing to pay for it. Local people catch lobsters by hand and sell them live to nearby resorts – sometimes several resorts might be bidding for fresh lobster, leading to overfishing. Some resorts refuse on principle to buy fresh lobster, so they get them frozen from the Persian Gulf or the West Australian coast – but frozen lobster is a travesty in itself, and certainly not worth big bucks and a bottle of wine.

A 1500ml bottle of mineral water is usually over US$2.50, sometimes US$4.50. A service charge of 10% can be added to your bar bill as well, and drinks from a minibar in your room will be even more expensive.

A bottle of ordinary Italian or French wine will cost from US$15 to US$45 at most resorts. House wines are typically an Australian 'bag in a box' riesling or cabernet sauvignon, and cost from US$2.50 to US$6 per glass. House wines are often in poor condition, especially red wines which aren't kept under refrigeration. If the wine is bad, send it back and don't sign the invoice.

A few resorts offer packages which include soft drinks, beer, basic spirits and house wine. For a moderate drinker this would be worth at least US$15 per day, but don't expect top-quality wine or real whisky.

An increasing number of resorts serve brewed coffee, but sometimes only at the bar, and it is charged as an extra (US$3 to US$5). At most resorts you still get instant coffee with breakfast.

Entertainment

Most resorts have some kind of entertainment a couple of evenings a week. Sometimes it's a band or a disco night, and other times a Maldivian cultural show, usually a *bodu beru* (big drum) performance with dancing. Fire dancers from Sri Lanka are popular. Some resorts, especially Italian ones, have 'animators' who organise games and amusements and fun activities almost nonstop. For the less animated there might be table tennis, chess, snooker or *carrom*, a South Asian board game played with counters.

RESORT DIFFERENCES

Resorts vary in more than cuisine, and not all the differences relate to price.

Comfort

The least expensive resorts might have very plain rooms, but they all have a private bathroom, a ceiling fan and high standards of cleanliness. Very few resorts have rooms without air conditioning and hot water (some of the older resorts still have a few).

Beyond the basics, as the room rate goes up, you'll get amenities like a small fridge, IDD telephone, minibar (ie, a fridge stocked with drinks), hair dryer, minisafe, satellite TV, CD stereo system and DVD player. The goodies are added in roughly that order, though some of the best rooms don't have a TV and some of the basic ones do. The quality of the furniture also increases with the price, as does the size of the room and the tastefulness of the decor.

Many resorts offer a range of rooms and prices – the best room at a budget resort might be bigger, better and more expensive than the standard rooms at a mid-range resort. Usually the most expensive rooms are the 'over-water bungalows' or 'water villas', built on stilts over a shallow lagoon and reached by a jetty. Some guests love them and they're often fully booked. But they can lack privacy, and the surrounding water is usually too shallow for a good swim, much less a swan dive from the sundeck.

The most expensive, luxury resorts offer every comfort you could want and every indulgence you could imagine. The very best ones have a wow! factor in the way they look and feel – like a walk-through work of art where no expense has been spared.

Character

You can choose between natural-look resorts with thatched roofs, sand floors, jungle-like vegetation and a tropical island feel; or modern places with tiled roofs, polished floors, well-maintained gardens, motel-style rooms and all mod cons (TV, minibar and all). The original Maldives resorts were in natural style, usually small and with not much more than a restaurant, bar and dive school. A second generation of resorts went modern, were usually bigger, and provided all sorts of recreational facilities – swimming pool, tennis court, gym, squash court, games room, motorised water sports. The latest resorts try to have it both ways, with swimming pools, elaborate spas, full facilities and a natural look, lots of trees and open, breezy buildings.

Natural does not mean cheap, and resorts go to great expense to achieve that primitive, rustic look. The simple sand-floor restaurant is time-consuming to maintain as all the sand must be dug out and replaced a couple of times a year. And that exuberant tropical vegetation requires careful cultivation, regular irrigation and sometimes soil imported from Sri Lanka.

Clientele

The larger, cheaper resorts attract younger people, more singles, and are more casual in style, with a lot of people out to have a good time. Smaller resorts are more intimate and cosy, quieter at night – they appeal to couples and honeymooners, but a single visitor could feel left out. Some resorts attract families and children, especially at certain times of the year.

A few resorts are overwhelmingly patronised by German speakers while others can have a high proportion of French or Japanese guests. Then there are the Italian resorts, operated by Italian holiday companies, with 100% Italian guests and excellent Italian food. They are usually 'club style' resorts and feature lots of group activities, often aided by 'animators' who ensure that everyone is involved in the fun.

All resorts offer scuba diving, but some appeal especially to hardcore divers, who dive all day, talk diving at dinner and collapse early into bed – at these places the nondiver may feel like a fish out of water.

Activities

Though you can dive from any resort, some are better for diving than others, and dive costs vary between resorts. Snorkelling is also much better at some resorts than others (see the individual resort reviews for comments). The Snorkelling & Diving special section has lots of information about Mal-diving in general. For very detailed information, check the website of the resort dive centre.

Most resorts offer windsurfing and catamaran sailing too, but the most suitable ones are those with a wide, deep lagoon and other islands you can sail to. Some have a wider choice of equipment and more comprehensive courses. Only a few resorts are near to surf breaks and only a couple are really suitable for surfers. A few have motorised water sports, and only some have tennis and squash courts, gyms and swimming pools. See the Activities section in the Facts for the Visitor chapter for more on things to do, and check resort websites for specific details.

Spas

Nearly every resort now has a spa of some sort, offering massages, beauty treatments, and various types of hands-on therapy. In some new, luxury developments, the spa is central to the 'concept' of the resort, and it's a fabulously lavish facility in a gorgeous setting (and well described in the resort's publicity). Many older resorts have just retro-fitted a couple of regular rooms with massage tables. The luxury spas tend to emphasise relaxation and beauty treatments, while some smaller spas have a more clinical atmosphere and promote the therapeutic benefits of the Indian, Ayurvedic techniques. Prices for a 55-minute massage run from about US$40 to US$60.

RESORT PACKAGES

It's cheaper to get a package deal than to travel independently, because the big travel companies get the best wholesale room rates, and can access discount group airfares and charter flights. The prices in this book are just a guide – what really counts is the deal you can actually get from your travel agent, tour company or online discounter.

The very cheapest resorts start at around US$70 per day in the low season for a standard double room with full board (ie, breakfast, lunch and dinner), which is very good value. Most resorts for most of the year will cost at least US$120 a day for a double room and full board; room and full board at a top-end resort could cost US$1000 or even more. Standard package prices are usually for one week's holiday including airfares and transfers, so it's hard to know the cost of the resort itself – most brochures give a rate for an extra night's stay, and this should give you some idea of the cost of room and board.

A bed tax of US$6 per person per night is included in all resort prices.

Price Structures

Even for a specific resort, the pricing structures are enormously complex, with multiple pricing periods, Christmas dinner surcharges, various meal plans, different room types, single supplements, and extra bed rates.

Pricing Periods Pricing patterns vary with the resort and the demands of its main market – some are incredibly detailed and complex with a different rate every week. The basic pattern is that Christmas–New Year is the peak season, with very high prices, minimum-stay requirements and surcharges for Christmas dinner and New Year's Eve. Early January to late March is high season, when many Europeans take a winter holiday. The weeks around Easter may attract even higher rates (but not as high as Christmas). From Easter to about mid-July is low season (and the wettest part of the year). July, August and September is another high season, for the European summer holidays. Mid-September to early December is low season again.

Specific markets can have their own times of high demand, such as the August holiday week for Italians, Chinese New Year in the Asian market or the end of Ramadan for some Middle-Eastern guests.

Meal Plans Most guests are on 'full board' packages that include accommodation and all meals. Some take a 'half-board' package, which includes dinner, bed and breakfast, and pay extra if they want lunch. Some resorts offer a 'bed-and-breakfast' plan, and guests pay separately for lunch and dinner. Very few have a 'room-only' deal, with no meals included. The resort restaurants are the only places to eat anyway, and they're not cheap. If you don't eat a big lunch, the half-board plan may be the most economic option in total. But unless you're a *very* light eater, the amount you'd save on a 'bed-and-breakfast' plan would be less than the extra cost of à la carte dinners.

Some resorts have an 'all-inclusive' plan, which includes soft drinks, beer, house wine, 'nonpremium' spirits (think Indian gin, Sri Lankan whisky), and maybe some water-sports equipment or excursions.

In a budget-resort package, the cost of meals would be about US$10 for breakfast, US$10 for lunch, and US$15 for dinner (so full-board will cost US$35 per person on top of the room-only rate). An 'all inclusive' plan might be an extra US$35 per person per day on top of the full-board rate. At a top-end resort, add as much as US$25 for breakfast, US$30 for lunch and US$55 for dinner.

Room Types Some resorts have just one type of room, which may be called 'Superior', 'Deluxe', or 'Super Deluxe'. Most bigger, newer resorts have several types of room, ranging from the cheapest 'Superior Garden Villas' to the 'Deluxe Over-Water Suite'. A

'Garden Villa' will not have a beach frontage, and a 'Water Villa' will be on stilts over the lagoon and twice the cost. More expensive rooms tend to be bigger, newer, better finished, and can have a bathtub as well as a shower, a minibar instead of an empty fridge, tea- and coffee-making facilities, a CD sound system or a jacuzzi.

Single Supplements & Extra Beds This book gives room rates for single/double occupancy, but most package-deal prices are quoted on a per-person basis, assuming double occupancy. Solo travellers have to pay a 'single-person supplement' for the privilege of having a room all to themselves.

Extra people can usually share a room, but there's a charge for the extra bed (at least US$15 for a child, US$30 for an adult) as well as additional costs for meals. In a package-tour price list, this appears as a supplement for children sharing the same room as parents, or for extra adults sharing a room.

For children two years and younger, usually just the US$6 bed tax is payable. From two to 12 years, the child supplement with full board will be from US$15 to US$30 in most budget to mid-range resorts, but much more in expensive resorts. Transfers from the airport are charged at half the adult rate. A more expensive, option is to get two adjacent rooms, ideally with a connecting door. You might get a discount on the second room.

Speciality Packages
Diving All Maldivian resorts offer scuba diving, so any package tour include diving. Some 'diving packages' may include dive costs in the tour price, as well as bonuses like a dive guidebook or a slightly higher baggage allowance, but do not offer any diving facilities or services that are unavailable to guests on a regular package. Some resorts are more focused on diving (see Diving under Recommended Resorts later in this chapter), but an advertised diving package may be just a travel agent promoting a resort that has no special attraction for divers.

Honeymoon A typical 'honeymoon package' includes a bottle of champagne on arrival, a fruit basket, and some flowers sprinkled over the king-size bed, but it's otherwise identical to a regular holiday package. Some travel agents charge extra for the honeymoon package while others offer it as a bonus (just tick the box marked 'honeymoon' on the booking form – some couples always tick this box in the hope of freebies, upgrades and better service). Almost every resort will have some complimentary extras for a honeymoon couple, but some resorts have a much more romantic ambience than others.

Spa Luxury resorts promote their spa facilities heavily and may advertise some special spa packages. All that pampering can certainly look attractive to the stressed-out city dweller! You might get priority reservations for the treatment of your choice and a small discount for using lots of spa services, but booking your trip as a spa package won't get you anything that's unavailable on the usual holiday. Most mid-range Maldives resorts offer massage and relaxation treatments – you don't have to book into the super-deluxe places.

Surfing The best surf tours are a genuine specialist travel package, offering services that are unavailable to the other resort guests – unlimited use of boats to the nearby surf breaks, a surf guide and access to the resort's own private reef break.

Extras
The cost doesn't end with the package tour price – extras add a lot to the cost of a Maldives holiday. Drinks will usually cost extra, apart from coffee or tea with meals and juice with breakfast. The price of drinks usually depends on the cost of the resort, although some cheap resorts charge top prices for drinking water. See Drinking under Maldives Resorts earlier in this chapter.

If you only take a half-board package, allow at least US$7 for a light lunch. Even with full board you can pay extra for a beach barbecue or a speciality restaurant meal.

Diving costs vary too, but a keen diver in a mid-price resort should allow maybe US$430 per week if they have their own equipment and US$540 if they're renting everything. This is based on about US$270 for a 10-dive package (or US$370 with equipment rental), plus US$12 per dive for the use of a boat, plus a little for tips and/or service charges. If you're a keen beginner, allow US$480 to US$600 for an open-water dive course. If you're here to dive, you won't count the cost and you won't regret it.

For windsurfing, night tennis, island-hopping excursions or snorkel hire, allow US$25 to US$35 per day. A short phone call home will add at least US$15 or so to your room bill, and Internet access isn't cheap either, from US$5 to US$12 for half an hour.

RECOMMENDED RESORTS

The best resort is the one that suits you best, that meets your needs, appeals to your taste and fits your budget. Here are some specific suggestions.

Families

Families have the most fun when kids can play with other kids their own age and their parents can relax with other parents. Try to come during school-holiday periods, when there are likely to be others on holiday too. Bigger resorts will probably get more kids than small resorts, and will have more room for energetic youngsters to run around. A few resorts boast a children's playground, some offer childcare and most will arrange a babysitter, but none is making a major pitch for the family market. Four Seasons and Kanuhuraa are top-end resorts with kids' clubs. Medhufushi, Filitheyo, Club Med Kani, Paradise Island, Laguna Beach, Bandos and Kuramathi are also quality, kid-friendly places. Meeru, Kuredu, Lily Beach and Sun Island could be as much fun for a lot less.

Singles

None of the resorts in the Maldives has a major singles scene. Bandos is a big resort, close to Male' and gets an interesting variety of guests, including expat workers, airline crews and day-trippers. Kuredu and Meeru are both big resorts with budget rooms and a relaxed atmosphere. Club Med Faru is a fun place with a no-kids policy, and it could be a good choice. Sun Island gets lots of guests from all over, and some of them have to be single. Ari Beach used to be *the* party island – it's now called White Sands and it's quieter, but still fun.

Romantic

If romantic means an intimate, private place with a lovely garden setting, secluded beach frontage, warm nights and cool scented breezes, then you'll find plenty of possibilities. The most romantic rooms have king-size, four-poster beds draped with diaphanous mosquito nets swaying under a slow ceiling fan. Natural finishes, subtle lighting and soft music help make the mood, as does an outdoor bathroom where you can splash in the moonlight.

A romantic resort can arrange a massage for two in a sumptuous spa, a dinner for two on a desert island, or a midnight snack in your room. To get the works, and if price is no object, look at Banyan Tree, Four Seasons, Soneva Gili, Taj Exotica, Coco Palm, Nika Hotel or the over-water rooms at the Hilton. For a slightly less expensive romance, try Kanuhuraa, Medhufushi, Mirihi, Makunudu Island or Kudahithi Relais. Even more cost-conscious romantics could consider the better rooms at less expensive resorts, like Baros, Villu Reef, Reethi Beach Resort, White Sands or Kuredu.

Over-Water Rooms

The Water Villa Suites at Soneva Gili are stunning, as are the Sunset Water Villa Suites at the Hilton. Medhufushi, Taj Exotica, Kanuhuraa, Mirihi, Coco Palm, Filitheyo, Olhuveli, Kuredo and White Sands all have something special over their lagoons. The new Cocoa Island may be a contender.

Back to Nature

Soneva Fushi is the masterpiece of designer back-to-nature, starting with a large, lush island and nestling in luxury rooms and suites with rustic finishes. Makanudu is much smaller and more low-key, but naturally delightful. Other, mostly upmarket resorts with natural appeal are Nika Hotel, Rihiveli, Medhufushi, Kanuhura, Filitheyo and Reethi Beach. Inexpensive resorts on natural looking islands include Palm Beach, Fihalhohi, Meedhupparu, Vilamendhoo and Asdu Sun Island.

High Style

If you'd like a resort that's straight from the pages of a glossy, designer magazine, with interiors and finishes that scream style and class, try Soneva Gili, Taj Exotica, Medhufushi, Four Seasons, Mirihi, Hilton, Kanuhuraa or Soneva Fushi.

Sheer Luxury & Total Indulgence

Looking for a combination of total comfort, impeccable service, fine cuisine, a lavish spa and really high prices? Go for the best rooms at Soneva Gili, Soneva Fushi, Four Seasons, the Hilton or Taj Exotica. Banyan Tree, Medhufushi and Kanuhuraa are close to perfection, but may not be expensive enough.

Food

The resorts with the very best cuisine are also the most expensive, notably the Hilton, Four Seasons, Soneva Fushi, Soneva Gili and Banyan Tree. Some slightly less expensive resorts also have excellent food, such as Taj Exotica, Coco Palm, Mirihi, Rihiveli, Filitheyo and Medhufushi.

Beaches

Many resorts have stunning beaches, including Meedhupparu, Kanuhuraa, Kuredu, Palm Beach, Soneva Fushi, Reethi Beach Resort, Royal Island, Coco Palm, Meedhupparu, Eriyadu, Angsana, Bandos, Baros, Banyan Tree, Soneva Gili, Club Med Kani, Rihiveli, Club Rannalhi, Fihalhohi, Sun Island, Bathala, Thudufushi, Veligandu, Villu Reef, Vakarufalhi, Fesdu, Filitheyo, Fun Island and the Hilton.

Diving

The best dive islands have great diving on a handy house reef, a lot of keen divers as guests and a totally dedicated dive centre. Ellaido, Bathala, Vadoo, Mirihi and Helengeli have all been known as hardcore divers islands. They've all upgraded their facilities and broadened their markets, but still have excellent house reefs and attract the serious divers. Biyadhoo and Villivaru are changing soon, but their house reefs will always have diver appeal. Eriyadu, Machchafushi, Vilamendhoo, Filitheyo, Reethi Beach, Embudu Village, Fesdu, Vakarufalhi and Kuredu all have great house reefs and keen divers. Dhigufinolhu and Velavaru lack good house reefs but compensate with first-class dive centres. For access to some of the best coral reefs in the country, untouched by coral bleaching, Equator Village is well worth the detour.

Snorkelling

The most interesting snorkelling is on reef edges where fish congregate, the coral growth is varied and the reef topography is most exciting. Any resort with an accessible edge on its house reef will be good (see the recommended diving resorts in the Diving section above), but some reefs are recovering from coral bleaching better than others. Kuredu has a complete program of snorkelling instruction and guided trips. Angsana and Banyan Tree are interesting for their efforts to regrow coral, and Lily Beach is helping turtles thrive round its shores. Equator Village has access to pristine coral reefs, but they're a 40-minute boat ride away. (See also the Snorkelling & Diving special section.)

Surfing

Dhonveli and Lhohifushi are the only two resorts that have a really good wave that you can reach from the shore. See Resort-Based Surfing under Activities in Facts for the Visitor chapter.

Water Sports

The best resorts for sailing and windsurfing have a wide lagoon that's not too shallow, and lots of equipment to choose from. Check out Kuramathi, Kanuhuraa, Meeru, Summer Island, Club Med Faru, Club Med Kani and Vilu Reef. Olhuveli, Reethi Beach and Kuredu are good choices too, and also offer kitesurfing.

Just about any resort will do sunset-, sunrise- or night-fishing trips, but it's a more authentically Maldivian experience at small, locally run resorts like Asdu Sun Island and Thulhagiri. Most resorts near Male' can arrange a big-game fishing trip, including Bandos, Baros, Club Med Faru, Full Moon, Kurumba, Laguna and Nakatchafushi.

The modern-style resorts are best for motorised water sports. You'll find jet skis and other not-so-cheap thrills at Fun Island, Holiday Island, Paradise Island, Royal Island and Sun Island.

Budget Resorts

A Maldives holiday can be affordable if you settle for an ordinary room and compromise on cuisine. You get the same sun and sea as the luxury resorts, and a friendly

Useful Tips

Contact the resort for specific, up-to-date information. Is there construction work happening on the island? Is the spa finished yet? Do they have a babysitting service?

Check the dive-centre website. They might provide a discount if you book your dives before your arrival. Email them for any specific dive information. Do they rent prescription face masks? Do they offer nitrox diving?

If the trip is a honeymoon, or second honeymoon, or if you will be celebrating an anniversary or birthday, let your travel agent or tour company know – the resort might surprise you.

Leave the resort phone number with your friends/family – calling the Maldives is expensive, but calling from a Maldives resort is astronomical.

informal atmosphere at Bathala, Thulhagiri, Asdu Sun Island, Giraavaru, Summer Island, Embudu Village, Kandooma, Club Rannalhi, Fihalhohi and Equator Village. For a budget room at a bigger resort, try Kuredu, Meeru, and White Sands. Some of the flash, modern resorts have inexpensive rooms, but allow some money for the extras at Sun Island, Fun Island and Holiday Island.

All-Round Appeal & Value

Some resorts are extra appealing and offer very good value for money. In approximate order of price, it is worth looking at Embudu Village, Fihalhohi, Kuredu, Meeru, White Sands, Fun Island, Helengeli, Olhuveli, Lily Beach, Club Med Faru, Rihiveli, Reethi Beach, Filitheyo, Madoogali, Mirihi, Makunudu, Kanuhura and Medhufushi.

Distinctive Resorts

A few resorts present their guests with some special quality or unusual features:

Kuramathi has three resorts on one island, a great lagoon and access to Rasdhoo village.

Dhonveli Beach provides unbeatable surfing services, a private surf break and Italian club ambience.

Soneva Gili stands out as a super-luxurious designer resort, which provides all of its guests with amazing over-water bungalows.

Taj Exotica serves all à la carte meals of epicurean quality – no buffets here.

Dhigufinolhu features fine food, a dedicated dive operation, and walkways to other resorts.

Club Rannalhi, an economical Italian club-style resort, welcomes non-Italians and hearty eaters.

Rihiveli is a charming, idiosyncratic, natural-style, French-influenced resort.

The Hilton has unforgettable cuisine, an unbelievable wine cellar and an in-house sommelier.

Equator Village, a recycled air base, offers free access to Maldivian villages and the best coral in the country.

Nika Hotel was the original, all natural, luxury resort with designer style, and it's still superb.

Sun Island is the biggest and the slickest of all. It's the resort with the lot.

DIGITAL RESOURCES

Check the Maldives tourist office website w www.visitmaldives.com to find exactly what activities and facilities are available at each resort.

The websites of Male'-based travel and tourism companies have information about many resorts, biased towards the ones they represent. Try w www.hellomaldives.com, w www.innermaldives.com, w www.capital travel.com, w www.crowntoursmaldives.com, w www.skorpion-maldives.com or w www .sunholidays.com.

PACKAGE-TOUR COMPANIES

Many companies, especially in Europe, sell holiday packages to the Maldives. Look for their brochures in your travel agent or contact them online.

The UK

First Choice (w www.firstchoice.co.uk)
Hayes & Jarvis (w www.hayesandjarvis.co.uk)
JMC (w www.jmc.com)
Kuoni (w www.kuoni.co.uk)
Thomas Cook (w ww1.thomascook.co.uk)
Thomson (w www.thomson-holidays.com)

Austria

Kuoni (w www.kuoni.at)
Neckermann (w www.neckermann.at)
TUI (w www.tui-reisecenter.at)

The over-water bungalows at Coco Palm Resort on Dhunikolhu island, South Maalhosmadulu Atoll

Ocean view at Club Med Faru, North Male' Atoll

Aerial view of a resort

The 'infinity pool' at Male's Four Seasons Resort, Kudahuraa island

Soneva Gili resort, Lankanfushi island

Room interior in an over-water bungalow

Budget rooms at a Maldivian resort

Belgium
Globus (**W** www.beltravel.net/
  globusreizen)
Jetair (**W** www.jetair.be)

France
Nouvelles Frontières (**W** www.nouvelles
  frontieres.fr)
Voyages Kuoni (**W** www.kuoni.fr)

Germany
ITS (**W** www.its.de)
Jahn Reisen (**W** www.jahn-reisen.de)
LTU (**W** www.ltu.de)
Meridian Reisen (**W** www.meridian.de)
Neckermann (**W** www.neckermann.de)

Italy
Club Vacanze (**W** www.clubvacanze.com)
Franco Rossi (**W** www.francorosso)
Turisanda (**W** www.turisanda.it)
Viaggi Kuoni (**W** www.kuonigastaldi.it)
Teorema (**W** www.teorematour.it)
Valtur (**W** www.valtur.it)

The Netherlands
Globas (**W** www.globas.com)
Sportreizen Service (**W** www.sportreizen.nl)

Spain
Kuoni (**W** www.kuoni.es)

Sweden
Apollo (**W** www.apollo.se)
Fritids Resor (**W** www.fritidsresor.se)

Switzerland
Kuoni (**W** www.kuoni.ch)
Manta Reisen (**W** www.mantareisen.ch)
PlanHotel (**W** www.planhotel.ch)
Tropic Tours (**W** www.tropic.ch)

Australia & New Zealand
Atoll Travel (**W** www.atolltravel.com.au)
Singapore Airlines (**W** www.siaholidays.com.au)

The USA & Canada
Singapore Airlines (**W** www.singaporeair.com)
Waterways Travel (**W** www.waterways.com)

Getting There & Away

Aside from a few yachties and cruise-ship passengers, most people arrive at the Maldives by plane.

AIR
In clear weather, the atolls and islands of the Maldives archipelago look stunning from the air – it's worth getting a window seat.

Airports
There's only one international airport in the Maldives – Male' International Airport (☎ 322075), on the island of Hulhule, 2km across the water from the capital.

Immigration and health checks are usually straightforward, especially if you are on the way to a resort with all the other passengers. Customs checks are quite thorough and involve an X-ray of all your luggage – if you have any alcohol it will be taken away, but you'll get it back when you leave.

As you leave the arrivals hall, you will see rows of counters with resort representatives and inbound tour operators. They pick out their own clients (the baggage tags are the obvious indicator), check them off their list and escort them to a boat or seaplane for transfer to the resort. The representative will usually collect all the air tickets from arriving passengers so that outward flights can be reconfirmed; tickets are returned to the passengers before they check out at the end of their stay. This is standard procedure and the tickets are always returned. Fully independent travellers (FITs) may be approached by independent travel agents, who should have an ID card and licence. Officially, touts are prohibited.

The tourist-information desk, airport shop and Bank of Maldives window are usually open for the arrival of incoming flights, but don't count on it if you are arriving late at night. The airport shop sells phonecards, and there are a few public card phones.

If you're heading into Male', go past the resort reps counters, continue over to the waterfront, and look for the next dhoni (traditional Maldivian boat) departing for town. They go every 15 minutes and charge Rf10.

Baggage Storage The airport baggage storage room is in the arrivals lobby, just to the right of the Maldives Tourist Promotion Board (MTPB) information desk. The cost is US$3 per piece per 24 hours. There's no left-luggage service in Male' itself, unless you get day use of a hotel room.

Tickets
Cheap fares are most likely to be offered in conjunction with a holiday package, especially during low season, and some of the cheapest are charter flights. It is still worth doing some research. Start early – some of the cheapest packages have to be bought months in advance. Look at the ads in newspapers, magazines and the Internet, watch for special offers and phone travel agents.

Once you have your ticket, write its number down, together with the flight number and other details. If the ticket is lost or stolen, this will help you get a replacement.

It's sensible to buy travel insurance as early as possible, to cover the cost of any delays that may occur before your scheduled departure.

Airlines Carriers with regular flights to the Maldives are Air Europe, Air Seychelles, Austrian Airlines, Condor, Edelweiss, Emirates, Eurofly, Indian Airlines, Lauda Air Italy, LTE International Airways, LTU, Malaysia Airlines, Monarch Airlines,

---

Warning

The information in this chapter is particularly vulnerable to change. Prices for international travel are volatile, routes are introduced and cancelled, schedules change, special deals come and go, and rules and visa requirements are amended. You should check directly with the airline or a travel agent to make sure you understand how a fare (and ticket you may buy) works, and be aware of the security requirements.

The upshot of this is that you should get opinions, quotes and advice from as many airlines and travel agents as possible before you part with your hard-earned cash. The details given in this chapter should be regarded as pointers and are not a substitute for your own careful, up-to-date research.

Qatar Airways, Singapore Airlines and SriLankan Airlines. See the Male' chapter for telephone numbers.

The Maldivian airline, Island Aviation, only does domestic flights.

Travellers with Special Needs

If you have special needs of any sort, you should let the airline know as soon as possible so that it can make arrangements. Remind them when you reconfirm your booking and again when you check in at the airport.

Most international airports will provide escorts from check-in desk to plane when needed, and should have ramps, lifts and wheelchair-accessible toilets. Aircraft toilets may present a problem, which travellers should discuss this with the airline and, if necessary, with their doctor. Deaf travellers can ask for airport and in-flight announcements to be written down for them

The UK

All scheduled flights will involve a stop in the Middle East, Sri Lanka or India, but some charter flights are direct. The cheapest fares will be as part of a tour package. You may be able to get flight-only fares on charter flights. Discounted return fares on scheduled airlines start at around £510 in low season, £600 in high season.

Any travel agent should have a number of Maldives packages to choose from. Independent travellers can shop for flights at big discount travel agents:

STA Travel (☎ 0870-1600599, W www.statravel .co.uk)

Trailfinders (☎ 020-79383939, W www.trail finders.co.uk)

Bridge the World (☎ 0870-4447447, W www .bridgetheworld.com)

Continental Europe

Most of the flights from Europe are charter flights available only to those on a package tour. Many other packages use scheduled flights, which are usually more comfortable, but slightly more expensive.

There are five direct flights per week from Germany to Male': Condor from Frankfurt and Munich; LTU from Dusseldorf, Frankfurt and Munich. Qatar, Emirates

and SriLankan have connections with a stop in the Middle East or Colombo. Fares start around €560 to €610 in low season, €850 plus in high season. Try STA Travel (☎ 01805-456422; W www.statravel.de) for student or budget fares. Also try your luck with a 'last minute' (stand-by) flight, occasionally available at most major airports in Germany.

From the Netherlands, most flights are via cities in Europe or the Middle East. Low-season fares are from about €860. NBBS (☎ 0900-1020300; W www.nbbs.nl), (now incorporated in MyTravel Reiswinkels) have brochures in MyTravel shops in many locations.

SriLankan Airlines has one direct flight a week from Paris, France; Emirates, Qatar and other airlines fly via the Middle East. Low-season fares are from around €700 to €800. Agencies for good fare deals include OTU Voyages (☎ 0-820-817-817; W www.otu.fr), with offices around the country; Nouvelles Frontières (☎ 0-825-000-825; W www.nouvelles-frontieres.fr); and Voyageurs du Monde (☎ 01 42 86 16 40; W www.vdm.com).

From Italy, Rome and Milan have some direct flights, but most are via Colombo or the Middle East. Low-season fares start around €680. CTS Viaggi (☎ 840-501150, W www.cts.it) is a student and budget airfare specialist with offices in major cities.

Zurich, Switzerland, has five direct flights per week. The best-known source of budget airfares is SSR (☎ 01-297 1111; W www.ssr.ch), which is affiliated with STA Travel. Low-season fares are around Sfl200.

From Austria there's one direct flight from Vienna per week, with others via Zurich, Colombo or the Middle East. The national student organisation, ÖKISTA, has travel services from STA Travel (☎ 01-401480; W www.statravel.at).

South Asia

There are frequent flights between Male' and its regional neighbours. From Colombo, Sri Lanka, return fares are around US$185 on SriLankan Airlines (W www .srilankan.lk).

There are no direct flights from Pakistan, but Emirates fly from Karachi via Dubai. From India, all flights to the Maldives are via Thiruvananthapuram (Trivandrum), in

Kerala, which has daily connections with Indian Airlines (w www.indian-airlines .nic.in) for a standard economy fare of Rs7265.

Southeast Asia

The best connections to Male' are from Singapore, which has daily flights with Singapore Airlines (w www.singaporeair.com) for about S$1010. There are also two flights weekly from Kuala Lumpur, Malaysia, with Malaysia Airlines (w www.malaysiaairlines .com.my).

Flights from other centres, including Hong Kong, Tokyo and Bangkok, will go via Singapore, Kuala Lumpur or Colombo. The most competitive places to buy tickets are discount travel agents in Bangkok, Singapore or KL.

Australia

The most convenient flights from Australia to the Maldives are with Singapore Airlines (w www.singaporeair.com), though from some cities this may involve a long stop (up to 14 hours) in Singapore. A discount three-month excursion fare from Melbourne, Sydney, Brisbane or Adelaide via Singapore to Male', is around A$1600 in the low season and over A$2000 in the high season (22 November to 31 January).

The cheapest flights are with SriLankan Airlines, via Singapore and Colombo or Kuala Lumpur and Colombo (a partner airline does the link out of Australia). A three-month excursion fare to Male' in low season is about A$1500.

For cheap tickets, try **Flight Centre** (☎ 131-600; w www.flightcentre.com.au) or **STA Travel** (☎ 1300-733035; w www.sta travel.com.au).

New Zealand

The most convenient route from New Zealand is a Singapore Airlines or Air New Zealand flight from Auckland or Christchurch to Singapore, changing there for a Maldives flight with Singapore Airlines. Shop for airfares at **Flight Centre** (☎ 0800-243544; w www.flightcentre.co.nz) **STA Travel** (☎ 0800-874773; w www.statravel.co.nz).

Middle East

Dubai has daily connections to Male', directly with or via Colombo with SriLankan.

Qatar Airways has seven flights a week from Doha to Male'.

Africa & Indian Ocean

From most of Africa, get a flight via the Middle East. South Africans can reach the Maldives via the Seychelles. Air Seychelles has a flight every Sunday from Mahe to Male'.

The USA & Canada

There are no direct flights from North America to the Maldives, which is almost exactly half a world away, hence the relatively small number of American visitors. From the west coast the most direct routes are via Singapore; from the east coast, it's better via Europe (Zurich, Frankfurt) and/or the Middle East (Dubai).

SEA
Boat

The occasional cruise ship drops by, but there are no regular passenger boats travelling to and from the Maldives. It might be possible to get on a cargo ship, but you'll have to be keen (and lucky).

Private Yacht

The Maldives has not been a popular stop for cruising yachties, but more are coming through and official policy is becoming more welcoming. Negatives are the maze of reefs that can make it a hazardous area, the high fees for cruising permits, the officialdom, the restrictions on where yachts can go, and the absence of lively little ports with cheap cafés and waterfront bars.

There are plans for a new, 100-berth marina for visiting yachts in the far north of the country, but facilities are minimal at the moment. Addu, in the far south, has a sheltered anchorage, a tourist resort and refuelling and resupply facilities.

The three points where a yacht can get an initial 'clear in' are Uligamu (Ihavandhippolhu Atoll) in the north, Hithadhoo/Gan (Addu Atoll) in the south, and Male'. Call in on VHF channel 16 to the NSS Coastguard and follow the instructions. If you're just passing through and want to stop only briefly, a 72-hour permit is usually easy to arrange. If you want to stay longer in Maldivian waters, or stop for provisions, you'll have to do immigration, customs, port authority and quarantine checks, and get a cruising permit. This can only be done in Male', but latest reports are that authorities in Uligamu and Addu can do most of the clear-in procedures.

If you want to stop at Male', arrive well before dark, go to the east side of Viligili Island, between Viligili and Male', and call the coastguard on channel 16. Officially, all boats require a pilot, but they don't usually insist for boats under 30m. Carefully follow the coastguard's instructions on where to anchor, or you may find yourself in water that's very deep, or too shallow. Then contact one of the port agents, like **AMSCO** (☎ 33878; ᴡ www.amsco.com.mv), **Island Sailors** (☎ 337539; ᴡ www.islandsailors.com/sub/requirements.htm) or **FIFO** (☎ 317641; ᴇ fifo@dhivehinet.net.mv), if they haven't already contacted you. They can arrange for port authority, immigration, customs and quarantine checks, and advise on repairs, refueling etc. They'll charge about US$175 for a two-week stay, including all government charges – it would be a nightmare to do it all without an agent's help. After the initial checks you'll be able to cross to the lagoon beside Hulhumale', the reclaimed land north of the airport. This is a good anchorage. The bigger stores, like STO People's Choice and Fantasy, have quite a good range of provisions at reasonable prices. The port agents can advise on other necessities like radio repairs, water and fuelling. Diesel fuel is about Rf5 per litre.

The cost of a cruising permit increases greatly with the length of stay – the first two weeks are free, the first month is US$200, the second month is US$300. Customs, port and inspection charges increase with the size of the boat. If you go cruising in the tourism zone you'll be able to stop at many of the resorts to eat, drink, swim, dive and spend your money, but you should always call the resort first. Usually you have to be off the island by sunset.

Before you leave Maldivian waters, don't forget to 'clear out' at Uligamu, Hithadhoo or Male'.

Getting Around

Transport between the many Maldives' atolls and islands is by limited domestic air services and local cargo boats. Transfers between the airport and the resorts are by seaplane, local boat (dhoni) or speedboat, and are arranged by agents as part of a holiday package. Boats and seaplanes can be chartered for special trips, though this is expensive.

The other option is a live-aboard 'safari boat' trip, cruising around the atolls with stops for diving and sightseeing (see the Safari Cruises section in the Facts for the Visitor chapter).

AIR
Domestic Air Services
There is a local airline **Island Aviation** (☎ 335544; Ⓦ *www.island.com.mv*) which runs daily flights between Male' and four small domestic airfields in the outer atolls. Its fleet comprises a 37-seat Dash-8 jet and a 16-seat Dornier 228 turbo-prop. The Dornier is fun to fly in, but has very limited cargo capacity (surfboards and diving gear may not get on your flight). Fares are in US dollars for foreigners, or in Maldivian rufiya for locals – the rufiya fares are much lower.

Island Aviation has one or two flights per day to Gan, in Addu Atoll, in the far south of the country. The foreigners fare is US$119/238 one way/return, and a direct flight takes about 1½ hours. If you book a package to the Equator Village resort on Gan, this flight will be included.

Sometimes the Gan flight makes a stop at Kaadedhoo Island (KDM), near Thinadhoo in Gaaf Dhaal Atoll; on other days there are direct flights between Male' and Kaadedhoo (US$94/188 one way/return; 70 minutes). This is the airfield that's used by surfers joining a safari trip in Gaaf Dhaal.

The other internal flight to the southern atolls goes Kadhoo Island (airport code KDO) in Laamu Atoll (US$64/128 one way/return; one hour) five times a week.

The only air connection to the northern atolls is to Hanimaadhoo Island in South Haa Daahl Atoll (airport code HAQ), which has daily flights (US$64/128 one way/return; one hour).

To/From Resorts
Maldivian Air Taxi *(MAT;* ☎ *315201;* Ⓔ *ma taxi@dhivehinet.net.mv)* is a Maldivian company managed by Danes using seaplanes made in Canada. MAT's standard aircraft is a 16-seat De Havilland Twin Otter. They take off from the lagoon just east of Male' airport and fly mainly to resorts in Ari Atoll. Usually they 'land' in a lagoon, tie up to a pontoon and the passengers are ferried to their resorts by dhoni. Note that cargo capacity on the seaplanes is limited. All passengers and baggage are weighed before loading, and some heavy items may have to wait for a later flight or be transferred by boat.

Trans Maldivian Airways *(*☎ *325708;* Ⓦ *www.tma.com.mv)* also uses De Havilland Twin Otters and also offers very good service. They have their own terminal building on the east side of the airport island, take off from the lagoon there, and 'land' at pontoons or near the resorts.

All seaplane transfers are made during daylight hours, and they offer a fantastic perspective on the atolls, islands, reefs and lagoons. The cost is from US$140 to US$250 return, depending on the distance and the deal between the resorts and the agents, and it's generally included in the package price. If there is an option of a boat transfer, the seaplane will be charged as an extra.

Charter flights for sightseeing, photography and emergency evacuation can be arranged. Call both companies for rates and availability.

SEA
You'll almost certainly spend some of your time in the Maldives on a boat. Dive trips and excursions are mostly within the sheltered waters of an atoll and will be very pleasant. If you're transferring from the airport to a resort outside North Male' Atoll, you'll be crossing much deeper, more open water and it might get a lot rougher.

The departure time and the duration of a trip depends on the weather and sea conditions. Skippers always allow lots of time for a trip and are very cautious. Boats that regularly carry passengers have life jackets, but radios, life rafts and rescue gear are installed only on fancier boats.

Dhoni

The dhoni is the traditional all-purpose vessel of the Maldives. Dhonis come in various sizes with various superstructures, but the hull is always basically the same shape. Most are now powered by diesel engines, but they sometimes have a sail as a backup, or to save fuel when the winds oblige.

The basic fishing boat, the *mas dhoni*, has been modified for use as a short-distance ferry between Male' and the airport, and to/from nearby resorts and islands. The motorised dhoni has a diesel engine, a fabric roof to keep off the sun and the rain, and a wooden bench running down each side. Passengers face each other and any luggage is stacked down the middle. Dhonis are used for most diving trips and island excursions. If the weather is rough, passengers and luggage can both get wet.

To/From Resorts Dhonis move at the leisurely pace of around 10km/h, but they're fine for transfers to resorts close to the airport. Dhoni transfers will cost about US$30 to US$60 depending on distance, and they're usually included in the basic package price.

Dhoni Charters In Male', go along the waterfront at the eastern end of Marine Drive (Boduthakurufaanu Magu), and you'll find many dhonis waiting in the harbour. Most of these are available for charter to nearby islands. The price depends on where you want to go, for how long, and on your negotiating skills – somewhere between Rf1000 and Rf1500 for a day is a typical rate, but if you want to start at 6am and go nonstop for 12 hours, it could be quite a bit more. You can also charter a dhoni at most resorts, but

All-Purpose, All-Maldivian Dhoni

The truck and bus of the Maldives is the sturdy dhoni, a vessel so ubiquitous that the word dhoni will soon become part of your vocabulary. Built in numerous shapes and sizes, the dhoni has been adapted for use as an ocean freighter, interatoll cruiser, local ferry, family fishing boat, excursion boat, dive boat, live-aboard yacht, delivery truck and mini fuel tanker. The traditional dhoni is thought to derive from the Arab dhow, but the design has been used and refined for so long in the Maldives that it is truly a local product.

Traditionally, dhonis have a tall, curved prow which stands up like a scimitar cutting through the sea breezes. Most Maldivians say this distinctive prow is purely decorative, but in shallow water a man will stand at the front, spotting the reefs and channels, signalling to the skipper and holding the prow for balance. It can interfere with boarding or loading, so it's often dispensed with on modern utility craft, or there is the removable prow-piece that slots into the front of the boat to look good, but lifts out of the way for loading. If you want to stand at the front of a dhoni, be aware that a removable prow-piece can be a slightly wobbly balancing post!

The flat stern is purely functional – it's where the skipper stands and steers, casually holding the tiller with his foot or between his legs. The stern platform is also used for fishing, and for one other thing – when a small dhoni makes a long trip, the 'head' is at the back. If nature calls, go right to the stern of the boat, face forward or backwards as your need and gender dictate, and rely on the skipper, passengers and crew to keep facing the front.

The details on a dhoni are a mix of modern and traditional. The rudder is attached with neat rope lashing, but nowadys the rope is always plastic, not coir (coconut fibre). The dhoni design required very little adaptation to take a diesel engine, and a motorised *ingeenu dhoni* has the same shallow draft as a sail-powered *riyalu dhoni*. The propeller is protected so it won't snag on mooring lines or get damaged on a shallow reef. Despite modern materials (cotton caulking instead of coir; red oxide paint as well as shark oil), a modern dhoni will still leak, just like a traditional one, so there is a bilge pump just infront of the skipper – it's a simple but effective gadget made from plastic plumbing pipes.

Most inhabited islands have a dhoni or two under construction or repair and you may see them on an excursion from a resort. The best dhoni builders are said to come from Raa Atoll and teams of them can be contracted to come to an island to make a new boat. Twelve workers, six on each side of the boat, can make a 14m hull in about 45 days, if their hosts keep them well fed. The keel is made from imported hardwood, while the hull planks are traditionally from coconut trees. A lot of the work is now done with power tools, but no plans are used.

it will cost more (maybe US$200 or US$250 per day) and only if they're not all being used for excursions or diving trips.

Speedboat

Resorts more than 10km or 15km from the airport usually offer transfer by speedboat, which costs from US$45 to US$105 depending on distance. This is generally included in the package price, unless there is the option of transfer by dhoni, in which case a speedboat is priced as an extra.

The boats range from a small runabout with outboard motor to a massive, multi-deck launch with an aircraft-type cabin.

International Sea Services Maldives *(ISSM; ☎ 321198; ℮ issm@dhivehinet.net.mv)* rents out speedboats for up to five passengers, from US$500 to US$700 a day depending on the size of the boat, how far you want to travel and for how long. The larger resorts, especially those near Male', can arrange big power boats too, usually for game-fishing trips.

Ferry Service

A new interisland ferry service is due to start operation. **Island Ferry Services** *(☎ 318252;* **ⓦ** *www.ifs.com.mv; Education Building, Boduthakarufaanu Magu)* will use 280-seat high-speed catamarans on three, once-weekly routes. The south-bound boat departs Male' at 5.30pm, makes a stop at Foammulah, and arrives at Hithadhoo, in Addu Atoll, at about 7am Tuesday (Rf495/990 one way/return to Hithadhoo; Rf485/970 to Foammulah). Going north, there's a service to Velidhoo, in Noonu Atoll; and another to Iguraidhoo, Ugoofaaru and Alifushi

(all in Raa Atoll). The services (and the website) were not quite up and running at the time of writing.

Vedi

A vedi is a large dhoni with a big, square-shaped wooden superstructure, used for trading between Male' and the outer atolls. Sail-powered vedis once made trading trips to Sri Lanka, India, Burma and Sumatra, but these days the vedis are diesel powered and used only for interatoll transport.

No vedi will take you as a passenger to an atoll unless you have a permit to go there. To get a permit, you must be sponsored by someone from that atoll, and it's best to have that person arrange transport. Vedis use Inner Harbour in Male', west of the fishing harbour.

Travel on a vedi is slow and offers basic food and no creature comforts. Your bunk is a mat on a shelf, the toilet is the sea and fellow passengers may include chickens. A trip down to Addu Atoll, the most southerly and distant atoll, will take at least two days and cost around Rf300.

Private Yacht

Visiting yachties who want to cruise around the Maldives must obtain a cruising permit. See the Getting There & Away chapter for information on 'clearing in' and getting a permit.

CAR & MOTORCYCLE

The only places where visitors will need to travel by road are Male' and the southernmost atoll, Addu. Taxis are available in both places.

Snorkelling & Diving

CHRIS MELLOR

MICHAEL AW

CASEY & ASTRID WITTE MAHANEY

Title Page: Schooling pennant butterflyfish, Felidhoo Atoll. (Photographers: Casey & Astrid Witte Mahaney)
Top: Underwater world of the Maldives
Middle: Pair of spotfin lionfish *(Pterois antennata)*
Bottom: Soft corals at Lion's Head, North Male Atoll

Just a few metres below the surface, it's a world of steep cliffs, big boulders and vast blue voids – a complete contrast to the uniform flatness of the islands and the sea. The water is filled with tiny plankton, huge whale sharks, graceful turtles, sluggish sea cucumbers and schools of psychedelic-coloured fish. Soft corals, sea fans, feather stars and sponges decorate the reefs, while little staghorns, brains and colourful polyp patches are colonising the old hard-coral blocks.

The dappled light in the sandy shallows is enchanting, and you'll see some silvery fish there. But the real revelation comes at the reef edge, where the coral slopes steeply into the blue-green depths and fish dart from crevices or cruise in the current. The reef slope can be covered in corals, anemones, sponges and sea squirts, or pitted with caves where lobsters lurk. Take a deep breath and duck-dive. Look out for eagle rays gliding beside you.

You'll need equipment and dive training to access some of the best dive sites in the world. The Maldives has handy house reefs for beginner dives, underwater pinnacles in the sheltered waters of an atoll; and outer-reef slopes, where the big ocean fish come to feed, for more challenging dives.

The warm water and great visibility let you dive all year long, but whale sharks, manta rays, turtles and tuna can be seasonal visitors. Many dive sites are known (and named) for spectacular underwater wildlife, but there's no guarantee that you'll spot them at any given place and time. Every dive is different, and uncertainty is part of the thrill.

SNORKELLING

Much of the marine life in the Maldives can be seen by snorkellers at depths of just a few metres. Because the water absorbs so much red and yellow light, most of the underwater world is a monochrome blue below about 5m, so snorkelling gear is all you need to see some of the best of it.

Where to Snorkel

Usually, an island is surrounded firstly by a sand-bottomed lagoon, then by the 'reef flat' or *faru*, a belt of dead and living coral covered by shallow water. At the edge of the reef flat is a steep, coral-covered slope that drops away into deeper water. These 'reef slopes' are the best areas for snorkelling – around a resort island this is called the 'house reef'. The slope itself can have interesting features like cliffs, terraces and caves, and there are clearly visible changes in the coral and marine flora as the water gets deeper. You can see both the smaller fish which frequent the reef flats and sometimes much larger animals that live in the deep water between the islands, but come close to the reefs to feed.

You can also take a boat from your resort to other snorkelling sites around the atoll. A *giri*, or coral pinnacle, that rises to within 5m of the surface, is ideal for snorkelling, which is not difficult if it's in sheltered waters inside an atoll. A *kandu*, or sea channel, will usually have excellent soft corals, schools of reef fish and large pelagic (open sea) species.

The best resorts for snorkelling have an accessible house reef, where the deep water is not far offshore, at least around part of the island. There are usually channels you can swim through to the outer-reef slope. To avoid grazing yourself or damaging the coral, always use these channels rather than trying to find your own way across the reef flat. Another option is to walk out on a jetty to the reef edge – all resorts have at least one jetty, though sometimes they don't extend right to the edge of the reef.

Resorts with excellent house reefs tend to be popular with divers too. Some of the best are Ellaido, Bathala, Vadoo, Mirihi, Biyadhoo, Eriyadu, Machchafushi, Vilamendhoo, Filitheyo, Reethi Beach, Embudu Village, Fesdu, Vakarufalhi and Kuredu. (See also the Choosing a Resort chapter.)

Resorts that don't have an accessible house reef will usually provide a couple of boat trips per day to a good snorkelling site nearby, but this is a lot less convenient. Many resorts offer island-hopping trips or snorkelling excursions that stop at really superb snorkelling sites. Full-day excursions usually cost around US$20 or so, but are definitely worth it. Kuredu Island resort has the most comprehensive snorkelling program, with guided snorkelling trips to many interesting sites, including a shipwreck. Sometimes snorkellers can go out with a dive boat, if the dive site is suitable and there's space on the boat.

Top Snorkelling Sites

If you stay in a resort with an interesting and accessible house reef, that will probably be your main snorkelling site. You can visit the same reef again and again, and get to know its nooks and crannies, its resident fish and its regular visitors.

A resort excursion can take you to the best snorkelling sites in your atoll, and if you're on a live-aboard safari boat you'll have an unlimited choice. The best snorkelling sites are also dive sites, with a lot of interest in the shallower water. Fit and experienced snorkellers can free-dive to 5m or more without too much trouble, and if the visibility is good they can appreciate any features down to about 10m. Many of the dive sites described in this book are also excellent for snorkelling:

North Male' Atoll
Lion's Head – outer-reef slope
Banana Reef – reef and kandu

South Male' Atoll
Vaadhoo Caves – kandu
Embudhoo Express – kandu
Kuda Giri – giri and wreck

Ari Atoll
Rasdhoo Madivaru –
  outer-reef slope
Orimas Thila – thila
Panetone – kandu
Manta Reef – reef and kandu

Baa Atoll
Milaidhoo Reef – kandu

Lhaviyani Atoll
Kuredhoo Express – kandu
Fushifaru Thila – thila

Felidhoo Atoll
Devana Kandu –
  kandu and thila
Fotteyo – kandu
Rakeedhoo Kandu – kandu

North Nilandhoo Atoll
Two Brothers – giri

South Nilandhoo Atoll
Macro Spot – giri

Addu Atoll
Maa Kandu – kandu and reef

Preparation

If you've never tried snorkelling before, you'll soon pick it up – many resorts give brief snorkelling lessons free of charge in swimming pools or in shallow parts of the lagoon. Every resort will have snorkelling equipment that you can rent, but this will cost US$5 to US$10 per day (much less by the week). It's definitely better to have your own. It's also cheaper in the long run and you can be sure that it suits you and fits properly. You can buy good-quality equipment at reasonable prices at the airport shop and in Male'. Most resort shops sell them too, but the range is smaller and the prices are higher. Ideally, you should bring your own set from home.

Mask Human eyes won't normally focus in water, but a face mask keeps an air space in front of your eyes so that you can focus under water. Any mask, no matter how cheap, should have a shatterproof lens. Ensure that it fits comfortably – press it gently onto your face, breathe in through your nose a little, and the suction should hold the mask on your face.

If you're shortsighted you can get the mask lens ground to your optical prescription, but this is expensive. Alternatively, get a stick-on optical lens to attach to the inside of the mask lens, or simply fold up an old pair of spectacles and wedge them inside the mask. You can wear contact lenses with a mask, but there is the risk of losing them if the mask is flooded – many people now use soft disposable contact lenses under their mask.

Snorkel The tube has to be long enough to reach above the surface of the water, but should not be either too long or too wide. If it is too big then you have more water to expel when you come to the surface. Also, each breath out leaves a snorkel full of used air, and if the snorkel is too big you will rebreathe a larger proportion of carbon dioxide.

Fins These are not absolutely necessary, but they make swimming easier and let you dive deeper, and they give a margin of safety in currents. Fins either fit completely over your foot or have an open back with an adjustable strap around your heel, designed for use with wetsuit boots.

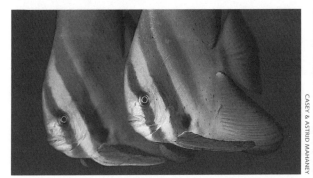

CASEY & ASTRID MAHANEY

Right: Batfish swimming in a kandu

Shirt A Lycra swim shirt or thin wetsuit top will protect against sunburn and minor scratches from the coral or rocks. Even a T-shirt will give some sun protection – sunburn is a real hazard.

Snorkelling Safely

Don't snorkel alone, and always let someone else know where and when you'll be snorkelling. Colourful equipment or clothing will make you more visible. Beware of strong currents or rough conditions – wind chop and large swells can make snorkelling uncomfortable, or even dangerous. In open waters, carry a safety balloon and whistle.

DIVING

The Maldives is a world-renowned scuba-diving destination, and with good reason. The enormous variety of fish life is amazing, and there's a good chance you'll see some of the biggest marine creatures – a close encounter with a giant manta or a 2m Napoleon wrasse is unforgettable, and the friendly sharks of the Maldives are legendary.

Combine this with warm water, visibility reliably over 25m and professional dive centres, and you'll know why divers come back again and again.

MICHAEL AW

Left: Diving over hard coral

Diving Safaris

On a diving safari, a dozen or so divers cruise the atolls in a live-aboard boat fitted out for the purpose. You can stop at your pick of the dive sites, visit uninhabited islands and local villages, find secluded anchorages and sleep in a compact cabin. If you've had enough diving, you can fish, snorkel or swim off the boat. Generally, bigger boats are more comfortable, more fully equipped and more expensive. For keen divers, a safari trip is a great way to get in a lot of dives at a variety of sites, and it will probably work out cheaper than a resort-based dive trip. See the Safari Cruises section in the Facts for the Visitor chapter for general information about cruises and choosing a safari boat.

Everyone on a diving safari should be a qualified diver. If you need to do a diving course, contact the boat operator in advance (you may need a minimum of two to four people for a course). Dive clubs can often get together enough members to fill a safari boat and design a program and itinerary that suits their needs. Ideally, everyone on board should be of a similar diving standard.

A diving safari should have a separate dhoni that has the compressor and most of the equipment on board. This means that compressor noise doesn't disturb passengers at night, and the smaller boat can be used for excursions near shallow reefs. All dive safari boats will have tanks and weights, and they'll be included in the cost of dives. Regulators, BCDs, depth gauges, tank pressure gauges and dive computers are available on most boats for an additional charge. It's best to bring your own mask, snorkel, fins and wetsuit. Ask about the availability of specialised equipment such as cameras, lights and nitrox. A video player is good for entertainment, and playing back dive videos. Facilities for recharging camera batteries are handy. Check **w** www.visitmaldives.com for reasonably up-to-date details on what each boat provides.

For safety, every dive-safari boat should have oxygen equipment, a first-aid kit and good radio and telephone communications with Male'. The divemasters should give thorough predive briefings and emergency plans, have a check list of every diver and do a roll call after each dive. It's good to have descent lines and drift lines available for use in strong currents, and to be able to hang a safety tank at 5m for deeper dives. Night diving requires powerful lights, including a strobe light.

Where to Dive

There are hundreds of recognised and named dive sites, and dozens accessible from nearly every resort. Many of the best dives are described in detail in *Diving & Snorkelling Maldives*, by Casey Mahaney & Astrid Witte Mahaney, published by Lonely Planet. In general there are four types of dive sites in the Maldives.

Reef Dives The edges of a reef, where it slopes into deep water, are the most interesting part of a reef to dive. Inner-reef slopes, in the sheltered waters inside an atoll, are generally easier dives and feature numerous smaller reef fish. Hard corals on inner-reef slopes were badly damaged by bleaching, but are growing back at various rates.

The reef around a resort island is known as its 'house reef', and only the guests of that resort are allowed to dive or snorkel on it.

At some resorts qualified divers can do unguided dives on the house reef. This is cheaper and more convenient than a boat dive, and gives divers a chance to get really well acquainted with the reef. House reefs can be terrific for night dives too. See the Diving section in Choosing a Resort chapter for more on the resorts with the best house reefs.

Outer-reef slopes, where the atoll meets the open sea, often have interesting terraces, overhangs and caves, and are visited by pelagics. Visibility is usually good, but surf and currents can make for a demanding dive.

Kandus These are channels between islands, reefs or atolls. Obviously, kandus are subject to currents and this provides an environment in which attractive soft corals thrive. Water inside an atoll is a breeding ground for plankton, and where this water flows out through a kandu into the open sea, the rich supply of plankton attracts large animals such as manta rays and whale sharks. During the southwest monsoon (May–November), currents will generally flow out of an atoll through kandus on the eastern side, while in the northeast monsoon (December–March), the outward flow is on the western side.

Thilas & Giris A thila is a coral formation that rises steeply from the atoll floor and reaches to within five to 15m of the water surface – often it's a spectacular underwater mountain that divers fly around like birds. The top of a thila can be rich in reef fish and coral, while the steep sides have crannies, caves and overhangs which provide shelter for many small fish, and larger fish come, in turn, to feed on the smaller fish.

A giri is a coral formation that rises to just below the water surface. It has many of the same features as a thila, but the top surface may be too shallow to dive.

Thilas and giris are found inside kandus, where the nutrient-rich currents promote soft-coral growth. They also stand in the sheltered waters inside an atoll, where the sea is warmer and slower moving.

MICHAEL AW

Hard-coral structures on sheltered thilas and giris suffered most from the 1998 coral bleaching, and have been the slowest to recover.

Wrecks While many ships have foundered on Maldivian reefs over the centuries, there are few accessible wrecks with any historical interest. Most were on outer-reef slopes and broke up in the surf long ago, leaving remnants to be dispersed and covered in coral. Any wreck sites of historical significance will require special permission to dive. The

Left: Halaveli wreck in Ari Atoll was deliberately sunk for diving.

diveable wrecks are mostly inside the atolls and are not very old. They are interesting for the coral and other marine life which colonises the hulk within just a few years. Quite a few of the wrecks have been sunk deliberately, to provide an attraction for divers.

Top Diving Sites

Some of the better-known dive sites are described in the chapters covering each atoll and marked on the maps. For examples of the different types of dive sites, look up:

Outer-Reef Dives
Lion's Head – North Male' Atoll
Dhidhdhoo Beyru – Ari Atoll
Shark Point – Addu Atoll

Kandu Dives
Embudhoo Express –
  South Male' Atoll
Guraidhoo Kandu –
  South Male' Atoll
Maa Kandu – Addu Atoll

Thila & Giri Dives
Helengeli Thila – North Male' Atoll
HP Reef – North Male' Atoll
Maayafushi Thila – Ari Atoll
Fish Head – Ari Atoll

Wreck Dives
Maldive Victory –
  North Male' Atoll
Halaveli Wreck – Ari Atoll
British Loyalty – Addu Atoll

Diving Seasons

January to April are generally considered the best months for diving, and should have fine weather and good visibility. May and June can have unstable weather – storms and cloudy days are common until September. October and November tend to have calmer, clearer weather, but visibility can be slightly reduced because of abundant plankton in the water. Some divers like this period because many large fish, such as whale sharks and mantas, come into the channels to feed on the plankton. December can have rough, windy weather and rain.

Learning to Dive

Diving is not difficult, but it requires knowledge and care, and a lot of experience before you can safely dive independently. It doesn't require great strength or fitness and if you can do things with minimum expenditure of energy, your tank of air will last longer. An experienced diver will use much less air than a beginner. Women often have an advantage because they don't breathe as much air as men.

There's a range of courses, from an introductory dive in a pool or lagoon, to a 'resort course' (which allows you to dive at that resort only), to an open-water course that gives an internationally recognised qualification. Beyond that, there are advanced and speciality courses, and courses that lead to divemaster and instructor qualifications. Courses in the Maldives are not a bargain, but they're reasonably priced and you are assured of high standards, good equipment and extremely pleasant conditions. On the other hand, if you do a course at home you'll have more time for diving when you get to the Maldives. A compromise is to do the theoretical stuff and introductory dives at home, so you just have to complete the open-water dives when you reach your resort.

An introductory dive, including equipment, will cost about US$30, which is sometimes credited towards a proper course if you decide to do so. Some resorts offer a free introductory dive to get you in.

A resort course is usually a couple of dives in sheltered water (pool or lagoon), plus a couple in open water, with some basic theory and your first logbook. This will cost from US$150 to US$200, depending on how much the course includes. Again, the cost and the training can sometimes be credited towards a more advanced course.

If you're at all serious about diving, you should do an open-water course. This requires about nine dives, usually five in sheltered water and four in open water, as well as classroom training and completion of a multiple-choice test. The cost in the Maldives is around US$380 to US$550. Sometimes the price is all-inclusive, but there are often a few extra charges – US$12 for each boat trip, US$50 for equipment hire, US$80 for logbooks, certificates, dive tables, course materials, 10% service charge etc. These can really add up. One resort advertised its open-water course for US$455, but by the time you include all the extras, it would cost you over US$600. You could do the course in as little as five days, but you really should allow six to nine. Don't try it on a one-week package – transfers and jet lag will take a day or so, and you shouldn't dive within 12 to 24 hours before a plane flight. Besides, you'll want to do some recreational dives to try out your new skills.

The next stage is an advanced open-water course, which will involve five dives (including one night dive). The cost will be US$250 to US$350, depending on the dive school. Then there are the speciality courses in night diving, rescue diving, wreck diving, nitrox diving and so on.

Dive Schools & Operators Virtually every resort has a professional diving operation and can run courses for beginners, as well as dive trips and courses that will challenge even the most experienced diver. The government requires that all dive operations maintain high standards, and all of them are affiliated with one or more of the international diving accreditation organisations – most are with PADI.

Certificates When you complete an open-water course, you receive a certificate that is recognised by diving operators all over the world. Certificates in the Maldives are generally issued by PADI, the largest and the best-known organisation, but certificates from CMAS, SSI and a number of other organisations are quite acceptable.

Equipment

Dive schools in the Maldives can rent out all diving gear, but most divers prefer to have at least some of their own equipment. It's best to have your own mask, snorkel and fins, which you can also use just for snorkelling. The tank and weight belt are always included in the cost of a dive, so you don't need to bring them – sealed tanks are prohibited on aircraft anyway, and you'd be crazy to carry lead weights. The main pieces of diving equipment to bring with you are described below.

Wetsuit The water may be warm (27°C to 30°C) but a wetsuit is still necessary for comfortable diving. A 3mm suit should be adequate, but 5mm is preferable if you want to go deep or dive more than once per day. Some resorts don't have a good selection of wet suits for rental, so this is a good item to bring if you can. When dive centres say 'full equipment rental', that doesn't usually include a wetsuit. Renting a suit will cost about US$5 per day.

Regulator Many divers have their own regulator, with which they are familiar and therefore confident about using, and a 'reg' is not cumbersome to carry. Rental will cost from US$3 to US$7 per dive.

Buoyancy Control Device (BCD) These are readily available for hire, costing US$3 to US$7 per dive, but bring your own if possible.

Depth Gauge, Tank Pressure Gauge & Timer These are usually available too, but if you have them, bring them.

Dive Computer Now generally preferred over dive tables, these are now compulsory in the Maldives. They're available for rent, from US$4 to US$7 per dive.

Logbook You'll need this to indicate to divemasters your level of experience, and to record your latest dives.

Other items you might need include an underwater torch (especially for cave and night dives), waterproof camera, compass and safety buoy or balloon, most of which are available for rental. Some things you won't need are a spear gun, which is prohibited, and diving gloves, which are discouraged since you're not supposed to touch anything anyway.

Diving Costs

The cost of diving varies between resorts, and depends on whether you need to rent equipment. A single dive, with only tank and weights supplied, runs from US$30 to US$50, but is generally around US$35 (night dives cost more). If you need to rent a regulator and a BCD as well, a dive will cost from US$40 to US$60. Sometimes the full equipment price includes mask, snorkel, fins, dive computer and pressure gauge, but they can cost extra. A package of 10 dives will cost from US$250 to US$300, or US$300 to US$400 with equipment rental. Other possibilities are five-, 12- and 15-dive packages, and packages that allow you as many dives as you want within a certain number of consecutive days. In addition to the dive cost, there is a charge for using a boat – about US$12 for half a day, US$20 for a full day. There may also be a service charge of 10% if diving is billed to your room.

Someone planning to do 10 dives in a week should budget around US$540, perhaps US$100 less if they bring all their own equipment.

Diving Health & Safety

Health Requirements Officially, a doctor should check you over before you do a course, and fill out a form full of diving health questions. See the Health section in the Facts for the Visitor chapter. In practice, most dive schools will let you dive or do a course if you're under 50 years old and complete a medical questionnaire, but the checkup is still a good idea. This is especially so if you have any problem at all with your breathing, ears or sinuses. If you are an asthmatic, have any other chronic breathing difficulties, or any inner-ear problems you shouldn't do any scuba diving.

Diving Safely In the Maldives the dive base will ensure you are aware of the following points to ensure a safe and enjoyable experience, whether scuba diving, skin diving or snorkelling:

- If you are scuba diving, you must possess a current diving certification card from a recognised scuba diving instructional agency. The resort dive base will check your card and provide training if you need it. A check dive is often required.
- Be sure you are healthy and feel comfortable diving.
- Obtain reliable information about physical and environmental conditions at the dive site. The dive base will always provide this.
- Be aware of local laws, regulations and etiquette about marine life and the environment.
- Dive only at sites within your experience level.

Be aware that underwater conditions vary significantly from one site to another. Seasonal changes can significantly alter any site and dive conditions. These differences influence the way divers dress for a dive and what diving techniques they use.

The following laws apply to recreational diving in the Maldives, and divemasters should enforce them:

- Maximum depth: 30m.
- Maximum time: 60 minutes.
- No decompression dives.
- Each diver must carry a dive computer.
- Obligatory three minutes safety stop at 5m.
- Last dive no later than 12 hours before a flight.

Decompression Sickness This is a very serious condition usually, though not always, associated with diver error. The most common symptoms are unusual fatigue or weakness; skin itch; pain in the arms, legs (joints or mid-limb) or torso; dizziness and vertigo; local numbness, tingling or paralysis; and shortness of breath. Signs may also include a blotchy skin rash, a tendency to favour an arm or a leg, staggering, coughing spasms, collapse or unconsciousness. These symptoms and signs can occur individually, or a number of them can appear at one time.

The most common causes of decompression sickness (or 'the bends' as it is commonly known) are diving too deep, staying at depth for too long, or ascending too quickly. This results in nitrogen coming out of solution in the blood and forming bubbles, most commonly in the bones and particularly in the joints or in weak spots such as healed fracture sites.

Other factors contributing to decompression sickness include excess body fat; heavy exertion prior to, during and after diving; injuries and illness; dehydration; alcohol; cold water, hot showers or baths after diving; carbon dioxide increase (eg, through smoking); and age.

Avoid flying after diving, as it causes nitrogen to come out of the blood even faster than it would at sea level. It's not a good idea to dive within 24 hours before a flight, and certainly not within 12 hours. Low-altitude flights, like a seaplane transfer to the airport, may be just as dangerous because the aircraft are not pressurised. There are various opinions about the risks and the time required to minimise them – a lot depends on the frequency, depth and duration of dives over several days before the flight. Seek the advice of an instructor when planning the dives during the final few days of your stay, and try to finish up with shallow dives.

Even if you take all the necessary precautions, there is no guarantee that you will not be hit by the bends. It's a diver's responsibility to be aware of their own condition, and that of their diving buddy, after a dive.

The only treatment for decompression sickness is to put the patient into a recompression chamber. That puts a person back under pressure similar to that of the depth at which they were diving so nitrogen bubbles can be reabsorbed. The time required in the chamber is usually three to eight hours. The treatment is usually effective, with the main problem being caused by delay in getting the patient to the chamber. If you think that you, or anyone else you are diving with, are suffering from the bends, get to a recompression chamber as soon as possible.

Ear Problems Many divers experience pain in the ears after diving, which is commonly caused by failure of the ears to compensate properly for changes in pressure. The problem will usually fix itself, but injuries are often caused when people try to treat themselves by poking cotton buds or other objects into the ear.

Emergencies The **Divers Alert Network** *(DAN;* ☎ *www.diversalert network.org)* operates a 24-hour diving emergency hotline in the US (☎ 1-919-684-8111). **DAN Maldives** *(☎ 440088)* is based at Bandos resort, in North Male' Atoll, where there's a recompression chamber and a complete divers health service. There's also a new recompression facility and fully staffed diving clinic at Kuramathi, in Rasdhoo Atoll at the far north of Ari Atoll. They are both commercial facilities.

Insurance In addition to normal travel insurance, it's a very good idea to take out insurance which gives specific cover for diving, and which will pay for evacuation to a recompression facility and the cost of hyperbaric treatment in a chamber. Evacuation would normally be by chartered speedboat or seaplane (both very expensive). Recompression treatment can cost thousands of dollars, especially since time required in the chamber could reach eight hours.

Some dive operations insist on diving insurance, or will provide it for about US$10 for three weeks. Others may include the coverage in their rates.

DAN can be contacted through most dive shops and clubs, and it offers a DAN TravelAssist policy that provides evacuation and recompression coverage.

MARINE ENVIRONMENT PROTECTION

The waters of the Maldives may seem pristine but, like everywhere, development and commercial activities can have adverse effects on the marine environment. The Maldivian government recognises that the underwater world is a major attraction, and has imposed many restrictions and controls on fishing, coral mining and tourism operations. Twenty-five Protected Marine Areas have been established, and these are subject to special controls.

You'll find dive operators throughout the country are overwhelmingly conservation-minded too. Diving techniques have been modified to protect the environment, and operators now use drift diving or tie mooring ropes by hand rather than drop anchors. The practice of feeding fish has been abandoned, and most operators are careful to ensure that unskilled divers are not taken on dives where they may accidentally damage coral.

Visitors must do their best to ensure that their activities don't spoil the experience of those who will come in the future. The following rules are generally accepted as necessary for conservation, and most of them apply equally to snorkellers and divers:

- Do not use anchors on the reef, and take care not to ground boats on coral. Encourage dive operators and regulatory bodies to establish permanent moorings at popular dive sites.
- Avoid touching living marine organisms with your body or dragging equipment across the reef. Polyps can be damaged by even the gentlest contact. Handling fish can remove the slimy coating which protects the animal's skin.
- Never stand on corals, even if they look solid and robust. If you must hold on, to prevent being swept away in a current, hold on to dead coral.
- Be conscious of your fins. Even without contact the surge from heavy fin strokes near the reef can damage delicate organisms. When treading water in shallow reef areas, take care not to kick up clouds of sand. Settling sand can easily smother the delicate organisms of the reef.
- Collecting lobster or shellfish is prohibited, as is spearfishing. Removing any coral or shells, living or dead, is against the law. All shipwreck sites are protected by law.
- Take home all your rubbish and any litter you may find as well. Plastics in particular are a serious threat to marine life. Turtles can mistake plastic for jellyfish and eat it. Don't throw cigarette butts overboard.
- Resist the temptation to feed fish. You may disturb their normal eating habits, encourage aggressive behaviour or feed them food that is detrimental to their health.
- Minimise your disturbance of marine animals. Chasing, grabbing or attempting to ride on turtles, mantas or any large marine animal can frighten them and deter them from visiting a dive site.
- Practise and maintain proper buoyancy control. Major damage can be done by divers descending too fast and colliding with the reef. Make sure you are correctly weighted and that your weight belt is positioned so that you stay horizontal. If you have not dived for a while, have a practice dive in a pool or lagoon before taking to the reef.
- Take great care in underwater caves. Spend as little time within them as possible as your air bubbles may be caught within the roof and thereby leave previously submerged organisms high and dry. Taking turns to inspect the interior of a small cave will lessen the chances of damaging contact.

Back from the Bleaching

It's true that coral bleaching killed nearly all of the hard coral in the Maldives, but that's not the end of the story. In a few places old coral has unaccountably survived, and you can occasionally be surprised by a big-table coral or a long-branching staghorn. Soft corals and sea fans were less affected by coral bleaching and have regrown more quickly. Magnificent soft-coral gardens thrive at many dive sites, especially around channels that are rich with water-borne nutrients, and a few fine specimens can be seen at snorkelling depths on many house reefs.

The underlying hard-coral structure is still there of course – new coral grows on the skeletons of its predecessors. The healthiest living coral has many metres, perhaps kilometres, of dead coral underneath. New coral is growing on reefs all over the Maldives, though the large and elaborately shaped formations will take many years to build. It's fascinating to observe the new coral growth – the distinctly coloured patches with the finely textured surface of a living, growing organism. The first regrowth often occurs in crevices on old coral blocks, where it's protected from munching parrotfish. The massive *Porites* type corals seem to come first, but they grow slowly – look for blobs of yellow, blue or purple that will eventually cover the whole block in a crust or a cushion or a brain-like dome. The branching corals *(Acropora)* appear as little purplish trees on a coral block, like a pale piece of broccoli. Growing a few centimetres per year (15cm in ideal conditions), they will eventually become big, extended staghorn corals or wide, flat-topped tables.

The recovery is not uniform. Some parts of a reef can be doing very well, with 80% or 90% of the old surfaces covered with new and growing coral, while 100m along the same reef, new coral growth cover is less than 20%. Reef formation is a very complex natural process, but surprisingly the marine ecosystem as a whole seems to be undamaged by the coral bleaching. Fish life is as abundant and diverse as ever.

FISH-SPOTTER'S GUIDE

You don't have to be a hardcore diver to enjoy the rich marine life of the Maldives. You'll see an amazing variety just snorkelling, walking in the shallows, peering off the end of a jetty. This guide will help you identify a few of the most colourful and conspicuous varieties; see the colour pictures after page 88. A point to remember is that even within the same species, colour and patterning can vary greatly over a fish's life cycle, as well as according to gender.

For a comprehensive online guide to the fish of the Maldives, go to Fish Watching in the Maldives at **w** www.popweb.com/maldive.

(1) & (5) Angelfish (*Pomacanthidae* family) Of the many species, there are 14 in the Maldives, mostly seen in shallow water, though some inhabit reef slopes down to 20m. They can be seen individually or in small groups. Small species are around 10cm, the largest around 35cm. They feed on sponges and algae. Regal (or empress) angelfish have bright yellow bodies with vertical dark blue and white stripes. The emperor, or imperial, angelfish (pictured) are larger (to 35cm) and live in deeper water, with almost horizontal blue and yellow lines and a dark blue mask and gill markings; juveniles are quite different in shape and markings. The shy blue-faced angelfish (pictured) also change colour dramatically as they age.

(2) Butterflyfish (*Chaetodontidae* family) There are over 30 species in the Maldives; they are common in shallow waters and reef slopes, singly, in pairs or small schools. Species vary in size from 12cm to 30cm, when mature, with a flattened body shape and elaborate markings. Various species of this carnivorous fish have specialised food sources, including anemones, coral polyps, algae and assorted invertebrate prey. Bennett's butterflyfish (pictured), bright yellow and 18cm long, is one of several species with a 'false eye' near the tail to make predators think it's a larger fish facing the other way. Spotted butterflyfish, which grow to 10cm long, are camouflaged with dark polka dots and a dark band across its real eye.

(3) Anemonefish (*Pomacentridae* family) Maldives anemonefish (pictured) are indigenous to the Maldives. They are around 11cm, orange, dusky orange or yellow, with differences in face colour and the shape and thickness of the head bar marking. Their mucus coating protects them from the venomous tips of sea anemone tentacles, allowing them to hide from predators in amongst the anemones' tentacles. In return for this protection, they warn the anemones of the approach of fish such as butterflyfish, which feed on the tentacle tips. Juveniles are lighter in colour than adults, and have greyish or blackish pelvic fins.

(4) Flutemouth (or cornet fish) (*Fistulariidae* family) One species of flutemouth (pictured) is very common in shallow waters in the Maldives, often occurring in small schools. They are very slender, elongated fish, usually around 60cm in length, but deep-sea specimens grow up to 1.5m. Flutemouths eat small fish, often stalking prey by swimming behind a harmless herbivore. The silver colouring seems almost transparent in the water, and it can be hard to spot flutemouths even in shallow sandy lagoons.

(6) Moorish idol (*Zanclidae* family) One species of moorish idol (pictured) is commonly seen on reef flats and reef slopes in the Maldives, often in pairs. Usually 15cm to 20cm long, the moorish idol is herbivorous, feeding primarily on algae. They are attractive, with broad vertical yellow and black bands, pointed snouts, and long, streamer-like extensions to the upper dorsal fin.

(7) Sweetlips (*Haemulidae* family) Only a few of the many species are found in the Maldives, where they inhabit outer-reef slopes. Some species grow up to 1m, but most are between 50cm and 75cm; juveniles are largely herbivorous, feeding on algae, plankton and other small organisms; older fish hunt and eat smaller fish. Oriental sweetlips (pictured), which grow to 50cm, are superb-looking with horizontal dark and light stripes, dark spots on fins and tail, and large, lugubrious lips. Brown sweetlips are generally bigger, duller and more active at night.

(8) Parrotfish (*Scaridae* family) More than 20 of the many parrot-fish species are found in the Maldives – they include some of the most conspicuous and commonly seen reef fish. The largest species grow to more than a metre, but those around 50cm long are more typical. Most parrotfish feed on algae and other organisms growing on and around a hard-coral structure. With strong, beak-like mouths they scrape and bite the coral surface, then grind up the coral chunks, swallowing and filtering to extract nutrients. Snorkellers often hear the scraping, grind-ing sound of parrotfish eating coral, and notice the clouds of coral-sand faeces that parrotfish regularly discharge. Colour, pattern and even sex can change as parrotfish mature – juveniles and females are often drab, while mature males can have brilliant blue-green designs. Bicolour par-rotfish (pictured) start life white with a broad orange stripe, but the mature males (up to 90cm) are a beautiful blue with hot pink highlights on the scale edges, head, fins and tail. Green-face parrotfish grow to 60cm, with the adult male identified by its blue-green body, bright green 'face' and white marks on fins and tail. Heavybeak (or steephead) par-rotfish can be 70cm long, and have a distinctive rounded head.

(9) Snapper (*Lutjanidae* family) There are 28 species that have been documented in the Maldives, mostly in deep water. Small species are around 20cm and the largest grow to 1m (snapper, themselves carnivorous, are popular with anglers as a fighting fish, and are excellent to eat). Blue-striped snapper (pictured), commonly seen in schools near inshore reefs, are an attractive yellow with blue-white horizontal stripes. Red snapper (or red bass), are often seen in lagoons.

(10) Rock cod (*Serranidae* family, *Cephalopholis* subfamily) Hundreds of species are currently classified as *Serranidae*, includ-ing rock cod and groper which are common around reefs. Smaller species reach 20cm; many larger species grow to 50cm and some to over a metre. Rock cod are carnivorous, feeding on smaller fish and invertebrates. Vermillion rock cod (or coral groper; pictured) are often seen in shallow waters and near the coral formations in which they hide; they are a brilliant crimson colour covered with blue spots, up to 40cm long.

(11) Stingray (*Dasyatidae* family) Several species, such as the black-spotted stingray (pictured) are often seen in very shallow water on the sandy bed of a lagoon where they are often well cam-ouflaged. Most rays seen inshore are juveniles, up to about 50cm across; mature rays can be over a metre across, and maybe 2m long including the whiplike tail. A barbed and venomous spine on top of the tail can swing up and forward, and will deliver a painful injury to anyone who stands on it.

(12) Reef shark (*Carharhinidae* family) Several smaller shark species frequent reef flats and reef edges inside Maldivian atolls, often in schools, while larger pelagic species (*Rhincodontidae* family) congregate around channels in the atoll rim at certain times of the year. Most reef species are small, typically 1m to 2m. Reef sharks hunt small fish (attacks on swimmers and divers are almost unknown). White-tips grow from 1m to 2m long and have white tips on dorsal fins. They are often seen in schools of 10 or more in the sandy shallows of a lagoon. Black-tips, distinguished by tips on dorsal fins and tail, grow to 2m. Grey reef sharks (pictured) are thicker in the mid-section and have a white trailing edge on the dorsal fin.

(13) Surgeonfish (*Acanthuridae* family) The surgeonfish is so named for the tiny scalpel-sharp blades that are found on the sides of their bodies, near their tails. When they are threatened they will swim beside the intruder swinging their tails to inflict cuts, and can cause nasty injuries. Over 20 species of surgeon, including the powder-blue surgeon (pictured), are found in the Maldives, often in large schools. The adults range from 20cm to 60cm. All species graze for algae on the sea bottom or on coral surfaces.

(14) Triggerfish (*Balistidae* family) There are over a dozen species in the Maldives, on outer-reef slopes and also in shallower reef environments. Small species grow to around 25cm and the largest species to over 75cm. Triggerfish are carnivorous. Orange-striped triggerfish (30cm) are common in shallow reef waters. Titan triggerfish have yellow and dark-brown crisscross patterning, grow up to 75cm and can be aggressive, especially when defending eggs, and will charge at divers. The clown triggerfish (pictured; up to 40cm) is easily recognised by its conspicuous colour pattern with large, round, white blotches on the lower half of the body.

(15) Unicornfish (*Acanthuridae* family) From the same family as the surgeonfish, there are several species of the *Nasinae* subfamily. They grow from 40cm to 75cm long (only males of some species have the horn for which the species is named). Unicornfish are herbivores. Spotted unicornfish are very common blue-grey or olive-brown fish with narrow dotted vertical markings (males can change their colours for display, and exhibit a broad white vertical band); their prominent horns get longer with age. Bignose unicornfish, or Vlaming's unicorn (pictured), have only a nose bump for a horn.

(16) Wrasse (*Labridae* family) Some 60 species of this large and very diverse family occur, some on reefs, others on sandy lagoon floors, others in open water. The smallest wrasse species are only 10cm; the largest over 2m. Most wrasse are carnivores; larger wrasse will hunt and eat small fish. Napoleonfish (or Napoleon wrasse, or humphead wrasse; pictured) are the largest wrasse species, often seen around wrecks and outer-reef slopes; they are generally green with fine vertical patterning. Large males have a humped head.

Moon wrasse, about 25cm, live in shallow waters and reef slopes, where adult males are beautifully coloured in green with pink patterning and a yellow marking on the tail. Cleaner wrasse have a symbiotic relationship with larger fish which allows the wrasse to eat the small parasites and food scraps from their mouths, gills and skin surface. At certain times, large numbers of pelagic species congregate at 'cleaning stations' where cleaner wrasse abound – a great sight for divers.

(1) Emperor angelfish *(Pomacanthus imperator)*

(2) Bennett's butterflyfish
(Chaetodon bennetti)

(3) Black-footed anemonefish
(Amphiprion nigripes)

(4) Flutemouth (or cornetfish) *(Fistularia commersoni)*

(5) Blue-faced angelfish
(Euxiphipops xanthometapon)

(6) Moorish idol
(Zanclus cornutus)

(7) Oriental sweetlips
(Plectorhynchus orientalis)

(8) Bicolour parrotfish
(Cetoscarus bicolor)

(9) Blue-striped snapper
(Lutjanus kasmira)

(10) Coral groper
(Cephalopholis miniatus)

(11) Black-spotted stingray *(Taeniura melanospila)*

(12) Grey reef shark *(Carcharhinus amblyrhynchos)*

(14) Powder-blue surgeonfish
(Acanthurus leucosternon)

(13) Clown triggerfish
(Balistoides conspicillum)

(15) Bignose unicornfish
(Naso vlamingii)

(16) Napoleon wrasse
(Cheilinus undulatus)

Male'

Small, quaint and densely settled, Male' (pronounced 'mar-lay') is very clean and friendly, and has a certain charm all of its own. It's by far the most important political, cultural and economic centre in the country, and well worth a visit if you want to meet Maldivians and get a feel for this small but rapidly developing nation.

The island of Male' is about 2km long and 1km wide, and completely covered with roads, buildings and a few well-used open spaces. New buildings are going up everywhere, new taxis and motor scooters crowd the streets, and the place feels like it will soon burst at the seams. Around the bustling waterfront and the slick, new office buildings, every second person is talking on a mobile phone and you'd think you're in a mini-Manhattan. But in the residential areas, in the heat of the day, it's more like a sleepy country town, where people stand in doorways, chat to their neighbours and walk slowly on the shady side of the street.

Officially, the population is around 74,000, but with foreign workers and short-term visitors from other islands there may be many more people than that in town. The resident population includes some 20,000 expatriates, perhaps 12% of them European, the others mostly workers from Sri Lanka, India and Bangladesh.

Land reclamation projects have more than doubled the original size of the island. Looking at a map, you can see the irregular street pattern which indicates the extent of the island early last century, when the population was around 5000. The streets laid out in a more or less rectangular grid are on reclaimed land, a block wide on the northern edge of the island, but covering a broad swath on the southern, eastern and western sides of the old centre. The most recent reclamation works, in the late 1990s, provided space for sports fields, outdoor entertainment areas and Artificial Beach at the eastern end of the island, and space for utilities along the southern shore.

Land reclamation and breakwaters now extend to the outer edge of the surrounding reef, and there is no possibility of enlarging the island any more. Further growth can only be accommodated by more high-rise

Male' Highlights

Grand Friday Mosque
The big, white mosque, with its gold dome and modern-style minaret, is the city's most handsome structure. On Friday at noon the faithful arrive in their hundreds, in silence and on foot.

Male' Markets
The Fish Market and the Produce Market both face the waterfront. The Maldives' main products are carried straight from the boats, including piles of coconuts, big bunches of bananas and thousands of fat, silver tuna.

Male' at Play
In the late afternoon as the temperature cools casual games of soccer, basketball, netball, volleyball and cricket almost overlap on the busy sports grounds at the east end of the island. Less structured sports include swimming, surfing, in-line skating and ice-cream licking.

Nightlife
After prayers, after dark, when the sun sets, the streets fill with people strolling, shopping and socialising. Older men go to tea shops, youngsters enjoy occasional outdoor concerts, and expatriates get a boat to the bar at the airport hotel.

The Whale Sub
This tourist submarine trip is like diving without getting wet. Check out a reef and eyeball the fish.

buildings, or on neighbouring islands. Nearby islands are already being used for the airport and other purposes, and the island of Viligili is being developed for housing. There's also an ambitious project to create a completely new island north of the airport, to accommodate more housing and commercial activities (see Hulhumale', in the Around Male' section at the end of this chapter).

Obviously, the population density and the rate of growth are causing problems in Male'. Charming old buildings are being demolished to make way for bigger, more modern ones, and the quality of ground water has declined severely. There are still some lovely streetscapes, overhung with shady trees, but the loveliness is imperilled by new construction, and the increasingly brackish water supply may not support trees for much longer. The first five-storey building went up in 1987 and the maximum permitted height has since increased from five storeys, to eight, to the current 12. Tall buildings are erected on tiny blocks of land, and many locals feel that bigger buildings have blocked out cooling breezes and made the climate less pleasant.

An interesting architectural feature is the rounded corners of walls and buildings, especially at street junctions. These make it easier for vehicles to negotiate tight corners, but they also soften the appearance of many buildings that would otherwise be undistinguished boxes. Many new, multistorey buildings also have rounded edges and are reminiscent of the Bauhaus style, but might also be called Male' Modern.

Increasing affluence has meant that there are more motorcycles and cars in Male'. Be prepared for traffic congestion when catching taxis.

HISTORY

Male' has been the seat of the Maldives' ruling dynasties since before the 12th century, though none left any grand, old palaces. Some trading houses appeared in the 17th century, along with a ring of defensive bastions, but Male' did not acquire the trappings of a city and had only a very limited range of economic and cultural activities. Visitors in the 1920s estimated the population at only 5000.

Growth started with the modernisation of the country in the 1930s, and the first banks, hospitals, high schools and government offices appeared in the following decades. It is only since the 1970s, with wealth from tourism and an expanding formal economy, that the city has really burgeoned and growth emerged as a problem.

ORIENTATION

Boats from the airport or from the resort islands pull into the congested inner harbour, along the north side of the island, beside the waterfront road, Boduthakurufaanu Magu. This road now goes right around Male', and is still sometimes known by its older name, Marine Drive. All streets in Male' now have an official name in the local language – a *magu* is a wide street, a *goalhi* is a narrow lane and a *higun* is a longer, wider *goalhi*.

The main square, Jumhooree Maidan, faces the waterfront, and many government and office buildings are nearby along Boduthakurufaanu Magu and in surrounding streets. Just to the south of the square is the big Islamic Centre and Grand Friday Mosque, with its golden dome and tall minaret. Chandanee Magu runs past the western side of the square and has quite a few shops and tourist-oriented businesses, as do Fareedhee Magu, Medhuziyaarai Magu, Orchid Magu and some smaller back streets nearby. The other principal street is

What's in a Name?

The full name of the country is Dhivehi Raajjeyge Jumhooriyyaa, or Dhivehi Raajje for short. In English it's officially 'Republic of Maldives', but generally it is called THE Maldives. Why the definite article? No-one seems to know, but it is probably carried over from references to the Maldive Islands and the Maldives Archipelago. The article is omitted in many contexts, like 'Visit Maldives Year'.

The capital of the country, and the name of its most important atoll, is Male', also written as Malé or Male. It's pronounced mar-lay, which suggests an acute accent. The most common local spelling is with an apostrophe on the end, used because the name is a contraction – it comes from the Malei dynasty, which ruled for 160 years from the time of conversion to Islam.

It was assumed that Maldivians adopted the apostrophe because they couldn't do an acute accent on an old English typewriter. Foreign publishers with fancy typesetting technology took the liberty of converting the apostrophe to an accent, which was soon accepted as correct. Modern Maldivian publishers, with the latest in word-processing and desktop-publishing software, prefer the apostrophe ending. Unfortunately, the accent ending is catching on, not because it is more correct to Maldivians, but because it is seen as being better English.

Majeedee Magu, which crosses the island from east to west. It has lots of shops for local people and they throng here in the evenings.

The fishing and commercial harbours are west of the main square. The New Harbour, at the southwest corner of the island, is used by safari boats and dhonis shuttling to the nearby island of Viligili. On the eastern side of the island, land reclamation has provided some much-needed space for recreation. In the evenings it's an especially popular place for walking, socialising, kite flying, soccer, cricket, basketball, volleyball and so on. The 'Artificial Beach' here offers an inviting semicircle of sea water, mainly for kids to splash in. A little farther south, a fair to middling right-hand wave attracts crowds of local surfers.

For the purposes of street and postal addresses, the capital is divided into four districts, from west to east: Maafannu, which covers most of the western end of the island; Machangolhi, which runs north–south across the middle of the island; Galolhu, a crowded residential maze in the southcentral part of Male'; and Henveiru, covering the east and northeast. These districts are not discernible to visitors, but the addresses are understood by taxi drivers (see also Post in the following Information section). Street numbers are rarely used – many premises are known by a building name.

Maps

The Maldives Tourism Promotion Board (MTPB) Resort/Hotel Guide brochure has an adequate map of Male'; it's given out free at the airport and at the MTPB office in town.

INFORMATION

Male' is changing rapidly due to constant rebuilding – government and commercial offices shift around and new developments spring up. If you're not sure where to go, take a taxi – the drivers seem to know every business, office and household in town. If you're wanting to see Male' before arriving at your resort, it's worth noting that there is no left-luggage service in Male'. See Baggage Storage in the Getting There & Away chapter.

Tourist Offices

The **MTPB** (☎ 323228) has an **information counter** (open 7.30am-2.30pm Sun-Thur) on the 4th floor of the **Bank of Maldives building** (Boduthakurufaanu Magu). It gives away free booklets and maps and can answer specific inquiries. The information desk at the airport is supposedly open when international flights arrive, but sometimes this isn't the case. Even when it's not staffed, look on the shelf out the front for some useful booklets.

Travel agents at the airport and in Male' may also supply information on resorts, safari trips and, to a lesser extent, the outer atolls. Note that the MTPB desk at the airport will refer you to the next available travel agent, not necessarily the one who can give you the best deal. (See Independent Travel in the Facts for the Visitor chapter before you start dealing with local agents.)

Money

Several banks are clustered near the harbour end of Chandanee Magu and east along Boduthakurufaanu Magu. They all change travellers cheques, usually for a US$5 transaction fee. Bank of Maldives doesn't charge a fee if you change travellers cheques for Maldivian rufiya, but does charge if you want US dollars. Most banks open from about 8am to 1.30pm Sunday to Thursday, maybe 9.30am to 12.30pm during Ramazan. The **Maldives Monetary Authority** (Chandanee Magu) can be crowded and slow. For faster service, try the **State Bank of India**, **Bank of Maldives** or **HSBC Bank**, all on Boduthakurufaanu Magu.

HSBC Bank has the only ATM that lets you withdraw money from banks affiliated with the main international banking networks. ATMs at Bank of Maldives, State Bank of India and other South Asian banks are only for their own account holders to access local accounts.

Some authorised moneychangers around town will exchange US dollars or euro travellers cheques, at certain times when the banks are closed. You can always try some of the hardware shops, souvenir shops and guesthouses. Most tourist businesses will accept US dollars in cash at the standard rate, and the main European currencies at reasonable rates.

The American Express agent is **Universal Enterprises Ltd** (☎ 322971, **W** www.unisurf .com; 39 Orchid Magu).

MALE'

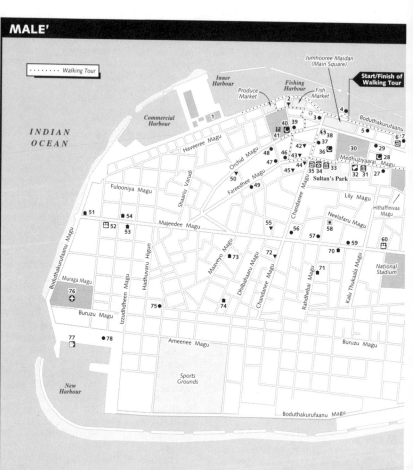

PLACES TO STAY
21 Nasandhura Palace Hotel; Trends
22 Maagiri Lodge
23 Mookai Hotel
24 Kam Hotel
25 Relax Inn
51 Villingili View Inn
53 West Inn
54 Male' Tour Inn
61 Buruneege Residence
62 Kai Lodge
65 Extra Haven Guesthouse
67 City Palace
70 Athama Palace Hotel;
   Mugulai Restaurant
71 Central Hotel
73 Transit Inn
74 Blue Diamond Guesthouse

PLACES TO EAT
2 Dawn Cafe
9 Thai Wok
11 Beach Restaurant

18 Queen of the Night
42 Nastha
43 Olive Garden
44 Seagull Cafe
45 Salsa Café
50 Twin Peaks Restaurant
55 Symphony Restaurant
66 Haruge
68 Mövenpick; Kiosks
69 EG Takeaway
72 Night Star Indian Restaurant

OTHER
1 Port Authority Building
3 Unixpo Jewels
4 President's Jetty
5 Ministry of Atolls Administration
6 Info Business
7 Atoll Surf
8 Bank of Maldives; Maldives
   Tourism Promotion Board
10 Indian High Commission
12 HSBC Bank

13 Airline Offices
14 Shell Beans
15 State Bank of India
16 Danish, Finnish, Norwegian &
   Swedish Consulates
17 Inner Maldives
19 Airport Dhonis
20 Post Office
26 Citizens' Majlis (Parliament Building)
27 Muleeaage
28 Hukuru Miskiiy (Old Mosque)
29 Immigration Department
30 NSS Headquarters
31 Esjehi Gallery
32 Sri Lankan High Commission
33 National Museum
34 Dhiraagu (Telecom
   Company Office)
35 Dhiraagu Cyber Café;
   Public Telephones
36 Islamic Centre & Grand
   Friday Mosque
37 Souvenir & Craft shops

MALE'

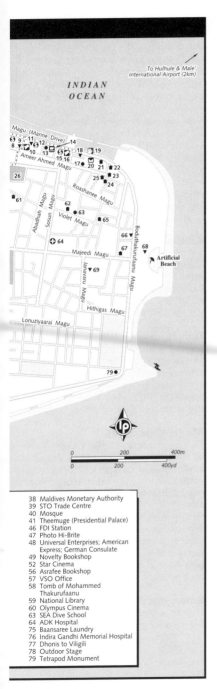

To Hulhule & Male'
International Airport (2km)

INDIAN
OCEAN

Magu (Marine Drive)

Ameer Ahmed Magu

Roashanee Magu

Abadhah Magu
Sosun Magu
Violet Magu

Majeedi Magu

Janaviru Magu

Hithigas Magu

Lonuziyaarai Magu

Boduthakurufaanu Magu

Artificial
Beach

0   200   400m
0   200   400yd

38 Maldives Monetary Authority
39 STO Trade Centre
40 Mosque
41 Theemuge (Presidential Palace)
46 FDI Station
47 Photo Hi-Brite
48 Universal Enterprises; American
     Express; German Consulate
49 Novelty Bookshop
52 Star Cinema
56 Asrafee Bookshop
57 VSO Office
58 Tomb of Mohammed
     Thakurufaanu
59 National Library
60 Olympus Cinema
63 SEA Dive School
64 ADK Hospital
75 Baansaree Laundry
76 Indira Gandhi Memorial Hospital
77 Dhonis to Viligili
78 Outdoor Stage
79 Tetrapod Monument

Post

The **post office** (Boduthakurufaanu Magu; open 7.30am-11pm Sun-Thur) is near the airport boat landing. There's a small post office at the airport too. Postal addresses in Male' often consist simply of the name of a house or building preceded by an abbreviation for the district (see under Orientation earlier in this chapter): M for Maafannu, Ma for Machangolhi, G for Galolhu, H for Henveiru.

Telephone & Fax

The Maldives telephone company, **Dhiraagu** (☎ 123; Medhuziyaarai Magu; open 7.30am-10pm Sun-Thur, 9am-6pm Fri & public holidays), near the intersection with Chandanee Magu, has an office where you can send telegrams and faxes. Phonecards are available here, and at many shops in Male'. There's a long row of public phones just around the corner in Chandanee Magu, and plenty of others throughout town.

Email & Internet Access

The **Dhiraagu Cyber Café** (Chandanee Magu; open 9am-1am Sat-Thur, 4pm-1am Fri & religious holidays), is just around the corner from the Dhiraagu office. It's a comfortable, air-conditioned place with modern equipment and quite quick connections. You have to pre-pay for your connection time, at rates that vary from Rf20 for 15 minutes to Rf45 for an hour. If you pre-pay for more time than you use, the extra minutes can be used at a later date. 'Happy hour' rates, available before 10am and after 10pm, are only Rf25 per hour. Dhiraagu has another Cyber Café at the airport, with similar opening hours and rates (but no happy hour).

Info Business Centre (Ameer Ahmed Magu; open 9am-midnight Sat-Thur, 2pm-midnight Fri) charges Rf30 per hour, any time, but the connections are slower than at Dhiraagu.

Travel Agencies

There's a plethora of travel agents in Male' – anyone with a table, chair and an Internet connection seems ready to call themselves an agent. Most of the smaller ones do nothing but try to sell an allocation of rooms at a resort or two. If you're an independent traveller looking for a resort or a safari tour, see Independent Travel in the Facts for the Visitor chapter, and be prepared to do some

Ode to a Tetrapod

A tetrapod is a concrete block with four, fat legs, each approximately 1m long, sticking out like the four corners of a tetrahedron. These blocks can be stacked together in rows and layers so they interlock together to form a wall several metres high, looking like a giant version of a child's construction toy. A tetrapod breakwater has gaps that allow sea water to pass through, but the structure is so massive and its surface so irregular that it absorbs and dissipates the force of the waves and protects the shoreline from the physical impact of a storm.

A severe storm in 1988 flooded Male's streets, but the worst damage was on the southern and eastern edges of the island. Huge waves broke up tons of landfill that was part of a land-reclamation scheme, and much of this land was re-reclaimed by the sea. Land reclamation is essential for new housing and services on the crowded island, but it encroaches on the surrounding coral reef: the narrower the reef is, the less protection it provides from the ocean's force.

The solution was to protect the whole island with a rim of tetrapod breakwaters, constructed as part of a Japanese foreign-aid project. In some places, the tetrapod walls are used to retain landfill, and have a path on top forming an attractive seaside promenade. In other places, tetrapod walls enclose an artificial harbour that provides a sheltered anchorage for small boats, and a safe spot for kids to swim.

shopping around – ask in town, or call one or more of the following:

AAA Travel & Tours	☎ 324933
Capital Travel & Tours	☎ 315089
Crown Tours	☎ 322432
Inner Maldives	☎ 326309
Island Holidays	☎ 320856
Sun Travel & Tours	☎ 325975
Voyages Maldives	☎ 325349

Bookshops
Most bookshops sell school books, magazines and stationery. The Maldives' main readers must be youngsters: the most well-stocked series are *Goosebumps*, *Sweet Valley High* and *Babysitters Club*, *Harry Potter* and *Archie* comics. **Asrafee Bookshop** *(Chandanee Magu)*, near the corner of Majeedee Magu, has a small range of English paperbacks. **Novelty Bookshop** *(Fareedhee Magu)* has some very good books on the Maldives (a selection are published by them).

Libraries
The **National Library** *(Majeedee Magu; open Sat-Thur)* is in a big, newly renovated building, and has quite a few English books. Nonresidents can't borrow books, but are welcome to sit and read in the library.

Laundry
Any hotel will take care of your laundry for a few dollars per item. Guesthouses will do it more cheaply, or arrange for someone to do it for you. Allow a couple of days if the weather is rainy. There are no laundromats (yet), and only a couple of dedicated laundry services – **Baansaree Laundry**, a few blocks northeast of the New Harbour, charges Rf5 for shirts, Rf8 for jeans and Rf10 for underpants!

Toilets
The few public toilets are reasonably clean, provide toilet paper and cost Rf2. One that's convenient to the shopping area is just west of the main square, on the street that goes behind the fish market. There's another on a side street near the airport-boat landing.

Medical Services
The government-run **Indira Gandhi Memorial Hospital** *(☎ 316647, Buruzu Magu)* is a modern public facility, well equipped and staffed with mostly Indian-trained doctors (all English speaking). **ADK Private Hospital** *(☎ 313553; Sosun Magu)* is a private facility with Western-trained doctors and dentists, excellent standards of care, and quite high prices. Both will make arrangements with travel insurance companies, and both have doctors trained to do a diving medical check.

Emergency
Hopefully you won't need to call the following numbers:

Ambulance	☎ 102
Fire	☎ 118
Police	☎ 119

WALKING TOUR

If you have an hour or so to spare in Male', this walking tour will take you past most of the main sights, plenty of shops and some good places to eat.

Start from the waterfront near **Jumhooree Maidan**, the main square, conspicuous for the huge Maldivian flag flying on its eastern side. The fountain here is illuminated in changing colours every evening. Tour boats from the resorts pull in here, near the carved wooden **President's Jetty**. Nearby are two old cannons, originally part of the defences built in 1632 to deter any Portuguese attacks. If you've come from the airport, your dhoni will pull in farther east, so just walk west towards the flag. Continue west along the waterfront and you'll pass the main fishing harbour – this is a great sight in the late afternoon when dozens of colourful dhonis are unloading fish by the hundreds, mostly large, silver tuna. On the left you'll find the **fish market**, with more fat fish than you've ever seen before. Further on is the **produce market**, trading the limited range of fruit and vegetables grown in the Maldives. Coconuts and bananas are the most plentiful produce, but look inside for the stacks of betel leaf, for wrapping up a 'chew'. Continue for a few more blocks along the waterfront, a bustling area with hardware shops and hang-outs for sailors and fishermen. Fishing and marketing are men's work here, and Maldivian women don't usually venture into these areas.

Ahead you'll notice a big, modern, white building, shaped like the bridge of a ship – this is the **Port Authority** headquarters. Retrace your steps, turn right after the produce market and turn down the street to your left one block inland. This passes behind the **Theemuge**, or Presidential Palace – notice the watchtowers on the corners with the narrow gun embrasures and remember that the last coup attempt was in 1988. Pass the back of the fish market, turn right at its southeast corner, walk one block, do a dogleg and walk another block. There are many shops and a few tea shops around here.

Turn right, on Orchid Magu, and continue on to the four-storey State Trading Organisation (STO) building, which houses a supermarket and various shops and offices. On the next corner is a charming, old-fashioned little **mosque**. Continue half a block to see the front of the presidential palace, then go

back to the corner and turn south. Go down to the end of the block and turn left onto Fareedhee Magu, walk another block and you'll reach Chandanee Magu, one of the main commercial streets. The two irregular blocks between Chandanee Magu and the STO building have most of the souvenir shops and various eateries. This area was once known as 'Singapore Bazaar', because of the number of shops selling cheap electrical goods, but now it's the **tourist shopping area**, and you'll be met with numerous invitations to 'come and see my shop'. Go east on Medhuziyaari Magu with the impressive **Grand Friday Mosque** on your left and the **National Museum** and **Sultan's Park** on your right (see separate entries later in this chapter). If you need a break, the park has a few shady seats, or drop into the Seagull Cafe, on the corner of Fareedhee Magu and Chandanee Magu, and have a fresh fruit juice at an outdoor table.

Continue east on Medhuziyaarai Magu, with the wall of the National Security Service (NSS) headquarters on your left (no photos please), past the **Esjehi Gallery** (see the separate entry later). The ancient **Hukuru Miskiiy mosque**, with its carved tombstones and fat, round minaret, is in the next block, and the **Muleeaage** is opposite (see the separate entry later in this chapter). Go another block to the new **Citizens' Majlis** (parliament), built with aid from Pakistan. Turn left and walk two blocks back to the waterfront, then turn right (east) to see a **dhoni jam** – the harbour here is crowded with boats, which go to the airport and anywhere else people charter them to. Turn around and go west along Boduthakurufaanu Magu, with banks, offices and government buildings on your left, and coastguard boats and luxury launches on your right. You'll soon be back at the square where you started.

ISLAMIC CENTRE & GRAND FRIDAY MOSQUE

Opened in 1984, and built with help from the Gulf States, Pakistan, Brunei and Malaysia, this *miskiiy* (mosque) once dominated the skyline in the middle of Male' – now it competes with many new multistorey buildings. From a boat coming into the Male's harbour, you can still see the gold dome glinting in the sun, although the gold is actually anodised aluminium.

The *munnaaru*, or minaret, with its space-age shape and distinctive zigzag decoration, was supposed to be the tallest structure in Male', but that title now goes to the telecommunications towers.

Visits to the Grand Friday Mosque must be between 9am and 5pm, but not during prayer times. (It closes to non-Muslims 15 minutes before prayers and for the following hour.) Before noon and between 2pm and 3pm are the best times to visit. Invading bands of casual sightseers are not encouraged, but if you are genuinely interested and suitably dressed, you'll get in. Men must wear long pants and women a long skirt or dress.

The main prayer hall inside the mosque can accommodate up to 5000 worshippers and has beautifully carved wooden side panels and doors, a specially woven carpet and impressive chandeliers. The Islamic Centre also includes a conference hall, library and classrooms.

HUKURU MISKIIY

Close by, Hukuru Miskiiy *(Medhuziyaarai Magu)* is the oldest mosque in the country, dating from 1656. (The name means Friday Mosque, but don't confuse it with the much bigger and newer Grand Friday Mosque.) The exterior is protected by a corrugated iron covering which doesn't look very attractive, but the coral-stone walls are intricately carved with patterns and Arabic script. The interior is superb and famed for its fine lacquer work and elaborate wood-carvings. One long panel, carved in the 13th century, commemorates the introduction of Islam to the Maldives. Visitors wishing to see inside are supposed to get permission from an official of the Ministry of Islamic Affairs (☎ 322266). However, most of the staff are officials of the ministry and, if you're respectful and well dressed, they may well give you permission on the spot.

The mosque was built on the foundations of an old temple which faced west to the setting sun, not northwest towards Mecca. Consequently, the worshippers have to face the corner of the mosque when they pray – the striped carpet, laid at an angle, shows the correct direction.

Overlooking the mosque is the solid, round, blue-and-white tower of the *munnaaru* – at first you may think it's a water tank, but the doors in the side are a giveaway.

House Names

Street numbers are rarely used in Male', so most houses and buildings have a distinctive name, typically written in picturesque English as well as in the local Thaana script. Some Maldivians prefer rustic titles like Crabtree, Forest, Oasis View and G Meadow (the G stands for Galolhu, which is the district that the house is in). Others are specifically floral, like Sweet Rose and Luxury Garden, or even vegetable, like Carrot, or the perplexing Leaf Mess. Marine titles are also popular, such as Sea Speed and Marine Dream, as is anything with blue in it – Blue Haven, Blue Seven and Bright Blue. The tropical sun gives rise to the likes of Sun Dance, Sunfront, Sunny Coast, Radiant and Plain Heat (or the cool alternative, Shady Side).

There are also exotic names like Paris Villa and River Nile; more obscure choices like Remind House, Pardon Villa, Frenzy and Mary Lightning; or those that sound like toilet disinfectants – Ozone, Green Zest, Dawn Fresh. For Anglophile ambiguity, it's hard to beat Aston Villa as a house name.

Shop names and businesses, on the other hand, often have an overt advertising message – People's Choice Supermarket, Fair Price, Goodwill and Neat Store. Premier Chambers is not a pretentious house name – it's where you'll find Male's first barrister.

Though it doesn't look that old, it dates from 1675. West of the mosque is a graveyard, with many elaborately carved tombstones. Those with rounded tops are for females, those with pointy tops are for males and those with gold-plated lettering are the graves of former sultans. The small buildings are family mausoleums and their stone walls are intricately carved. Respectful and respectably dressed tourists are welcome to walk around the graveyard.

MULEEAAGE & MEDHU ZIYAARATH

Across the road from the Hukuru Miskiiy is a blue-and-white building with colourful gateposts. This is the Muleeaage, built as a palace in the early 20th century. The sultan was deposed before he could move in and the building was used for government offices for about 40 years. It became the president's residence in 1953 when the first republic was

Lacquered and decorated box

Grand Friday Mosque, Male'

Local produce market, Male'

Schoolchildren, Male'

Buddhist-influenced stone head, Male' Museum

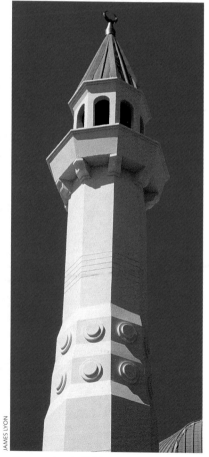
Mosque minaret, Male'

Aerial view of Male'

proclaimed, but President Gayoom moved to a new official residence in 1994. At the eastern end of the building's compound, behind an elaborate blue-and-white gatehouse, the Medhu Ziyaarath is the tomb of Abu Al Barakaath, who brought Islam to Male' in 1153.

NATIONAL MUSEUM

Heading west from the Muleeaage is the National Museum (Medhuziyaarai Magu; adult/ child under 12 yrs US$3/1; open 8am-6pm Sun-Thur, closed government holidays). Housed in a small, three-storey building, it is the only remaining part of the original sultan's palace – the rest was demolished in 1968 at the beginning of the second republic.

The museum has a small collection, but it's quite well displayed and most exhibits are labelled in English. A useful, illustrated guide to the museum, sold at the entrance for Rf50, has colour pictures and more detailed descriptions of the exhibits. Many of the exhibits are things once owned by the sultans – clothing, utensils, weapons and a throne. Some of the fabrics are beautiful, especially the rich brocades. Excellent, traditional lacquer work is displayed on large bowls and trays used to bring gifts to the sultan. Weapons include *bonthi* sticks, which were used in martial arts, and a *silvan bonthi*, used by a husband to punish an unfaithful wife.

Especially interesting are the pre-Islamic stone carvings collected by Thor Heyerdahl and others from sites all over the country. They include a fine Buddha's head, and various phallic images. Most of them are labelled, but little is really known about the significance or historical context of these fascinating finds.

SULTAN'S PARK

The park (open 8am-6pm Fri) surrounding the museum was once part of the grounds of the sultan's palace. It is a small, shady retreat from the streets.

ESJEHI GALLERY

Just east of the Sultan's Park, one of Male's oldest buildings houses a small gallery and artists' workshop (☎ 320288; Medhuziyaarai Magu) dedicated to the preservation and promotion of traditional and contemporary Maldivian arts and crafts. The building dates from the 1870s and was originally the home of a nobleman. It's quite small, but has handsome rooms, beautifully preserved wooden panels and some fine carving. Occasional exhibitions feature, and sometimes sell, the work of local artists. Even if there's no exhibition, there's a good chance of meeting and talking with members of Male's arts community.

TOMB OF MOHAMMED THAKURUFAANU

In the back streets in the middle of town, in the grounds of a small mosque, is the tomb of the Maldives' greatest hero, the man who liberated the country from Portuguese rule and was then the sultan from 1573 to 1585. Thakurufaanu is also commemorated in the name Boduthakurufaanu Magu (*bodu* means big or great).

MOSQUES

There are more than 20 *miskiiys* in Male'; some are simple coral buildings with an iron roof and others are quite stylish with elegant minarets. Outside there is always a well or some sort of outdoor bathroom, because Muslims must always wash before they pray. Visitors usually can't go inside, but there's no need to – the doors are always wide open, and you can clearly see that the interior is nearly always devoid of furniture or decoration.

TOURIST SUBMARINE

The **Whale Submarine** (☎ 333939; W www .submarinesmaldives.com.mv; adult/child/ family US$75/38/170) is one of the newer tourist attractions in town – actually it's just outside of town, in a floating dock between Male' and Viligili. The outing starts with a short boat ride from either the airport (where Whale Submarine has a prominent display) or from the waterfront near the main square in Male'. At the submarine dock (the 'Whale House') you pay your money, have a cool drink and board the sub.

The sub takes a few minutes to get to its dive spot, then descends to about 35m while passengers gaze out through large, lens-like windows. A variety of fish come very close to the windows, attracted partly by the food that the sub dispenses – surgeon fish, blue-striped snapper, and unicorn fish are among the most commonly seen, but you have an excellent view of smaller creatures too, such as lionfish and anemonefish. The sub goes very close to a reef wall, and its lights illuminate crevices and show up colours that wouldn't be visible in natural light. The commentary on board is not especially helpful, so if you're keen on marine biology, bring along your own fish-identification chart or field guide to coral reefs.

Many resorts near Male' will arrange a Whale Sub excursion, or you can make a reservation yourself by phone. There are up to eight trips per day, including two night dives. Underwater time is about 45 minutes, but allow 1½ hours for the whole trip. Quite a few people fit in a submarine trip if they have a few hours to spare at the airport before their departure flight. The sub maintains normal surface pressure inside, so it's quite safe to fly straight afterwards.

PLACES TO STAY

Accommodation in Male' is quite expensive by Asian standards, with the most basic places starting at US$25 and quite ordinary air-con rooms costing around US$50. Foreigners, unless they have a resident permit, must pay a bed tax of US$6, which is always included in the price. A few guesthouses, used mainly by locals, quote their prices in rufiya; others are priced in US dollars. Guesthouses typically have only a few rooms, and the better ones fill up fast, so it's worth telephoning ahead.

Places to Stay – Budget
Blue Diamond Guesthouse (☎ 326125; *Badifasgandu Magu; singles/doubles with fan US$25/35*), on a small street south of

Circumnavigating Male'

If you have some spare time and energy, it is possible to walk right around Male' island on Boduthakurufaanu Magu. You can even run around it – it's often used as a training track for football clubs, squads of National Security Service (NSS) troops and individual fitness fanatics. The less energetic should allow at least 1½ hours for an easy, 4.5km clockwise trek; and don't try it in the heat of the day because there's very little shade. It's most pleasant in late afternoon when lots of local people are out playing games or promenading.

Starting at the main square, walk east along Boduthakurufaanu Magu past the busy harbour, and continue around to the east side of the island. The reclaimed land here still looks a little barren, but the trees are growing and will soon provide greenery and shade. Every evening you'll see people here playing cricket, soccer, volleyball, basketball and, if you're lucky, that Maldivian speciality *bashi* (traditional girls' team game played with a tennis ball, racket and net). **Artificial Beach** is actually a sheltered, sea water pool, used by children, their mothers and minders. Kiosks here sell ice creams, snacks and caffè latte. Continue south along the waterfront walking path and you'll have a good view of the Male' surf scene, at its best from March to November.

Near the southeast corner of Male' is the **tetrapod monument** to Male's sea defences, acknowledging the contribution of the Japanese aid programme to this construction project. Also nearby are some of the old **cannons** that were once part of Male's military defences.

The south side of the island looks a little utilitarian. You'll see some large buildings housing the power plant, petrol storage and Male's first petrol stations. The garbage depot is also here – note the large signs exhorting people to recycle containers and segregate their waste.

Continuing west on Boduthakurufaanu Magu will eventually bring you past some more new sports grounds and then to the **New Harbour**, where many commercial boats are repaired and resupplied. A rectangular space by the harbour is the venue for an outdoor concert on Thursday evenings – traditional drum groups and popular rock bands belt it out over a powerful sound system, while lots of small shops provide refreshments and snacks at outdoor tables.

Boduthakurufaanu Magu is interrupted by the harbour, but it resumes on the west side of the island, at the conspicuous **Indira Gandhi Memorial Hospital**. The west coast, protected by a tetrapod wall, offers good views west over the busy shipping channel to the neighbouring island of Viligili – the northwest corner is a good place to watch the sun set. Continuing around to the north side of the island, Boduthakurufaanu Magu passes the **Commercial Harbour**, where containers and freight are unloaded, and there are some associated workshops and warehouses. Then there's the fishing harbour and the fish market, and soon you're back on the main square.

Majeedee Magu, has small, simple rooms with private bathroom, cool showers, drinking water and breakfast. It's in a residential part of town, interesting for its authentic local ambience, but not very convenient for shops, restaurants or transport. The Maldivian family management is friendly and quite efficient, and the place is popular with Voluntary Service Overseas (VSO) workers and various visitors on limited budgets.

Extra Haven Guesthouse (☎ 327453, 775614; singles/doubles with fan US$20/30, with air-con US$35/40), in the back streets at the east end of town, attracts a mixed clientele of visiting workers and budget travellers. The air-con rooms are small and nothing fancy, and the fan-cooled rooms are even smaller and plainer, but they're all clean and have bathrooms. Some have an outlook over the town. There's satellite TV in the lobby and fresh water is available.

West Inn (☎ 317152; Majeedee Magu; singles/doubles with fan US$25/30) is a new place with small, clean, dark rooms off a narrow balcony. Rooms have quite good bathrooms, but no other comforts. It's at the west end of the island, a long way from the airport jetty and the main shopping areas.

Male' Tour Inn (☎ 326220; Shaheed Ali Higun; singles/doubles with fan US$25/30) has small, unattractive rooms, with cleanish bathrooms. Also at the west end of the island, it's mainly used by visiting workers.

Places to Stay – Mid-Range

This type of accommodation in Male' starts at around US$35/45 for singles/doubles with breakfast, and offers much better standards than the budget places. Most rooms will have air-con, a phone and hot water in the bathroom, and the better ones will have a TV. You might get a discount at some of these places if you stay more than a few days.

Transit Inn (☎ 320420; e transit@dhiveh inet.net.mv; Maaveyo Magu; singles/doubles US$35/45) has 10 spacious, clean, white rooms with air-con, fan, TV and a big, tiled bathroom. All rooms are pleasant and appealing but some have a better outlook than others. Rates include a cooked breakfast, there's a good café out front, and plenty of other eateries nearby. It's a well-run establishment, and quite often full.

Buruneege Residence (☎ 330011, 763789; w www.frontline.com.mv; Hithaffinivaa Magu;

singles/doubles US$35/45) is the only place with any old-style charm – it's in an old building with rooms set around an inner courtyard. The rooms themselves are thoroughly modernised, and have air-con, private bathroom, TV and phones, but no particular character. It's not far from the airport ferries, and handy to the centre of town.

Athama Palace Hotel (☎ 313118; e ath amapalace@yahoo.com; Majeedee Magu; singles/doubles US$35/45) has 15 rooms on various levels, all with air-con, fan, satellite TV and bathrooms with hot water. The decor may not appeal to everyone, but the rooms are good value for money and some have a panoramic view of the town. The lobby is up a spiral staircase above an Indian restaurant.

Kai Lodge (☎ 328742; e kailodge@dhiv ehinet.net.mv; Violet Magu; singles/doubles US$44/55, apartments US$100), a few blocks inland from the airport-ferry landing, has clean, comfortable rooms with bathroom, hot water, IDD phone, satellite TV and air-con; some have a balcony. Breakfast is US$5 extra. A couple of two-room apartments accommodate four people.

Villingili View Inn (☎ 318696; e villiview@ dhivehinet.net.mv; Majeedee Magu; standard singles/doubles US$45/55, deluxe US$60/75), at the far west end of Majeedee Magu, has only a couple of rooms with views over the water to Viligili island – most have no outlook at all. It's a long way from the town centre. The rooms have all mod cons, including air-con and satellite TV, and the price includes breakfast at the attractive restaurant.

Maagiri Lodge (☎ 322576; e maagiri@ dhivehinet.net.mv; Boduthakurufaanu Magu; singles/doubles US$48/63) is very convenient for the airport-ferry harbour and not far from Artificial Beach. It's a rambling building with a bit of character and a restaurant in front. The rooms are smallish, but well equipped with fan, air-con, telephone, hot water and local TV, and some have a view over the water. The staff are friendly and people enjoy staying here, but it's not great value for money – try asking for a discount.

City Palace (☎ 312152; e citymale@dhiv ehinet.net.mv; Filigas Higun; singles/doubles/ triples US$50/65/76) is a new place near the east end of Majeedee Magu, and Artificial Beach. The quite nicely decorated rooms are comfortable and have IDD phones, satellite TV, and minibars without alcohol. Some rooms overlook town, and the top-floor restaurant looks east to the sea.

Places to Stay – Top End

Four of Male's top-end hotels are on the northeast corner of the island, handy to the airport dhonis, and a fifth one is in the middle of town – all are comfortable, but none outstanding. Note that alcohol is not served at any of the Male' hotels. All these hotels have air-con, IDD phones, satellite TV, hair dryers, in-house restaurants and services for business travellers.

Kam Hotel (☎ 320611, fax 320614; e kam hotel@dhivehinet.net.mv; Ameer Ahmed Magu; singles/doubles from US$60/77) is a modern, multistorey building right beside the Relax Inn (see later), just a block or so from the airport-ferry landing. The compact but comfortable rooms have all the usual facilities, and some have great views of the harbour and the airport. Rates include breakfast and the use of a small swimming pool.

Relax Inn (☎ 314531, fax 314533; w www .relaxmaldives.com; Ameer Ahmed Magu; standard singles/doubles from US$64/78), cheek by jowl with the Kam, is another modern, multistorey hotel. Standard rooms have full facilities and great views; the executive rooms include a jacuzzi and a bidet. The hotel has a gym, rooftop spa, two restaurants, a billiard room and karaoke. Rates include breakfast.

Mookai Hotel (☎ 338811, fax 338822; e mookai@dhivehinet.net.mv; Meheli Goalhi; singles/doubles US$66/77) is the newest place in town, just across the road from the Kam Hotel. It offers very well-finished rooms and suites for transit passengers, business travellers and long-term stayers. A feature is the rooftop pool, with a wonderful outlook over the sea and nearby islands.

Nasandhura Palace Hotel (☎ 323380, fax 320822; e nasndhra@dhivehinet.net.mv; Boduthakurufaanu Magu; singles/doubles US$70/80) is just across the road from the airport-ferry landing and has a handsome lobby and a popular garden restaurant. Rooms are comfortable, motel style with all mod cons – some of the upstairs rooms have a sea view. Popular with business people, Nasandhura Palace houses a business centre, conference facilities and 24-hour coffee shop.

Central Hotel (☎ 317766, fax 315383; w www.centralmaldives.com; Rahdhebai Magu;

singles/doubles from US$61/70, junior suite singles/doubles US$88/98) is right in the centre of the island, just south of Majeedee Magu – the big, neon sign is easy to spot. It's some distance from the airport jetty, but the hotel provides free transfers. The rooms are a bit small, some are oddly shaped, but all are well furnished and fully equipped, and all rooms on the upper floors offer good views over the town. Junior suites are more spacious, and apartments are available for longer stays.

Hulhule Island Hotel (☎ 330888; fax 330777; e sales@hih.com.mv; Hulhule island; singles/doubles US$157/169, suites US$193), on the airport island about 400m north of the arrivals hall, is nearly always full with transit passengers and air crews. All the rooms have great views over the water to Male', as well as all the usual amenities. The swimming pool, restaurants, and bars serving alcohol are a big attraction for foreigners living in Male'. Many transit passengers take a room on a 'day use' basis, until 11pm, for US$120.

PLACES TO EAT

Basically, there are four sorts of places to eat in Male': tea shops, serving Maldivian food, the kiosks and coffee shops specialising in ice creams, snacks, juices and coffee, Indian and Sri Lankan eateries, and modern restaurants, serving a range of European and Asian dishes.

Tea Shops

Tea shops are frequented by Maldivian men – it's not the done thing for a Maldivian women to be in one, but there's no law against it. Foreign women use them sometimes, generally with a male companion, and there's no problem. Some traditional tea shops have broadened their menus, installed air-conditioning and improved their service – you should feel quite comfortable in these places. Tea shops are a great place to meet local people, and they're very cheap. A bigger and slightly better tea shop might be called a café or 'hotel'.

Tea shops have their goodies displayed at a counter behind a glass screen, and customers line up and choose, cafeteria style – if you don't know what to ask for, just point. Tea costs around Rf2 and the *hedhikaa* (finger food snacks) are Rf1 to Rf3. You can fill yourself for under Rf10. At meal times they also serve 'long eats', such as soups, curried fish and *roshi* (unleavened bread). A good meal costs from Rf12 to Rf25. Often you can phone the local tea shop and it will deliver short eats.

Tea shops open as early as 5am and close as late as 1am, particularly around the port area where they cater to fishermen. During Ramazan they're open till 2am or even later, but closed during the day.

There are dozens of tea shops in Male', mostly inconspicuous establishments without a big sign out the front. They all have similar food, prices and decor (plastic tables and chairs). The following suggestions are a sample, and include places with a good atmosphere in different parts of town.

Queen of the Night (*Boduthakurufaanu Magu*), a very popular spot facing the waterfront near the east end of Boduthakurufaanu Magu, has tables next to the street where men play *carrom* (a snooker-like board game) and chess until all hours. The tables in the back and upstairs are always busy with guys grabbing some short eats.

Beach Restaurant (*Boduthakurufaanu Magu*), also facing the waterfront, is one of the newer, more elegant tea shops. It offers a selection of curries (Rf10), noodles (Rf32), steaks (Rf65) and snacks, as well as the usual short eats. It's air-conditioned, and often shows international news and sports on its TV. The ground floor room is for tea and snacks; go upstairs for a full meal.

Nastha, in the tourist-shopping area, on a side street west of Chandanee Magu, has an air-conditioned section upstairs, with comfortable seating and a good selection of short and long eats. The downstairs section is not air-conditioned and is thick with cigarette smoke.

Dawn Cafe (*Haveeree Higun*) is one of the bigger tea shops in the area around the fish market. You can get a brilliant meal here. Try it on Friday afternoon when people come in after going to the mosque.

Kiosks and Cafés

Mövenpick (*Artificial Beach*), the first international name-brand eatery in the country, is a kiosk serving delicious Swiss ice cream (from Rf10 for a single scoop), peach melba (Rf25) and caffè latte (Rf12).

Shell Beans (☎ *333686; Boduthakurufaanu Magu; sandwiches Rf28*) is more a coffee bar than a restaurant, but it serves a good range

of tasty pastries, sandwiches and snacks as well as espresso and cappuccino. The fresh bread and cakes come daily from the Bandos resort bakery. It's a new place, with Latin music and contemporary decor aimed at attracting Male's fashionable younger set.

Seagull Cafe (☎ *323 792; cnr Chandanee Magu & Fareedhee Magu; full meals from Rf90*) is one of the most pleasant and popular places, with its delightfully shaded outdoor eating area. It serves sandwiches and snacks (Rf25 to Rf50), delicious juices (Rf25), full meals, such as instant noodles or a T-bone steak (Rf20 to Rf50) and fine coffee (Rf25). Its speciality is the range of ice creams and exotic sundaes starting at Rf35.

Salsa Café (☎ *310319; Keneree Magu; main courses around Rf30*) features a mostly open-air dining area, with a garden setting and cooling fans. On a back street near the shopping area, it's a new place already popular with expats. The menu features Maldivian, Asian and European dishes, all well prepared and presented. The breakfast buffet (7.30am to 10am) includes Maldivian *mas huni* (mixture of tuna, onion, coconut and chilli) and *roshi* as well as cornflakes, fried eggs and fresh fruit – all you can eat for Rf25.

Indian & Sri Lankan

A few eateries cater mainly to visiting workers from South Asian countries. These places are very inexpensive, reasonably hygienic and totally authentic.

Night Star Hotel (*Chandanee Magu; meals under Rf25*) serves truly excellent Indian food in very unpretentious surroundings – try the tandoori fish or the chicken biryiani.

EG Takeaway (☎ *336552; Janavaru Magu; main courses Rf15*) does Sri Lankan dishes as well as some Indian standards, and it has a few stools and narrow tables if you want to eat in. The 'egg hopper' (Rf2) is a cup-shaped pancake with a fried egg that you can fill with curry, rice and other spicy stuff. The rice pudding (Rf5) shows the English influence on Sri Lankan cuisine.

Mugalai (*Majeedee Magu; main courses Rf20*), on the ground floor of the Athama Palace Hotel building, is a very good Indian restaurant with an air-conditioned interior and a few outdoor tables. Considerably fancier than Night Star, it's popular with more affluent Indian visitors – you see some colourful saris here.

MALE'

Restaurants

A Male' restaurant menu will often include Indian, Indonesian and Thai dishes, as well as pizza, pasta, hamburgers, grilled steak, seafood and Maldivian fish curry. The food is usually palatable, often good, but rarely outstanding. Nearly everything is imported, including the prawns and the lobsters, which will be the most expensive items. The customers are mostly businesspeople, young Maldivian couples, sundry expats and day-trippers from nearby resorts. Some places have a starchy ambience, with stiff table-cloths and chilly air-con, but more casual outdoor eating is becoming popular.

None of the Male' restaurants serve alcohol, but some serve nonalcoholic beer for about Rf10 to Rf20 per can. Nearly every restaurant has now acquired an espresso machine, and you can get a good cup of coffee, a cappuccino or a café latte almost anywhere.

Symphony (☎ 326277; off Majeedee Magu; main courses Rf25-45), a longtime favourite for Male' residents, has dim lighting, chilly air-con and a smart look. The menu has a not-too-inspiring selection of grills, rice, noodles, pasta and curry dishes, but the servings are sizable, the French fries are crisp and the coffee is good.

Thai Wok (☎ 310007; Ameer Ahmed Magu; main courses Rf35-50), with its spacious upstairs dining room and tasteful decor, is one of the classiest places in town. Authentic-tasting Thai favourites include tom yum soup (50 Rf for two) and pad thai (50 Rf).

Haruge (☎ 337733; Boduthakurufaanu Magu; main courses Rf45-65), facing Artificial Beach on the east side of the island, has a snack bar at street level (Rf10 to Rf20), while upstairs is a delightful, open-sided eating area decorated with Maldivian antiques and marine artefacts. The menu is varied, with pasta, grills, Asian fare, and a choice of Maldivian dishes – all well prepared and nicely spicy. But it's the friendly management, the interesting Maldivian and international clientele, and the sea views that make this a really fun place to eat.

Olive Garden (☎ 312231; Fareedhee Magu; pizzas Rf40-70) is a mainly Italian restaurant serving pasta and very tasty pizzas. But in true Male' style it also serves soup, salad, burgers, fried noodles, hot curries and fresh seafood. The lighting is dim, the air-con arctic, and the espresso strong.

Twin Peaks (☎ 327830; Orchid Magu; pizzas Rf100-140) is a well-established Italianish restaurant serving pretty good pizzas, pastas, seafood, ice cream and cappuccino. It's quite a smart place and popular with local business people and expats who get a big discount (tourists arriving with a guide pay premium prices).

Hotel Restaurants

Most hotels have their own restaurants, and during the fasting month of Ramazan these might be the only places serving meals between sunrise and sunset. Hotel restaurants include those on the top floors of **Relax Inn** and the **Kam Hotel**, both offering good views and OK food, though the service may be variable. Most main courses will cost at least Rf45. The restaurant at the **Central Hotel** has no view and average food. **Terrace Restaurant**, at the City Palace Hotel, is more economical and has been recommended by some readers.

Trends (☎ 323380; Boduthakurufaanu Magu, main courses Rf50-100), at the Nasandhura Palace Hotel, is an outdoor restaurant offering a varied menu of European, Indonesian, Chinese and Indian dishes. Thai dishes are recommended after 10.30pm, when the Thai chef comes in.

Airport Restaurants

At the airport there's an expensive snack bar, with lots of white, plastic tables, where you can get a Rf40 salad roll or a Rf30 Coke. Outside the terminal building, facing the dhoni dock, is the **Satellite Restaurant**, which serves Maldivian dishes to Maldivian customers at very reasonable prices, but may charge foreigners higher prices for burgers, fish and chips or more elaborate meals. If you're waiting around the arrivals area, beware of people selling overpriced soft drinks for US$3 to US$5 a can.

Hulhule Island Hotel (☎ 330888), about 400m north of the arrivals hall, has a couple of upmarket places to eat. The **Faru Coffee House** is open 24 hours and serves assorted light meals – burgers (US$7), pasta (US$9), sushi (US$6 to US$9), fish fillet (US$11) and fried chicken (US$13). The **Gadhoo Seafood & Grill** does excellent steaks and fresh seafood for international hotel prices (allow at least US$25 for a meal). Unlike other eateries in Male', these places can serve beer (US$3) or wine with your meal.

Supermarkets

People's Choice and the **supermarket** in the STO building offer a good selection of packaged food and some fresh fruit and vegetables. These stores are handy for self-catering, which is another option during Ramazan.

ENTERTAINMENT

There may be no bars, nightclubs, dance halls or discos in town, but Male' is a surprisingly lively place from about 8pm to late in the evening. Majeedee Magu bustles with late-night shoppers and cafés full of people.

Two cinemas have thriving businesses, though both have suffered from the increasing popularity of VCRs, DVDs and satellite TV.

Star (Majeedee Magu; tickets about Rf25), at the west end of Majeedee Magu, is the place to see an American action movie or a Hindi epic.

Olympus (Majeedee Magu), across from the stadium, specialises in Maldivian movies, made for TV, shown on video and usually imitative of Hindi love stories. Neither the Olympus nor Star is air-conditioned.

The weekend begins on Thursday night, often with an outdoor concert for young people on the outdoor stage down by New Harbour. Some performances may be less than totally professional, but the audience is enthusiastic and it can be a wild night – Maldivians get unbelievably excited dancing and singing, without any help from alcohol or ecstasy.

Airport Restaurants

The airport island has **Hulhule Island Hotel** (☎ 330888; Hulhule island) which attracts expats in the evening, to swim in the pool, drink in the bar or enjoy a good meal. (Maldivians are not allowed to drink alcohol there.) The hotel runs a free transfer boat 14 times a day, from beside the President's Jetty in Male'. Evening departures are at 5.15pm, 5.45pm, 7.15pm, 8.15pm and 9.15pm – call the hotel for other times. Day use of the swimming pool costs US$20, including one drink.

Giraavaru Resort (☎ 440440; Giraavaru island), a small, nearby resort, provides a free transfer boat at 9am on Friday for those who want to spend a day there, paying for

drinks, meals and activities. Officially, it's for VSO workers, but other foreign residents can call the resort and ask to be put on the list.

SPECTATOR SPORTS

National Stadium (Majeedee Magu) hosts the biggest football matches (tickets Rf15 to Rf25) and the occasional cricket match. More casual games can be seen any evening in the sports grounds at the east end of the island and near New Harbour.

SHOPPING

Most of the shops selling imported and locally made souvenirs are on and around Chandanee Magu, Fareedhee Magu and Orchid Magu. Many of the tourist shops have a very similar range of stock, but it's worth browsing in several if you're looking for something special.

The most popular purchases are T-shirts, sarongs, cotton clothing, postcards, picture books, small handcraft items (carved fish, lacquer boxes, coconut-shell spoons), and trinkets from India, Sri Lanka, Thailand and Indonesia. Prices are negotiable; they are generally cheaper in Male' than in resorts, but more expensive than on village islands. Typical tourist shops on Chandanee Magu include **Lemon**, **Bamboo** and **Najee Artpalace**.

Male' is definitely the best place to shop for more unusual antiques and Maldivian craft items – look for old, wooden measuring cups, coconut graters, ceremonial knives, and finely woven-grass mats. **Antique & Style** and **Gloria Maris**, both upstairs on the east side of Chandanee Magu, are worth visiting. For less conventional souvenirs, such as giant fish-hooks, boat balers, hookahs (water pipes) and medicinal herbs, look in the local hardware, chandlery and general stores along the waterfront west of the fish market and down Fareedhee Magu.

For quality jewellery, including sapphires and rubies from Sri Lanka, try **Unixpo Jewels**, at the north end of Chandanee Magu, and **Walton Jewels**, farther south on the same street. Take note that sapphire salesmen can be very persuasive.

The best range of surfboards, accessories and surf wear is at **Atoll Surf** (☎ 334555; Boduthakurufaanu Magu). Several photographic shops stock quality film – **Photo Hi-Brite** (*Fareedhee Magu*) for Kodak products, **Villa Photo** (*STO Trade Centre, Orchid Magu*) for Agfa, and **FDI Station** (*Fareedhee Magu*) for Fuji.

GETTING THERE & AWAY
Air

All international flights to the Maldives use Male' International Airport, which is on a separate island, Hulhule, about 2km east of Male' island. Domestic flights and seaplane transfers to resorts also use Hulhule.

Most visitors won't need to contact their airline because their tour operator will reconfirm outward flights. Airline offices in Male' include:

Air Europe	☎ 318459
Austrian Airlines	☎ 318459
Condor	☎ 323116
Emirates Airlines	☎ 315466
Indian Airlines	☎ 310111
Island Aviation	☎ 335544
Lauda Air	☎ 318459
LTU International Airways	☎ 323116
Malaysia Airlines	☎ 332555
Monarch	☎ 323617
Qatar	☎ 334777
Singapore Airlines	☎ 314803
SriLankan Airlines	☎ 328456

Boat

Boats on excursions from the resorts will dock on Boduthakurufaanu Magu near the President's Jetty, opposite the main square. If you want to get out to a resort, it may be better to go to the airport and take a transfer boat with a group of new arrivals. Dhonis to/from the airport dock at the east end of Boduthakurufaanu Magu. This is also the best place to charter a dhoni for a short trip or for a day. To charter, ask at the small ticket booth facing the harbour.

Dhonis to nearby Viligili use the New Harbour on the southwest corner of Male'.

Safari boats and private yachts usually moor between Male' island and Viligili, or in the lagoon west of Hulhumale', the new island north of the airport. Safari-boat operators will normally pick up new passengers from the airport or Male', and ferry them directly to the boat.

For information about the new fast-boat service to the outer atolls, call **Island Ferry Service** (☎ *3188252*).

GETTING AROUND
To/From the Airport

Dhonis shuttle between the airport and Male' all day and most of the night, departing promptly every 15 minutes. At the airport, dhonis leave from the jetties just north of the arrivals hall. In Male' they arrive and depart from the landing at the east end of Boduthakurufaanu Magu. The crossing costs Rf10 per person.

Taxi

The numerous taxis offer a few minutes of cool, air-conditioned comfort and a driver who can usually find any address in Male'. Many streets are one way and others may be blocked by construction work or stationary vehicles, so taxis will often take roundabout routes.

Fares are the same for any distance – Rf10 if you phone first and they pick you up; or (officially) Rf15 if you hail one on the street (in practice, many charge only Rf10 even from the street). Taxis may charge Rf5 extra for luggage, and they cost Rf20 after midnight. You don't have to tip. There are quite a few taxi companies, but don't worry about the name of the company – just call one of these numbers: ☎ 323132, 325757, 322454, 322122, 321414, 325656 or 329292.

Bicycle

A bicycle is a good way to get around, but there's no place to rent one. Your guesthouse might be able to arrange something. Be sure to lock it up and always use a light at night.

AROUND MALE'
Diving Sites

While the waters around Male' are said to be thick with rubbish and wrecked bicycles, there is some excellent diving within easy reach. The **SEA dive school** (☎ *316172*; **w** *www.seamaldives.com.mv; Violet Magu*) is a very well-regarded operation that does dive courses and dive trips for locals and the expat community. It charges US$35 for a single dive with full equipment, US$30 with tank and weights only (including the boat trip). If you do nine dives, the 10th dive is free. A PADI open-water course is US$420, including dives, equipment and certification.

The water sports centre at **Hulhule Island Hotel** (☎ *330888; Hulhule island*) advertises

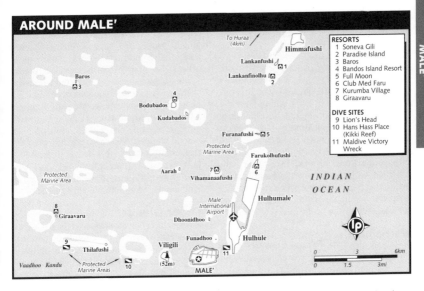

AROUND MALE'

To Huraa (4km)

Himmafushi

Lankanfushi ⌂ 1

Lankanfinolhu ⌂ 2

Baros
⌂ 3

Bodubados ⌂
4 ⌂
Kudabados ⌂

Furanafushi ⌂ 5

Protected
Marine Area
Farukolhufushi
⌂ 6

Protected
Marine Area

Aarah ⌂
7 ⌂
Vihamanaafushi

INDIAN
OCEAN

Male'
International
Airport
Hulhumale'

8 ⌂
Giraavaru

Dhoonidhoo ⌂

Funadhoo ⌂
Hulhule

9
Thilafushi
Viligili
⌂
(52m)

Hulhule
11

Vaadhoo Kandu
Protected
Marine Areas
10
MALE'

0   3   6km
0   1.5   3mi

RESORTS
1 Soneva Gili
2 Paradise Island
3 Baros
4 Bandos Island Resort
5 Full Moon
6 Club Med Faru
7 Kurumba Village
8 Giraavaru

DIVE SITES
9 Lion's Head
10 Hans Hass Place
(Kikki Reef)
11 Maldive Victory
Wreck

some of the cheapest dive rates in the country – US$35 for a single dive with equipment provided, US$25 with tank and weights only (including the boat trip), and US$315 for a PADI open-water course.

Some of the best dives are along the edges of Vaadhoo Kandu (the channel between North and South Male' Atolls), which has two Protected Marine Areas. There is also a well-known wreck.

Hans Hass Place Also called Kikki Reef, this is a demanding wall dive beside Vaadhoo Kandu in a Protected Marine Area. There is a lot to see at 4m or 5m, so it is good for snorkellers and less-experienced divers if the current is not too strong. There's a wide variety of marine life, including many tiny reef fish and larger species in the channel. Further down are caves and overhangs with sea fans and other soft corals, where divers must take care to avoid damaging the reef.

Lion's Head This Protected Marine Area was once a popular place for shark feeding, and though this practice is now strongly discouraged, grey reef sharks and the occasional turtle are still common here. The reef edge is thick with fish, sponges and soft corals; although it drops steeply, with numerous overhangs, to over 40m, there is still much to see at snorkelling depth.

Wreck of the Maldive Victory This is an impressive and challenging dive because of the potential for strong currents. This cargo ship hit a reef and sank on Friday 13 February 1981 and now sits with the wheelhouse at around 15m,

and the propeller at 35m. The ship has been stripped of anything movable, but the structure is almost intact and provides a home for a rich growth of new coral, sponges, tubastrea and large schools of fish.

Viligili

Just over a kilometre to the west of Male' is the island of Viligili (also spelled Villingili), a one-time resort closed down to make room for a telecommunications station and residential development. Currently about 4300 people live here, in individual family houses and a few multistorey blocks of flats. Potentially it's a very attractive place, with lots of greenery and open space, and a wonderful alternative to the crowded capital – quite a few families have settled here, but it doesn't have the cachet of the main island.

Male' residents come here on weekends and holidays. There are sandy beaches on the northeast shore, with views across the busy harbour to Male'. Kids play soccer and volleyball under the trees, and a small water-sports centre, open on busy days, rents out windsurfers and jet skis. There's a tea shop or two if you're hungry, and some places selling ice creams. **Sun Down**, a tea shop/restaurant near the ferry landing, has been recommended.

Viligili is easy to get to. Just catch one of the frequent dhoni ferries from New Harbour on the southwest corner of Male' (15 minutes, Rf3).

Hulhule

This island was once densely wooded with very few inhabitants – just a graveyard and a reputation for being haunted. The first airstrip was built here in 1960, and in the early 1980s it had a major upgrade to accommodate long-distance passenger jets. Airport facilities have expanded to keep pace with the burgeoning tourist industry and now include a sizable terminal, workshops, administrative buildings, staff housing and a new hotel (see Places to Stay earlier in this chapter). Seaplanes 'land' in the lagoon on the east side of the island.

Hulhumale'

Between the airport and the island of Farukolhufushi about 1.8 sq km of reef has been built up to create a new island – the first phase of an ambitious project to relieve the pressure of growth on Male'. Sand and coral was dug up from the lagoon and pumped into big heaps on the reef top. Then bulldozers pushed the rubble around to form a quadrilateral of dry land about 2km long and 1km wide, joined by a causeway to the airport island. It's built up to about 2m above sea level, which is a metre higher than Male', to provide a margin of protection against the possibility of sea-level rises.

The project began in 1997, the first phase of land reclamation is done, palm trees are growing, and the first apartment blocks are going up. The Hulhumale' Development Unit, reporting to the President's Office, has commissioned state-of-the-art urban planning and design from international consultants. Housing for the first thousand or so residents will be ready by 2004, along with a community hospital, school and big, new mosque. Most of the funding is from the government and from international commercial loans – this is not a foreign-aid project. One of the challenges is to introduce a new land ownership system, so residents can have an equity in their own homes, and the value of the new real estate can be used to underwrite future development. The traditional land tenure system won't work for developing a new island.

When the first-phase land is fully developed, in 15 to 20 years, it will accommodate 50,000 people and have waterfront esplanades, light industrial areas, government offices, shopping centres, bus services, boulevards of palm trees, a marina and a national stadium. The basic layout has been carefully planned, but the details are still flexible, allowing for some natural, organic growth through multiple private developments. The second phase, a long-term proposal, involves reclaiming a further 2.4 sq km of land (engulfing all of Farukolhufushi, the Club Med island) and bringing the total population of Hulhumale' to around 100,000 people.

Other Islands

With so many small islands in the Maldives, it's not uncommon for individual islands to be allocated to specific activities or uses. One example is **Funadhoo**, between the airport and Male', which is used for fuel storage – it's a safe distance from inhabited areas, and convenient for both seagoing tankers and smaller boats serving the atolls.

West of Viligili, one of the fastest-growing islands in the country is **Thilafushi**, also known as 'Trash Island'. It's where the capital dumps its garbage. The land is earmarked for industrial development, and its three conspicuous, round towers are part of a cement factory, which has just been built.

The island of **Dhoonidhoo**, just north of Male', was the British governor's residence until 1964. The house is now used for detaining people who may disrupt Maldivian society (officially, there are no political prisoners in the Maldives).

Slightly further north, **Aarah** is a small island used as the president's holiday retreat.

Another 3km further north, the island of **Kudabados** was saved from resort development and became the **Kuda Bandos Reserve**, to be preserved in its natural state for the people's enjoyment. It has a few facilities for day-trippers, but is otherwise undeveloped – a small island encircled by a white beach. Tourists come here on 'island-hopping' trips from nearby resorts. Maldivian families and groups come on weekends and holidays – the Bandos Resort's Male' office (☎ 325529) arranges a boat most Fridays for local people for about Rf30, including the Rf10 entry fee.

North & South Male' Atolls

Because of their proximity to the capital and, more importantly, to the international airport, the islands of North and South Male' Atolls were the first to be developed for tourism – there are more than a dozen resorts within 15km of the airport. Some of these resorts are excellent, and most have had at least one major upgrade since they were first established. The advantages of a resort close to Male' include saving time, trouble and expense in transferring from the airport, and the ease with which you can make an excursion to the capital. Surprisingly, the number of resorts does not really affect the appeal of the area – you will see lights across the water at night, boats passing all day and planes flying overhead, but most of these inner resorts still feel secluded and relaxed.

Some excellent dive sites are found on these atolls, though all the corals have been affected by coral bleaching. Sites close to Male' have been heavily used, but generally they are in very good condition. Some of the most interesting sites are on either side of Vaadhoo Kandu, the channel that runs between North and South Male' Atolls. At the outer edge of the atolls, the dive sites are accessible from only a few resorts or by safari boat, and you'll probably have them all to yourself. Gaafaru Falhu Atoll, north of North Male' Atoll, has at least three diveable shipwrecks.

Some of the Maldives' best surf breaks are in North Male' Atoll. They can be reached by boat from nearby resorts, some of which are ideal for surfers. The smaller breaks in South Male' Atoll are accessible by boat, but none of the resorts is especially suitable for surfers. (See Surfing under Activities in the Facts for the Visitor chapter for more details.)

Some resorts make their beaches and facilities available, at a price, for day use by Male' residents. A few have facilities for conventions and business meetings, and most will cater for group social functions, but no resorts are currently catering for, or encouraging, individual day visitors.

The administrative atoll of Kaafu comprises South Male' Atoll, North Male' Atoll, the small atoll of Gaafaru Falhu to the north of that, and the island of Kaashidhoo, which is even further north. Kaafu extends for over 150km from north to south and has dozens of sandbanks and islands, of which only nine are officially inhabited. These have a total population of 13,400. The capital of Kaafu is the island of Thulusdhoo in North Male' Atoll. Male', the capital of the Maldives (see the Male' chapter), is in the south of North Male' Atoll, but is not part of the Kaafu Atoll administration.

KAASHIDHOO

Though in the Kaafu administrative district, the island of Kaashidhoo is way out by itself, in a channel between much larger atolls. The island has a clinic, a new secondary school, and over 1500 people, which makes it one of the most populous in Kaafu. Some of the ruins here are believed to be remains of an old Buddhist temple. Local crops include watermelon, lemon, banana, cucumber and zucchini, but the island is best known for its *raa* – the 'palm toddy' made from the sap of a palm tree, drunk fresh or slightly fermented.

Local boats going to or from the northern atolls sometimes shelter in the lagoon in Kaashidhoo in bad weather. Dive boats on longer trips might stop to dive Kaashidhoo East Faru, a good place to see large pelagic (open-sea) marine life.

GAAFARU FALHU

This small atoll has just one island, also called Gaafaru, with a population of 850. The channel to the north of the atoll, Kaashidhoo Kuda Kandu, has long been a shipping lane, and several vessels have veered off course and finished on the hidden reefs of Gaafaru Falhu. There are three diveable wrecks – SS *Seagull* (1879), *Erlangen* (1894) and *Lady Christine* (1974). None is anywhere near intact, but the remains all have good coral growth and plentiful fish. Dive trips are possible from Helengeli and Eriyadhoo, but most visitors are from live-aboard dive boats.

NORTH MALE' ATOLL

Kaafu's capital island is **Thulusdhoo**, on the southeastern edge of North Male' Atoll, with a population of about 850. It's an industrious island, known for *bodu beru* drums, traditional dancing and a government warehouse for salted fish. Contemporary products include T-shirts, Coca-Cola and modern fibreglass versions of the traditional Maldivian boat, the dhoni.

The island of **Huraa** (population 700) is visited by tourists on island-hopping trips, but it's not yet as touristy as other North Male' islands. The newly opened Four Seasons Resort on the next island, Kudahuraa, should help to boost the local economy. Huraa's dynasty of sultans, founded in 1759 by Sultan Al-Ghaazi Hassan Izzaddeen, built a mosque on the island.

Many tourists visit **Himmafushi** on excursions arranged from nearby resorts. The main street has two long rows of shops, where you can pick up some of the least expensive souvenirs in the country. Carved rosewood manta rays, sharks and dolphins are made locally.

If you wander into the back streets, you quickly get away from the tourist strip to find an attractive, well-kept village with many modern amenities. The local population, some 880 people, derive a substantial income from tourist shopping and working in nearby resorts.

A sand spit has joined Himmafushi to the once separate island of **Gaamaadhoo**, where there used to be a prison. The surf break here, aptly called **Jailbreaks**, is a great right-hander (see Surfing under Activities in the Facts for the Visitor chapter), accessible by boat from nearby resorts.

The island of **Girifushi**, which has a military training camp, is off limits.

Further north, **Dhiffushi** is one of the most appealing local islands, with approximately 900 people, three mosques and two schools. Mainly a fishing island, it has lots of greenery and grows several types of tropical fruit. Tourists from Meeru Island Resort are regular visitors.

Diving

North Male' Atoll has been well explored by divers and has many named sites. Some are heavily dived, especially in peak seasons. Consult with the resort dive operator to pick the most suitable dives for a given day, with regard to your abilities and interests. The following is just a sample of the best-known sites, listed from north to south:

Helengeli Thila Also called Bodu Thila, this long narrow thila on the eastern edge of the atoll is famous for its prolific marine life. Reef fish include surgeonfish, bannerfish, butterflyfish and dense schools of snapper and fusilier. Larger fish and pelagics are also common – sharks, tuna, rays, jacks and a resident giant groper. Soft corals are spectacular in the cliffs and caves on the west side of the thila at about 25m. The large hard coral formations here are recovering from coral bleaching quite quickly, possibly because of the strong, nutrient-rich currents.

Shark Point Also called Saddle, or Kuda Faru, this dive site is in a Protected Marine Area and is subject to strong currents. Lots of white-tip and grey reef sharks can be seen in the channel between a thila and the reef, along with fusiliers, jackfish, stringrays and some impressive caves.

Blue Canyon The alternative, less picturesque name is Kuda Thila, which means 'small thila'. A canyon, 25m to 30m deep and lined with soft, blue corals, runs beside the thila. The numerous overhangs make for an exciting dive, but require good buoyancy control. This site is recommended for experienced divers.

Bodu Hithi Thila & the Peak Bodu Hithi is a prime manta-spotting site from December to March, with a good number of sharks and many reef fish. The soft corals on the sides of the thila are in excellent condition. If currents are moderate this site is suitable for intermediate divers, and the shallow waters atop the thila offer superb snorkelling. Nearby, the Peak is another great place to see mantas in season; it is also home to some large Napoleon wrasse.

Rasfari The outer-reef slope here drops down to a depth of more than 40m, but a couple of thilas rise up with their tops at about 25m. Grey reef sharks love it here – you might see 20 or 30 of them, as well as white-tip sharks, barracuda, eagle rays and trevally. It's a Protected Marine Area.

Colosseum A curving cliff near a channel entrance forms the Colosseum, where pelagics perform. Shark and barracuda are often seen here. Experienced divers do this as a drift dive, going right into the channel past ledges and caves, with soft corals and the occasional turtle. Even beginners can do this one in good conditions.

Aquarium As the name suggests, this site (a coral rock formation about 15m down) features a large variety of reef fish. A sandy bottom at 25m can have small sharks and rays, and you might also see giant wrasse and schools of snapper. It's an easy dive and suitable for snorkelling.

Kani Corner Across the kandu from the Aquarium, this corner is the start of a long drift dive through a narrow channel with steep sides, caves and overhangs decorated with soft corals. Lots of large marine life can be seen, including sharks, barracuda, Napoleon wrasse and tuna. Beware of fast currents.

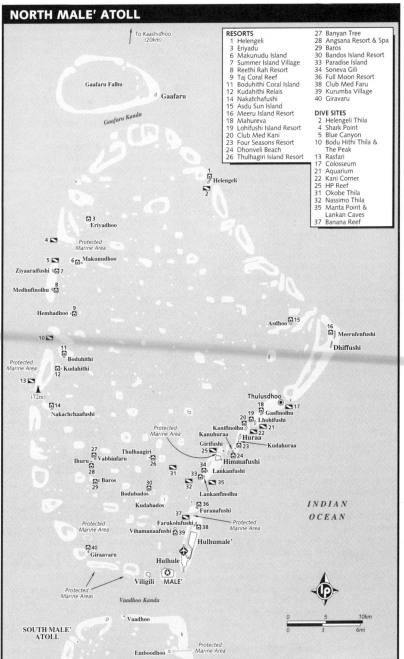

NORTH MALE' ATOLL

To Kaashidhoo (20km)

Gaafaru Falhu

Gaafaru

Gaafaru Kandu

RESORTS
1 Helengeli
3 Eriyadu
6 Makunudu Island
7 Summer Island Village
8 Reethi Rah Resort
9 Taj Coral Reef
11 Boduhithi Coral Island
12 Kudahithi Relais
14 Nakatchafushi
15 Asdu Sun Island
16 Meeru Island Resort
18 Mahureva
19 Lohifushi Island Resort
20 Club Med Kani
23 Four Seasons Resort
24 Dhonveli Beach
26 Thulhagiri Island Resort

27 Banyan Tree
28 Angsana Resort & Spa
29 Baros
30 Bandos Island Resort
33 Paradise Island
34 Soneva Gili
36 Full Moon Resort
38 Club Med Faru
39 Kurumba Village
40 Giravaru

DIVE SITES
2 Helengeli Thila
4 Shark Point
5 Blue Canyon
10 Bodu Hithi Thila &
  The Peak
13 Rasfari
17 Colosseum
21 Aquarium
22 Kani Corner
25 HP Reef
31 Okobe Thila
32 Nassimo Thila
35 Manta Point &
  Lankan Caves
37 Banana Reef

NORTH & SOUTH MALE' ATOLLS

1 Helengeli
2

3 Eriyadhoo

4 Protected Marine Area

5   6 Makunudhoo
Ziyaaraifushi 7

8 Medhufinolhu

9 Hembadhoo

10

11 Boduhithi
Protected Marine Area Kudahithi
12
13
(72m)

14 Nakachchaafushi

15 Asdhoo
16 Meerufenfushi
Dhiffushi

Thulusdhoo
18   17
19 Gasfinolhu
20   Lhohifushi
21
Kanifinolhu 22
Kanuhuraa Huraa
Girifushi 23
Kudahuraa
24
34 Himmafushi
Thulhaagiri
27
Ihuru Vabbinfuru
28 26 31 33 Lankanfushi
Baros 30 32
29 35
Bodubados Lankanfinolhu
Kudabados
36
37 Furanafushi
Farukolufushi
Vihamanaafushi 39 38
Protected Marine Area
Giraavaru 40
Hulhumale'
Hulhule
Viligili MALE'
Protected Marine Areas
Vaadhoo Kandu

INDIAN OCEAN

Protected Marine Area

SOUTH MALE' ATOLL

Vaadhoo

Protected Marine Area
Emboodhoo

0   5   10km
0   3   6mi

HP Reef This thila, also called Rainbow Reef or Girifushi Thila, sits beside a narrow channel where currents provide much nourishment for incredibly rich growths of soft, blue corals, and support a large variety of reef fish and pelagics. The formations include large blocks, spectacular caves and a 25m vertical swim-through chimney. It is a Protected Marine Area.

Okobe Thila Also called Barracuda Giri, the attraction here is the variety of spectacular reef fish that inhabit the shallow caves and crannies, including lionfish, scorpionfish, batfish, sweetlips, moray eels, sharks and big Napoleon wrasse.

Nassimo Thila This demanding dive follows the north side of a fine thila, also known as Paradise Rock, which has superb gorgonians and sea fans on coral blocks, cliffs and overhangs. Numerous large fish frequent this site.

Manta Point & Lankan Caves The best time to see the mantas for which Manta Point is famous is from May to November. Coral outcrops at about 8m are a 'cleaning station', where cleaner wrasse feed on parasites from the mantas' wings. Cliffs, coral tables, turtles, sharks and numerous reef fish are other attractions, as are the nearby Lankan Caves.

Banana Reef This Protected Marine Area has a bit of everything: dramatic cliffs, caves and overhangs; brilliant coral growths; big predators such as sharks, barracuda and groper; and prolific reef fish including jackfish, morays, Napoleon wrasse and blue-striped snapper. It was one of the first dive sites in the country to become internationally known. The reeftop is excellent for snorkelling.

Resorts

Most of the resorts in North Male' Atoll are reached by speedboat from the airport. Though some of the closest ones use a traditional dhoni (which can be a little slow-going!), some of the most distant ones offer optional seaplane transfers. Unless otherwise noted, airport transfers to the following resorts are by speedboat.

Budget Resorts

Summer Island Village *(Ziyaaraifushi island; ☎ 443088; W www.summerislandvillage.com; singles/doubles US$120/140; airport transfer fast dhoni 1½hr US$75; 108 rooms)* is popular mainly with German and British guests who find the all-inclusive packages good value – the price includes some activities, all meals, house wine, spirits and beer. Fully independent travellers (FITs) can get good deals here too.

The lagoon is wide and shallow, so the resort is more suited to windsurfing,

water-skiing and sailing than to snorkelling or swimming. The island has quite good beaches on two sides, though some stretches are protected by somewhat unattractive breakwaters.

Landscaping work has improved the appearance of this once sparsely vegetated island; though the corrugated iron roofs are a little obtrusive, new cream paintwork has softened the look of the buildings. Rooms are clean and functional, and have air-con but no other frills. Some guests like the upstairs rooms, but the single-storey bungalows have a better beach outlook – room numbers 50 to 74 have the best position. The 16 water villas cost an extra US$45 and have satellite TV, a fridge, phone and a glass panel in the floor so you can see the fish. Meals are buffets with a modest selection of curry, fish, salads and vegetables. Weekly theme nights feature Asian and international cuisine.

There are some great dive sites within about 5km – a single dive with equipment costs US$46; an open-water course costs US$490. The new Spa Lanka has 45-minute Thai-style treatments for US$55, or you can get three sessions for US$135. A daily snorkelling trip is included in the package (excluding equipment), as are table tennis, volleyball and badminton. But the main activity at this resort is taking it easy, hanging out on the beach or in the bar.

Asdu Sun Island *(Asdhoo island; ☎ 445051; W www.asdu.com; singles/doubles US$90/130; airport transfer 1½hr US$80; 30 rooms)* is one of the original Maldives resorts – small, natural and very easy-going (don't confuse it with the new Sun Island Resort in Ari Atoll, which is just the opposite). The rooms are characterised by what they *don't* have – there's no TV, air-con, or hot water, just louvre windows, ceiling fans and refreshing showers. International direct dial (IDD) phones are the only concession to modernity.

Parts of the island could do with a facelift, but the beaches are fine, the snorkelling is good and fishing trips are popular. It's an inexpensive resort, and the diving and drinks are very reasonably priced. All meals are a set menu – nothing elaborate, but the food is plentiful and well prepared, with lots of fresh fish. Many guests are on packages from Italy, and there's a sprinkling of FITs who sometimes get very cheap rates here.

Meeru Island Resort *(Meerufenfushi island; ☎ 443157; ⓦ www.meeru.com; standard singles/doubles US$110/130; airport transfer 50min day/night US$70/130; 227 rooms)*, at the eastern corner of North Male' Atoll, was an old-style budget resort, totally redeveloped in the late 1990s. As well as the old white-tiled standard rooms, it has new 'land villas' that are boxy prefabricated pine bungalows with air-con, telephones, good bathrooms and an all-timber finish (they cost up to US$30 more than standard rooms). Other new rooms are also very woody, and have a more interesting pentagonal design and better finish. Some are built with balconies over the water, and they're more expensive again. The two honeymoon suites (about US$440 in high season) are large, lavishly equipped, and stand on stilts over the lagoon 60m from shore – a small boat is provided for access.

Meerufenfushi means 'Sweet Water Island', and its wells were used to replenish passing boats. The ground water sustained lush, natural vegetation, but much of the 28-hectare island is now used for growing fruit and vegetables. Most guests are from Britain, Germany, France, Italy and other parts of Europe, many of them young (mostly couples), as well as families. There might be 50 or more kids on the island over Christmas and in August – there's lots of space for them and the pool is popular. The resort doesn't organise much entertainment, but the bars are busy most evenings, especially because many of the guests are on all-inclusive packages.

Facilities include a huge round restaurant with sand floors and a soaring thatched roof. Buffet meals featuring a huge variety of dishes are served here. There are also three bars (draught beer is US$3), two coffee shops serving à la carte snacks (the pizzas are great, from US$8 to US$10), and a seafood restaurant on an old sailing ship moored at the jetty. Other attractions include tennis courts, badminton, a golf driving range, a gym, and a spa offering massage and beauty treatments.

Snorkelling near the island is not good, but boats go to the edge of the house reef every two hours. All the usual water sports are offered – fishing trips are popular, and the vast lagoon is perfect for learning sailing and windsurfing. Meeru has its own safari boats, and two- or three-day cruises can be done from the resort. Inexpensive excursions go to the fishing village on neighbouring Dhiffushi. Those interested in Maldivian history and culture will also appreciate the small **museum** at Meeru where there's a huge blue whale skeleton on display.

Many of the visitors to Meeru are keen scuba divers, and the **Ocean-Pro** dive school (ⓦ www.oceanpro-diveteam.com) is a large and efficient operation. A single dive is US$30 with tank and weights only, or US$42 including full equipment rental, plus US$10 per dive for the boat trip. A US$2 discount applies after seven dives, and there's a good six-day, no-limit dive deal. An open-water course costs US$520. A whole slew of great dive sites are accessible in the channels within 5km. Once known only as a budget resort and dive destination, Meeru now caters to a wide variety of interests and budget levels – it's a big resort but it's not crowded and has retained its personal, friendly feel.

Thulhagiri Island Resort *(Thalhaagiri island; ☎ 445930; ⓔ reserve@thulhaagiri.com .mv; singles/doubles US$146/152; airport transfer 30min US$65; 69 rooms)* was once a Club Med resort, but is now independently managed and attracts guests from Germany, Switzerland, France and many other countries, including a few FITs. It's an appealing resort – the main buildings have some style and rustic charm while the island itself is small, pleasantly green and shady. The beach is beautiful on one side of the island, but non-existent on the other, and the house reef is too far out for convenient snorkelling. The small swimming pool may appeal to children. The rooms are cosy cottages with woven palm ceilings, air-con, phone, hot water, satellite TV and minibar. The 17 new over-water villas have four-poster beds, colourful fabrics and coffee-making facilities – they're nice, but not especially great value at around US$320 a double in high season.

All meals are buffets, and they're very good for a resort in this range, offering plenty of variety and quality ingredients. The dive centre is small, friendly and efficient and charges US$46 for a boat dive with all equipment, US$36 with tank and weights only. Open-water courses cost US$450. The 'learn to windsurf' package includes eight hours of instruction and one week's unlimited use of a sailboard for US$275. Overall, this resort is a good value choice for quiet relaxation or inexpensive activities.

NORTH & SOUTH MALE' ATOLLS

Giravaru *(Giraavaru island; ☎ 440440;* **w** *www.giravaru.com; singles/doubles US$115/ 135; airport transfer dhoni 45mins US$35, speedboat 15min US$50; 65 rooms)* is on a small island with very nice beaches, and though it's heavily developed, the palm-thatched buildings and the vegetation growing on every available space help it retain a natural feel. A very friendly place, it attracts guests from Italy, Britain and other parts of Europe, as well as a few expatriate workers enjoying a break from Male'.

The Giraavaru people are believed to be descended from the earliest inhabitants of the Maldives. About 30 years ago the population on the island declined to the point where it no longer included the 40 adult males required to support a mosque, so the islanders all moved to Male' and Giraavaru became available for resort development.

Some of the buildings are looking a little worn, but rooms have all been upgraded and have air-con, phone, fridge and TV – they're much better on the inside than they look from the outside. For a small resort, the restaurant offers an excellent buffet selection with an especially good choice of seafood and pasta dishes.

At the new Indus Ayurvedic Spa you can enjoy a traditional Indian healing massage in a simple setting; other activities include tennis, billiards, water-skiing, fishing and various excursions. The sailing and windsurfing courses are good value. Nearby Vaadhoo Kandu has some excellent dive sites which the enthusiastic **Planeta** dive centre *(**w** www.planetadivers.com)* will take you to for US$56 per dive, including boat trip and equipment. An open-water course will cost about US$500. The house reef is accessible and excellent for snorkelling. This resort is conveniently close to the capital, but still has a great get-away-from-it-all ambience.

Mid-Range Resorts

Helengeli *(Helengeli island; ☎ 444615;* **w** *www.helengeli-maldives.com; singles/ doubles US$110/165; airport transfer speedboat 2hrs US$110, seaplane 20min US$220; 50 rooms)* is the most northerly resort in North Male' Atoll and popular with keen divers – almost 40 dive sites are accessible from here, and most of them are used only by Helengeli guests and the occasional passing safari boat.

The 2km-long house reef is excellent, so you need not venture far for snorkelling, and qualified divers can do unguided scuba dives from the beach. Nearby Helengeli Thila is considered one of the best dive sites in the country. Dive costs are around US$53 for a boat dive with all equipment provided, or US$41 with tank and weights only. It's US$2 less after the seventh dive, and there's a good six-day, unlimited dive deal. An open-water course costs US$524, but most divers coming here are already qualified. The **Ocean-Pro** dive base *(**w** www.oceanpro-diveteam.com)* aims for personalised service and tries to keep guests with the same dive guides for their whole stay.

The resort was extensively renovated in 1996, and has 50 modern rooms with air-con, hot water and open-air bathrooms. All rooms face the water; the best swimming beach is at the western tip of the island. Helengeli is a fair-sized island with plenty of natural vegetation, an uncrowded feel and secluded accommodation. The restaurant alternates between set-menu meals and buffets, including a weekly beach barbecue – the variety of food may sometimes be limited, but the atmosphere and service are good. There's no windsurfing, sailing or other water sports, but a few excursions are offered. Evening entertainment is very low-key, consisting mainly of a few drinks at the delightful beachfront bar, and an early night in preparation the next day's diving activity.

Eriyadu *(Eriyadhoo island; ☎ 444487; singles/doubles US$198/294;* **w** *www.aaa -resortsmaldives.com/eriyadu/; airport transfer 50min US$80; 57 rooms)*, like other resorts in the far north of North Male' Atoll, has access to plenty of uncrowded dive sites. Many of the guests here are divers, and the **Werner Lau Dive Center** *(**w** www.wernerlau.com)* is a very professional operation. A single boat dive is US$50 with all equipment, US$46 with tank and weights only, but the six-day no-limit dive package will cost about US$460/530. An open-water course is about US$560. The house reef is accessible and good for snorkelling and diving, with lots of reef fish and larger marine life commonly seen.

The island itself is quite heavily developed, but the buildings are interspersed with lots of shady trees and shrubbery, and there are fine, white beaches all around. Rooms

Playing badminton on the beach

Sailing around the islands

Soaking in the shallows near dhonis

Catamaran sailing off Farukolufushi island

Men on the deck of a sailing boat at sunset

Dhonis moored at port

Beach cocktail party at sunset, Kudahuraa island

have polished timber floors, TV, minibar and other mod cons. The sand-floor restaurant serves most meals in buffet style, with a varied selection of European dishes, curries and seafood. Most of the guests are German, Italian and Swiss, with a few Brits and Japanese. The usual water sports and (expensive) excursions are available, as is some low-key evening entertainment, but this resort is mainly for diving, snorkelling and relaxing on the beach.

Makunudu Island (*Makunudhoo island;* ☎ *446464;* ⓦ *www.makunudu.com; singles/ doubles US$310/340; airport transfer 50min US$160; 36 rooms*) is a very tasteful, top-end, luxury resort with just 36 individual thatched-roof bungalows. All rooms face the beach and feature natural finishes, varnished timber, textured white walls, open-air bathrooms, and all facilities except television. The service is of a high standard and the food is excellent, thanks to the French chef. Breakfast and lunch are buffets while most dinners are a choice of thoughtfully prepared set menus, served in the delightful open-sided restaurant. Beach barbecues are a weekly event and breakfast can be served in your room.

The island is small, with lots of palm trees, natural vegetation, pure white beaches and a blue lagoon – it's picture perfect. Guests are mainly German, British, French and Italian couples who come to relax, or who are on their honeymoon. There are excellent dive sites in the area, the house reef is great for snorkelling, and an introductory dive is free. Single boat dives cost US$48/54 without/with equipment, and an open-water course is US$450. Dive groups tend to be small and friendly. Windsurfing and sailing are free, as are shorter excursions. If you've come in your own yacht, you'll find a safe anchorage here. If you want a small, exclusive, natural-style resort, Makunudu is one of the very best in the Maldives.

Reethi Rah Resort (*Medhufinolhu island;* ☎ *441905;* ⓔ *rrresort@dhivehinet.net.mv; airport transfer 45min; 60 rooms*) was one of the first resorts in the country and for many years it offered basic, back-to-nature style bungalows and a delightfully casual restaurant. Now that's all changing – the lease has been taken over and the whole resort is being redeveloped, almost certainly

as a modernised, more upmarket operation. It should reopen in 2004.

Taj Coral Reef (*Hembadhoo island;* ☎ *441948;* ⓦ *www.tajhotels.com/resort/coral _maldives/new.htm; singles/doubles US$225/ 280; airport transfer 45min US$95; 65 rooms*) is a very modern and efficiently run resort, with swimming pool, gym, spa and massage centre, and very good food. The beachfront rooms are big, comfortable and fully furnished with TV, in-house movies, minibar and the works. The 35 over-water bungalows are even bigger (and cost about US$50 more).

It all looks very new and neat, the main restaurant is enclosed and air-conditioned – no sand floors here. All meals are buffet, with theme nights featuring Chinese, Italian, Maldivian or other cuisines. In addition, a small, à la carte beach restaurant specialises in Indian food. A lot of landscaping work has been done, but the effect is more manicured than natural. The gardener conducts a regular tour if you're interested in tropical horticulture. Beach erosion is a problem in places, and unsightly walls dot the lagoon around half the island, though there's an interesting and accessible house reef on the other side, and a good beach at one corner.

The **Blue In dive centre** (ⓦ *www.blue inmaldives.com*) has first-class equipment, and charges about US$58 for a dive with everything included. An open-water course costs around US$500. A special diving attraction is the Hembadhoo Wreck, a 16m tugboat that was sunk just offshore, and now has a rich growth of soft corals and abundant fish.

Taj Coral Reef is a very well-managed resort, recommended for those who want a spacious room with all mod cons.

Boduhithi Coral Island (*Boduhithi island;* ☎ *443981;* ⓔ *boduvcz@clubvacanze.com.mv; singles/doubles €241/328; airport transfer 55min €62; 103 rooms*) is very much a club-style resort, with lots of activities, fine Italian food and a virtually 100% Italian clientele. Rooms are attractive and a good size, with high wooden ceilings and all facilities except a TV. The 21 over-water bungalows cost an extra €26/52. Rates include all meals, drinks with meals, most excursions and activities, two dives per day for qualified divers and an introductory dive for beginners. An open-water diving course costs US$400 extra.

The island is quite densely developed, but has lots of trees, two very nice beaches and an accessible house reef for snorkelling. Organised activities include aerobics, water aerobics, beach dancing, volleyball competitions and more. Every night there's a discotheque, trivia quiz, cabaret game or some other entertainment.

Nearly all guests are on one-week package tours from Italy, but independent agents in Male' may have the occasional cheap room here in the low season. This is a typically sociable and energetic Italian resort.

Kudahithi Relais (Kudahithi island; ☎ 444613; e kudahithi@clubvacanze.com. mv; singles/doubles €393/476; airport transfer 55min €62; 7 rooms) is one of the smallest, most exclusive resorts in the country. Each individual bungalow is decorated with a theme – Balinese, Maldivian, Sheik's Room, Maharani Room, Rehendi Room, Safari Lodge and Captain's Cabin – with authentic antiques, rich fabrics and designer tiles. Some face the beach and others have a private jetty. The cuisine is international, with a bias to Italian and fresh seafood. An open bar, excursions and activities are included in the price – guests use the dive and water sports facilities at nearby Boduhithi. Though you wouldn't come here for the activities or the nightlife, Kudahithi is the ultimate, intimate, romantic hideaway.

Nakatchafushi (Nakachchaafushi island; ☎ 443847; w www.unisurf.com/nakachafushi; singles/doubles US$180/220; airport transfer 45min US$65; 51 rooms) has a swimming pool and stylish thatched buildings in a tropical garden setting, shaded by palm trees and dripping with bougainvillea. But it's very much a modern-style resort and the look is carefully cultivated rather than Robinson Crusoe.

The attractive round rooms have tile floors, air-con, cane furniture and plenty of privacy. The main restaurant does set-menu or buffet meals – the twice-weekly barbecue buffet is good. A coffee and snack shop (serving pizza and seafood), an Asian restaurant (that does a weekly Mexican buffet) and a beach grill offer lots of options – to sample them, take a bed and breakfast or half-board plan. For entertainment, there's a disco and a weekly live band, but don't expect a wild party scene.

The big lagoon on the north side is good for swimming and windsurfing, while the house reef near the southern shore is easily accessible for snorkelling. The efficient dive centre charges about US$50 for a boat dive with all equipment, and US$500 for an open-water course.

Guests are mostly from Britain, Germany and elsewhere in Europe, and many of them are repeaters. It's ideal for a quiet, comfortable, hassle-free holiday.

Mahureva (Gasfinolhu island; ☎ 442078; singles/doubles €188/237; airport transfer 40min free; 40 rooms) caters exclusively to the Italian market with transfers, most activities and some drinks included. All bookings are by the week, through the Italian tour company Valtur (☎ 39-6-47061, fax 39-6-4706334, w www.valtur.it). Rooms are all air-con with hot water, but have no TV, no phone and no keys. The packages are all inclusive, the atmosphere is animated, and the pasta is al dente.

Lohifushi Island Resort (Lhohifushi island; ☎ 443451; w www.lohifushi.com; singles/doubles US$105/160; airport transfer dhoni 1½hr US$40, speedboat 25min US$70; 127 rooms) is quite a big, modern resort on a long, narrow island. The standard rooms are fan-cooled, but have phones and hot water. Most of the rooms are 'superior' or 'deluxe', cost at least US$10 to US$20 more, and have air-con (a deluxe room may not be worth the extra money). There are tennis and squash courts (US$10 per hour), a football field, a volleyball court, a small swimming pool, a children's play area and a Japanese-style spa/massage centre.

As well as the usual sailing, windsurfing and water-skiing, there's a very surfable left-hand wave off the southeast corner of the island called Lohi's, overlooked by a surfers' bar and viewing deck. Other breaks are accessible by boat (US$7.70 per person for three hours, minimum four persons) – boats should be booked at least a day ahead, and aren't always punctual. Rooms 152, 153 and 154 are close to the surf, but all the others are a fair hike away. Fishing enthusiasts can choose between sunrise fishing, night fishing and big-game fishing. Snorkellers can walk out on the jetty to get to the edge of the house reef, but for great snorkelling you'll need to take a boat trip.

Plenty of good dive sites are accessible, and the resort is quite popular with divers. The dive base charges US$39 for a single dive or US$370 for a 10-dive package with equipment provided, plus US$10 for each boat trip. A PADI open-water course will cost about US$460.

The large main restaurant serves buffet breakfast, set-menu lunch, and buffet dinner with weekly Maldivian theme nights. The best cuisine is in the Chinese and Italian speciality restaurants, and these cost extra, even for those on full-board packages. Entertainment is provided six nights a week, with discos, karaoke, live bands, crab races, cultural performances and 'animators' to help people enjoy themselves. There are several bars, charging US$3 for a beer and US$3 to US$5 for spirits.

The guests are generally a good international mix, from the UK, Switzerland, Germany, France, Japan and elsewhere. Lohifushi is quite a big resort and somewhat impersonal, but the cheaper rooms are quite good value if you don't spend too much on the extras.

Club Med Kani *(Kanifinolhu island; ☎ 443152; ᵂ www.clubmed.com; singles/doubles US$172/288; airport transfer 30min $US45; 209 rooms)* is a good-value, all-inclusive Club Med resort. This one has three room categories – beachfront rooms cost a little more than garden rooms, and over-water rooms are even more expensive. They're all comfortably furnished and feature lots of natural timber, air-con, phone and minibar. The meals are very good (though perhaps not quite as varied as at Club Med Faru – see later in this section), with accompanying wine, beer or soft drinks included in the package price. Drinks at the bar cost extra (US$3 to US$8).

The island itself is quite large and well vegetated, and the beachside bar and entertainment areas are particularly spacious. The wide lagoon is a good place to learn sailing or windsurfing (both included in the price), but not so good for snorkelling (though snorkelling trips to other reefs are also included). Fitness sessions, one daily scuba dive, volleyball and other games and activities are all included, but you pay extra for excursions and spa treatments (from US$25). The surf break on the east side of the island is an undemanding right-hander, but it's difficult to reach from the shore and Club Med doesn't provide any boats or guides for surfers. You are allowed to bring children here (unlike Club Med Faru), but there's no kids' club, and no special facilities or activities for children.

Dhonveli Beach *(Kanuhuraa island; ☎ 440055; ᵂ www.dhonvelibeach.com; singles/doubles US$131/210; airport transfer 30min US$60; 50 rooms)*, formerly Tari Village, is being completely renovated and virtually rebuilt. Most of the guests come from Italy, enjoying club-style activities like daily aerobics and evening 'animation'. From March to November there is also a sizeable contingent of surfers, from Australia, the USA, Europe, South Africa and elsewhere. It's an unusual mix, but it works.

The island is small, with scrubby natural vegetation and a few big banyan trees, but extensive landscaping is under way around the main beach, the new bar and the swimming pool. The beach on the north side of the island is great for swimming and sunbathing, as well as being safe for children. On the south side of the island, the island's private surf break is a consistent left-hander called Pasta Point. Outdoor tables here are great for a beer and a view of the surfing action.

The new rooms are fully equipped and come in various sizes, with designs that are more imaginative than at many resorts. All meals are buffet style and feature a fair selection of good quality food (Italian tastes are well provided for!). Kanuhuraa is not a big diving destination, but there are lots of good dive sites nearby (the Protected Marine Area at HP Reef is very close). A boat dive is US$61 with full equipment, US$46 with tank and weights only. An open-water course costs US$274. The house reef is not good for snorkelling.

There are no FITs here. All Italian guests book through the Italian agent Teorema (ᵂ www.teorematour.it). Surfing packages to Dhonveli can be booked only through an accredited agent such as Atoll Travel (ᵂ www.atolltravel.com; see Surfing under Activities in the Facts for the Visitor chapter), at a special rate that includes exclusive access to Pasta Point plus unlimited boat trips to other breaks in the area with experienced local surf guides. When the renovations are finished, this will be one of the classiest and most convenient surfing resorts anywhere.

Angsana Resort & Spa *(Ihuru island;* ☎ *443502;* **w** *www.angsana.com/maldives; singles/doubles US$380/429; airport transfer 30min US$90; 45 rooms)*, a sister resort to the nearby Banyan Tree, has been recently renovated and upgraded. With its canopy of palm trees and surrounding white beach, it conforms exactly to the tropical island stereotype and often features in photographs publicising the Maldives. The house reef forms a near perfect circle around the island, and is brilliant for snorkelling and shore dives. Look near the jetty for the 'barnacle', the oldest of several metal structures on which a small electric current stimulates coral growth. The best dive sites are some distance away on the edges of the atoll – take a boat dive trip for US$83 with all equipment or US$60 with tank and weights only. An open-water course is US$575.

The rooms are all redecorated in contemporary style, with black furniture, lime green accents and designer bathrooms – some have a private spa. There's a modern look in the restaurant too, but most guests prefer to eat dinner on the deck overlooking the sea. The spa is less opulent as the one at Banyan Tree (see under Top-End Resorts, later), but the therapists have done the same training and the treatments are almost identical. Angsana offers a very Banyan Tree–mix of cuisine, comfort and indulgence, but it's considerably less expensive, and not quite so classy.

Baros *(Baros island;* ☎ *442672;* **w** *www .unisurf.com/baros; singles/doubles US$205/ 245; airport transfer 25min US$75; 75 rooms)* is a longstanding favourite with many British and German guests. It's an attractive island, small but well vegetated, with good beaches and a good house reef (but you have to go out through gaps in the sea wall to reach the reef edge). A wide lagoon on one side is perfect for windsurfing, and you can feed stingrays here at sunset. Dive costs are lower than at many comparable resorts – US$38 for a single boat dive with all equipment, US$5 less if you have your own, and good discounts for multidive packages. An open-water course is US$494.

Standard rooms are smallish thatched cottages by the beach, with natural finishes and air-con, but no TV. The 16 octagonal over-water bungalows have wide balconies and lovely furnishings; they cost about US$100 more. Food and service are excellent – most

guests are on half-board packages to take advantage of the choice of restaurants. A live band plays four nights a week in the bar, but Baros is basically a pretty quiet resort, ideal for those who want to relax in very attractive surroundings.

Bandos Island Resort *(Bodubados island;* ☎ *440088;* **w** *www.bandos.com; singles/ doubles US$127/168; airport transfer 20min US$43; 225 rooms)* opened in 1972, has expanded several times since, and is now one of the biggest resorts in the country. Facilities are extensive – a 500-seat conference centre, coffee shop, several restaurants, disco/bar, tennis courts, billiard room, sauna, gym, swimming pool, beauty salon and spa-massage service. The childcare centre is free during the day, and only about US$5 per hour in the evening. With all these facilities, the island is quite intensely developed and resembles a well-manicured town centre rather than a typical tropical island.

Sailing and windsurfing are available, along with a full range of motorised water sports, and an active big-game fishing centre (US$800 per day for four). Fine, narrow beaches surround the island, and the house reef is handy for snorkelling and diving. Lots of fish and a small wreck can be seen here. The state-of-the-art dive centre does trips to about 40 dive sites in the area, and offers a full range of courses, including nitrox and re-breather training. A single dive costs about US$60, including all equipment, boat and service charges, US$9 less with your own equipment. An open-water course will run to about US$528. The diving health clinic here has a decompression chamber available to anyone who needs it (though it's very expensive).

Bandos caters for day-trippers (or evening visitors) from Male', but currently does not provide a regular boat – call the resort if you want to arrange something. Airline crews and travel agents often use Bandos for short-term stays, as well as guests from all over Europe and Asia, so there can be a very mixed group here.

Rooms are modern, with red-tiled roofs, white-tiled floors, air-con, hot water, hairdryer, minibar and IDD phone. 'Junior suites' are good for families. The main Gallery Restaurant does three international buffet meals daily. Other eateries include the 24-hour Seabreeze Café with à la carte curries and pasta, and the Harbour Grill for steak and seafood. The Sand Bar hosts live bands, disco nights, cultural shows or karaoke several nights a week. This is one of the liveliest resorts in the country, with a very varied clientele and something for everyone, from convention organisers to hard-core divers.

Paradise Island (*Lankanfinolhu island;* ☎ *440011;* Ⓦ *www.villahotels.com; singles/ doubles US$155/175; airport transfer 20min US$45; 260 rooms*), one of the biggest resorts, offers a complete range of facilities and services. The guests are from all over, including Europe, Japan, Taiwan and Russia. Some very cheap package holidays offer Paradise at bargain prices, but the cost of extras can be quite high.

Rooms are very clean and modern, with white tiles, white walls, air-con, bidet and satellite TV. Over-water bungalows are a bit bigger and up to US$100 more expensive. Full board is only US$10 per person more than half board and probably worth it. The main restaurant does a very good buffet for every meal. Full-board guests get a 15% discount at the speciality restaurants, which are good, but pricey, The Sunrise restaurant does seafood (fresh fish from US$15), Ristorante Al Tramonto is Italian (pastas around US$18); Fukuya Teppanyaki is Japanese (sashimi around US$20); and the coffee shop serves snacks 24 hours (US$7 to US$10).

The island is nicely landscaped and has good beaches and a swimming pool. Some rooms are a long way from the restaurant, and some don't have much of a view. Activities include gym, squash, badminton, tennis, billiards etc – everything costs extra except darts and table tennis. There's no spa as such, but there is a massage centre; 50-minute sessions cost from US$60. Snorkelling is not good in the shallow lagoon and a snorkelling trip by boat will cost US$16 per person, plus US$10 to rent mask, snorkel and fins.

The **Delphis dive centre** (Ⓦ *www.delphis .com.mv*) charges US$53 for a boat dive with tank and weights, or US$15 more with full equipment. An open-water course is US$612.

There's entertainment every night, from karaoke to crab races, but your bar bill might add up (a beer costs US$4 and a glass of cask wine costs US$6.50). If you budget for the extras, you can have an enjoyable, inexpensive holiday in Paradise!

Maldivian Multinationalism

As an island nation, the Maldives is almost exclusively a producer of fish and coconut products; everything else is imported. Thus the tourism industry must ship in everything needed for a resort except the sunshine, the sea and the island itself, which always remains Maldivian property. The diversity of imports can be surprising. A Maldivian island can be leased to a Sri Lankan company to develop a resort for the Italian market, with pasta imported from Australia, wine from South Africa, fruit from New Zealand, beer from Singapore, plumbing from Germany, air-conditioners from Japan, hairdryers from Canada, labourers from Bangladesh, dive masters from Austria, and prices in US dollars. When it comes to doing business, Maldivians are anything but insular!

Full Moon Resort (*Furanafushi island;* ☎ *442010;* Ⓦ *www.unisurf.com/fullmoon; singles/doubles US$170/210; airport transfer 20min US$33; 156 rooms*) is close to Male', and the ambience is more upscale country club than remote tropical island. Rooms are either in white concrete, motel-style two-storey blocks with green-tiled roofs, or somewhat boxy water villas built over the lagoon. They are equipped with every mod con except a TV. There's no attempt at the rustic look here, but every square centimetre is cultivated with tropical plants or carpeted with well swept white sand.

The Thai restaurant, Mediterranean restaurant and the Italian grill/pizza place serve more interesting food than the buffets at the main restaurant, so it might be best to take a bed and breakfast package and bring extra cash to spend in the speciality restaurants.

A full range of facilities is squeezed onto this small island, including an inviting free-form swimming pool, tennis courts, gym, spa and business centre. There are no motorised water sports, and the lagoon is unsuitable for snorkelling. The efficient dive centre charges about US$50 for a boat dive with all equipment, and US$500 for an open-water course. Windsurfing and sailing are available, as is big-game fishing, but this is not a resort for the hyperactive. Most guests are here for a short and relaxing holiday, and Full Moon provides it.

Club Med Faru (*Farukolufushi island; ☎ 443021;* W *www.clubmed.com; singles/ doubles US$172/288; airport transfer 20min $US30; 152 rooms*) is particularly good value because holiday packages include wine, beer, water or juice with meals, as well as sailing, windsurfing, canoeing and one scuba dive per day. Club organisers (called 'GOs') promote all sorts of games and activities to keep guests happy. Most of the guests are French, but there's a wide mix of European, Asian and other nationalities, and GOs speak French, English, Japanese and Chinese. About 40% of the guests are singles, and the rest are couples – no children are allowed at the resort.

Snorkelling trips, exercise sessions and amateur stage shows are all part of the package. Spa sessions are not included, but prices are less than at most resorts – US$22 for a half-hour 'smooth down', US$44 for a 50-minute Balinese massage. Another good-value extra is the PADI open water diving course for US$290. Excursions also cost extra, from a Rf210 Male' tour to a Rf3200 seaplane trip to a deserted island.

The meals are all buffet style, with a huge variety of excellent food, including Japanese, Indian, Chinese and European dishes, home-made ice cream and French cheese. Drinks at the bar are extra, purchased with coloured tickets which you buy from the front desk; it works out at about US$3 for a soft drink, US$4 for a beer, and at least US$5 for spirits. Rooms are in two-storey blocks, have terra-cotta tile floors, rounded windows and a bit of character (but no phone or TV).

At some stage Club Med might have to move from Farukolufushi to make way for the Hulhumale' development (see the Male' chapter), but on current plans it should be here until at least 2007. In the meantime, a second Club Med has opened on the island of Kanifinolhu, roughly 17km further north (see under Mid-Range Resorts, earlier).

Kurumba Village (*Vihamanaafushi island; ☎ 442324;* W *www.unisurf.com/kurumba; singles/doubles US$170/210; airport transfer 15min US$33; 171 rooms*), established in 1972, was the first resort in the Maldives. It's also the closest resort to Male', catering for business conferences and conventions as well as day-trippers from the capital, and the usual visiting holiday makers. If you're sensitive to aircraft noise, you may find it a little too close

to the airport. It's a good-sized island with manicured beaches, cultivated gardens, lots of palm trees, several restaurants, a spa, and a full range of recreational and conference facilities. Kurumba was slated for a major renovation in 2003, so its facilities, services and prices may be subject to change. For post-renovation information, contact the ever-efficient local operator, Universal Enterprises (☎ 323080, 38 Orchid Magu, Male').

Top-End Resorts

Banyan Tree (*Vabbinfaru island; ☎ 443147;* W *www.banyantree.com/maldives; singles/ doubles US$546/637; airport transfer 25min US$98; 48 rooms*), part of the international Banyan Tree Group, offers understated luxury, while upholding its pro-environment policies. Accommodation is in superbly finished beachfront or garden villas with conical roofs and stylish, spiral-shaped floor plans inspired by the shape of a sea shell. Each villa has a king-sized four-poster bed, ceiling fans, marble bathroom and tastefully carved wooden furniture. Bamboo screens provide every villa with a private garden area, though they can make parts of the island feel a little fenced in.

Guests come from all over Europe and Asia, and the superb buffet meals satisfy their varied tastes. Lunch under the palm trees is a delight, with barbecued fish, succulent steak, fresh salads and delicious desserts – even a cheese platter. The restaurant and bar are both casually elegant, open-sided spaces with sand floors and quality furniture.

This was one of the first resorts to have a spa, billed as a 'sanctuary for the senses', where Thai-trained therapists offer everything from a 60-minute tamarind and oatmeal body rub (US$50) to a three-hour Hawaiian Lomi Lomi for two (US$310). For the more active, night fishing, windsurfing, sailing and snorkelling are included in the price. The house reef is great for snorkelling and diving, but the very best dive sites are some distance away on the edges of the atoll. A single boat dive costs US$83 with all equipment or US$60 with tank and weights; an open-water course is US$575.

On one side of the house reef, look for the 'lotus' – a saucer-shaped metal framework about 20m across, dotted with small corals and electrified with a low-voltage current. It's an experiment in promoting rapid coral regeneration, monitored by the resident marine scientist. The resort also runs a turtle nursery, tags young turtles for research, and promotes environmental education in local schools. Banyan Tree is a wonderful resort for romance, relaxation, eating and being pampered – if it's environmentally proactive, so much the better.

Four Seasons Resort *(Kudahuraa island; ☎ 444888; w www.fourseasons.com; singles/ doubles US$532/629; airport transfer 25min US$90; 106 rooms)* is one of the finest luxury resorts in the country. The island itself is quite small but the beaches are wide and white, there are plenty of palm trees, and the landscaping has made the most of every square metre. It has been beautifully developed with public areas that are expansive but not pretentious, a gorgeous horizon pool and sumptuous Bali-style beach villas. A spine-like jetty at the southern end of the island gives access to the 36 over-water bungalows. All rooms have fine furnishings and full facilities (including a tastefully concealed television and DVD player) while some feature outdoor bathrooms, private plunge pools and even more spacious accommodation.

The main Café Huraa restaurant serves the buffet breakfast (including freshly baked pastries and exotic tropical fruits), lavish buffet lunch, and à la carte dinners featuring Asian and Continental cuisine. Japanese dishes are a speciality, and theme nights focus on Italian, Thai, Mexican and other styles. The Baraabaru Restaurant serves South Asian cuisine including gourmet vegetarian and Maldivian specialities, while the Reef Club beachside grill does Mediterranean dishes and fine seafood. Light meals and snacks are available in the bars and lounge, and special dinners can be arranged on the beach or in the rooms. The food is a real highlight here, and the wine list will complement any meal.

The Island Spa, on its own tiny island, provides a tranquil setting for an extensive menu of massage and beauty treatments from India, Thailand and Indonesia. A window beneath the massage table lets you gaze into the water while the masseuse works her wonders.

Other facilities include a library, gym and water-sports centre. The well-equipped dive base offers a single dive, including all equipment, guide and boat, for about US$70; a 10-dive package is US$650 and an open-water course is US$620. Nitrox is available for about US$10 more per tank. The wide, shallow lagoon is not very interesting for snorkelling, but there are excursions to nearby reefs. Other outings go to the fishing village on a neighbouring island, to Male' for shopping and sightseeing, and for big-game fishing. The Kudamas Kids Club provides a full programme of activities for children.

Four Seasons markets a variety of special packages for those who want romantic getaways, spa treatments or diving holidays. There's even an underwater wedding package! This is a top-quality resort, totally dedicated to giving guests a perfect holiday experience.

Soneva Gili *(Lankanfushi island; ☎ 440304; w www.sixsenses.com/soneva-gili; singles/ doubles US$1015/1125; airport transfer 15min US$100; 44 rooms)* opened in 2001, is setting new standards for super-luxury, high-concept resorts. The small island was completely redeveloped with gorgeous thatched pavilions for reception and restaurant spaces, and hundreds of mature palm trees transplanted from other islands. All guests stay in imaginative timber and glass villas built over the shallow lagoons. Each villa has a large bedroom, equally large bathroom, open-sided lounge area, floating sun deck and rooftop terrace. The architecture is rustic-modern, beautifully furnished, and finished with natural wood, palm thatch, linen and rope, highlighted with bare metal, polished stone, and glass bricks. Large windows and open-air spaces look out over the lagoon, offering a wonderful indoor-outdoor ambience combining personal privacy and a harmony with sea and sky. The larger 'residences' have a kitchenette and space for a second bedroom, while the seven 'Crusoe Residences' are stand-alone islands in the lagoon, accessed by personal boats.

The cuisine is truly superb, with an emphasis on fresh ingredients, fine seafood and impeccable presentation. Buffet meals are served in the elegant sand-floored restaurant, or under the stars at the sumptuous beach barbecue. À la carte service is available in your villa, by the pool, or in just about any other al fresco setting you'd like. There's an extensive wine list, as well as a wide selection of beers, spirits and cocktails in the over-water bar (or anywhere else). Breakfast includes your choice of a dozen blends of tea and coffee.

NORTH & SOUTH MALE' ATOLLS

The attention to detail is remarkable, in everything from the centimetre-thick bath towels to the subtle outdoor lighting and the heavy ironstone crockery. The service is excellent but unobtrusive, and many thoughtful touches are included in the package – a free bicycle to get around the island, and a manager's sunset drink party in the lagoon, where guests sip champagne in ankle-deep water.

The Six Senses Spa, in its own tranquil over-water villa, offers a full range of holistic, beauty and body treatments. Free activities include tennis, boules, board games and use of an extensive CD and DVD movie library. The diving and water-sports centre provides individual attention and personalised tuition – small diving groups and the use of speedboats means that even distant dive sites are accessible. Dive costs are quite expensive, like most things at Soneva Gili, but the guests here are prepared to pay – and get the very best of quality, service and style.

SOUTH MALE' ATOLL

There are only three inhabited islands, all on the eastern edge of the atoll, and all have been inhabited for a long time. The biggest and most populous island is **Maafushi** (population 1860) which has a prison and a reformatory, providing skill training and rehabilitation for wayward youths. A State Trading Organisation (STO) warehouse here buys salted fish from the local fishing villages and packs it for export.

Guraidhoo island, with around 1220 people, has a lagoon with a good anchorage, used by both fishing dhonis and passing safari boats. Sultans from Male' sought refuge here during rebellions from as early as the 17th century. Island-hopping visitors come here from the resorts, and a score or so of shops sell them souvenirs, sarongs and cool drinks.

The island of **Gulhi**, north of Maafushi, is not large but is inhabited by around 630 people. Fishing is the main activity, and there's also a small shipyard.

Diving

Some of the best dive sites are around the Vaadhoo Kandu, which funnels a huge volume of water between the North and South Male' Atolls. Various smaller kandus channel water between the atoll and the surrounding sea, and also provide great diving. Some typical, well-known sites include:

Velassaru Caves These rugged caves and overhangs, on the steep wall of the Vaadhoo Kandu, have very attractive coral growth. You may see sharks, turtles and rays on the bottom at around 30m. This dive is not for beginners, but if the current isn't too strong there's excellent snorkelling on the reef edge.

Vaadhoo Caves There is a row of small caves here, and a bigger one with a swim-through tunnel, as well as excellent soft corals, gorgonians, jackfish and the odd eagle ray. If the current is strong, this is a demanding dive; if not, it's great for snorkelling.

Embudhoo Express This is a 2km drift dive through the Embudhoo Kandu, which is a Protected Marine Area. With the current running in, rays, Napoleon wrasse and sharks often congregate round the entrance. The current carries divers along a wall with overhangs and a big cave. The speed of the current makes for a demanding dive, but also provides the ideal environment for soft corals and a large variety of fish. The reef top is good for snorkelling.

Kuda Giri Also called Yacht Thila, the attraction here is the hulk of a small freight ship, deliberately sunk here to create an artificial reef. Sponges and cup corals are growing on the wreck, and it provides a home for morays, gropers and large schools of batfish. A nearby thila has recovering coral growth and lots of reef fish to be seen at snorkelling depths. Sheltered from strong currents, this a good site for beginners and for night dives.

Vaagali Caves This is an exciting dive and not especially demanding. It's in a less-exposed location and has many caves on its north side, at around 15m, filled with sponges and soft corals. There is good coral regrowth and lots of fish on the top of the reef, much of it visible to snorkellers.

Guraidhoo Kandu A central reef splits this kandu into two channels, with many possibilities for divers, even those with less experience. There are numerous reef fish, larger pelagics near the entrance and mantas when the current is running out. The kandu is a Protected Marine Area.

Resorts

Most resorts in the South Male' Atoll are reached by speedboat from the airport, but some of the closer, cheaper resorts may offer a slower, less expensive transfer by dhoni. Unless otherwise specified, all transfer prices are by speedboat.

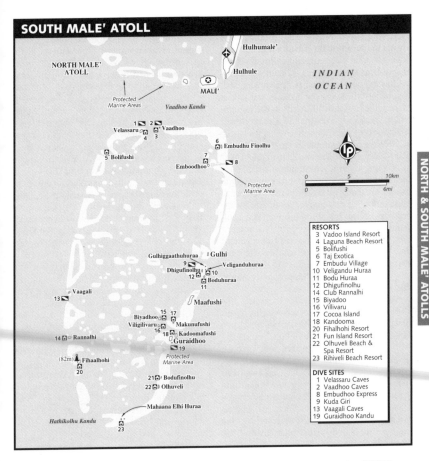

SOUTH MALE' ATOLL

NORTH MALE'
ATOLL

Protected
Marine Areas

Vaadhoo Kandu

Hulhumale'

Hulhule

MALE'

INDIAN
OCEAN

1   2   Vaadhoo
Velassaru   4   3
5 Bolifushi

6 Embudhu Finolhu

7
Emboodhoo   8

Protected
Marine Area

NORTH & SOUTH MALE' ATOLLS

0   5   10km
0   3   6mi

Gulhiggaathuhuraa   Gulhi
9   Veliganduhuraa
Dhigufinolhu   10
12   Boduhuraa
11

Vaagali
13

Biyadhoo   15 17
Viligilivaru   Makunufushi
16 18 Kadoomafushi
Guraidhoo

Rannalhi
14

19

Protected
Marine Area

(82m)   Fihaalhohi
20

21 Bodufinolhu
22 Olhuveli

Mahaana Elhi Huraa

Hathikolhu Kandu

23

Maafushi

RESORTS
3 Vadoo Island Resort
4 Laguna Beach Resort
5 Bolifushi
6 Taj Exotica
7 Embudu Village
10 Veligandu Huraa
11 Bodu Huraa
12 Dhigufinolhu
14 Club Rannalhi
15 Biyadoo
16 Villivaru
17 Cocoa Island
18 Kandooma
20 Fihalhohi Resort
21 Fun Island Resort
22 Olhuveli Beach &
     Spa Resort
23 Rihiveli Beach Resort

DIVE SITES
1 Velassaru Caves
2 Vaadhoo Caves
8 Embudhoo Express
9 Kuda Giri
13 Vaagali Caves
19 Guraidhoo Kandu

Budget Resorts

Embudu Village *(Emboodhoo island;
☎ 444776; **W** www.embudu.com; singles/
doubles US$84/132; airport transfer dhoni
45min US$40; 124 rooms)* is one of the bigger
budget to mid-range resorts with a friendly,
informal atmosphere and predominantly
European guests. Most are couples, along
with families at Christmas and a high proportion of repeat guests. The island has lots of
shady trees, some nice beaches and a very
accessible house reef.

All accommodation is on a full-board basis
with the 'standard' rooms being fan-cooled,
but still very acceptable. Superior rooms,
with air-con, hot water, fridge and phone,
cost about US$20 more. There are also 16
deluxe over-water bungalows (US$210).

An 'all-inclusive' option, for US$22 per
person per day, includes most drinks and
excursions.

The restaurant is a spacious, sand-floored,
open-sided pavilion serving all meals as buffets. The food is amazingly good for an inexpensive resort, with a varied, well-presented
selection and very fresh fruit and vegetables.
Entertainment is organised one night per
week, but the main attraction is watching
the sunset from the casual beach bar – a beer
is about US$3.

Diving is popular here, thanks to the
very professional **Diverland** (**W** www
.diverland.com) and the great dive sites in the
area. A single boat dive is US$45 with tank
and weights only, US$49 with all equipment
(good discounts for multidive packages).

An open-water course costs US$420; nitrox and rebreather courses and facilities are available. Windsurfing is also popular, and there's a good range of excursions to Male' and various other islands. Massage is available at the new, somewhat improvised, spa. If you're not looking for luxuries and lots of extra frills, Embudu Village is a really excellent and enjoyable resort.

Kandooma (*Kadoomafushi island;* ☎ *444452;* ⓦ *www.kandooma.com; singles/doubles US$55/72; airport transfer 35min US$70; 102 rooms*) is one of the least expensive resorts in the country, even after some recent improvements. A fancy swimming pool has been built, and a spa can't be far away. It's not the prettiest island, but it's quite big, and landscaping work is making it more attractive. Sand pumped from the lagoon has enhanced the beaches. Guests are mostly German, British and Italian couples, with quite a few singles in June, July and August, and children during holiday times.

Some nearby channels, including the Guraidhoo Kandu Protected Marine Area, offer excellent diving. A single boat dive is US$41 with tank and weights, or US$55 with full equipment provided, but after six dives the prices drop to US$36 and US$46. An open-water course is US$419. The **Aquanaut dive centre** (ⓦ *www.aquanaut -tauchreisen.de*) offers discounts of between 10% and 15% for advance bookings. There's no handy house reef for snorkelling, but there are two free boat trips a day to good snorkelling sites.

The big, cafeteria-like restaurant serves reasonable food; lunch and dinner alternate between set-menu meals and a buffet (with limited selection). Drinks are cheaper than in most resorts – a beer is US$2.50 and a decent bottle of wine is US$14. Organised entertainment is limited to two disco nights per week, one crab race and a cultural show, but the bar can be pretty lively. The standard rooms are clean and have cold freshwater showers, but no air-con, telephone or TV. The better rooms have air-con, a nicer view, and cost about US$10 more. Kandooma is the quintessential cheap and cheerful resort.

Fihalhohi Resort (*Fihaalhohi island;* ☎ *442903;* ⓦ *www.fihalhohi.info; singles/ doubles US$100/120; airport transfer 75min US$90; 128 rooms*) is an enjoyable, unpretentious Maldivian-run resort. The island is attractive with waving palm trees and beautiful beaches, and the buildings are modest with a natural look. Guests are a mix of Swiss, German and British; most are couples and quite a few bring children in August and over Christmas.

The house reef is very good for snorkelling, and is also used for night and individual dives. The Ocean Venture dive centre charges US$47 for a single boat dive with tank and weights, US$59 with all equipment. Open-water courses are US$460. A nitrox course is US$210, and nitrox dives cost US$4 extra. Diving excursions in a luxury yacht are an interesting alternative to the usual dive boats.

Meals are mostly buffet, and for variety there's a fun theme meal almost every night, from Middle Eastern to Mexican, flambé to fish and chips. Rooms have been progressively upgraded; all have hot water, but a few have no air-con. Deluxe rooms, in two-storey blocks, have extras like a hairdryer, safe and minibar. Fihalhohi is a fun resort, and a good choice for families, FITs and divers.

Club Rannalhi (*Rannalhi island;* ☎ *442688;* ⓦ *www.aitkenspencehotels.lk; singles/doubles US$110/150; airport transfer 45min US$90; 116 rooms*), on the western edge of the atoll, is an Italian club-style resort. It's an attractive island with tall palm trees, fine beaches and good snorkelling on the house reef, but it's so built up that there's hardly any open space left. The rooms are in two-storey blocks, modern and well finished with all the amenities, and there are 16 spacious water bungalows. The big, airy restaurant serves all buffet meals, and they're very good – plenty of pasta of course, and exquisite cakes and pastries.

Many of the guests dive, sometimes commuting to the dive sites in South Ari Atoll. A single boat dive costs about US$40 with tank and weights, US$55 with all equipment. Open-water courses are inexpensive at US$350. Snorkelling is good on the house reef, especially the excellent coral growth on the thila 100m off the service jetty. The main attraction, though, is the programme of activities, which start with morning aerobics, continue with volleyball and dance competitions, and finish late at night with amateur theatrics and karaoke. Nearly all guests come through the Italian agent Viaggi del Ventaglio (Club Venta), but there's also a sprinkling of French, British and FITs. Club

Rannalhi has a an enthusiastic, animated ambience, but guests who prefer to do their own thing can still have a fine holiday here.

Fun Island Resort (*Bodufinolhu island; ☎ 444558;* w *www.villahotels-maldives.com; singles/doubles US$115/130; airport transfer 45min US$80; 100 rooms*) is a modern resort on a long, narrow island with brilliant beaches. Rooms are in motel-like blocks, and equipped with air-con, hot water, phone and minibar. The main restaurant serves up good quality buffet meals three times a day, as well as theme nights like the beach barbecue. Nightlife is low key, with the occasional live band or disco night as highlights. The over-water bar is especially nice at sunset.

The lagoon is very wide and not great for snorkelling, but you can walk to the end of the jetty to reach the edge of the house reef. Diving is not hugely popular here, despite the many good dive sites around. The **Delphis dive school** (w *www.delphis.com.mv*) charges US$52 for a single boat dive with tank and weights, US$62 with all equipment. An open-water course is about US$608. A full range of water sports is available, including jet skis and other motorised activities. Windsurfer rental is US$14 per hour. As well as the usual range of excursions by boat, you can wade to a couple of nearby uninhabited islands at low tide. Considering the quality of the rooms and meals, Fun Island is very good value for money, though the cost of extras can add up.

Mid-Range Resorts

Laguna Beach Resort (*Velassaru island; ☎ 445903;* w *www.unisurf.com/laguna; singles/doubles US$180/220; airport transfer 20min US$45; 129 rooms*) is a modern resort offering full facilities and efficient service. Despite the quite dense development, the island is very attractive with lots of trees and gardens and very pretty beaches. Some rooms are in two-storey blocks, others are individual bungalows with a split-level design; there are also over-water suites for about US$150 extra. All of them are bright white and equipped with everything from coffee-making facilities to satellite TV.

The main restaurant buffets have a large selection of fine, but not outstanding, dishes. For a change, try the special Italian or Chinese restaurants, or the outdoor barbecue/grill. The bar has entertainment almost every night in the form of live bands, a cultural show or a disco. Guests are mostly from Europe – a mixture of young couples, older couples and families. The resort offers childcare and a children's swimming pool, as well as rooms with interconnecting doors which are good for families.

Excellent dive sites are nearby, on both sides of the Vaadhoo Kandu. The dive centre charges about US$50 for a boat dive with all equipment, and US$500 for an open-water course. Snorkelling is wonderful on the edge of the house reef, but it's hard to get to and subject to currents. The lagoon is good for learning windsurfing and sailing, and excursions to Male' and other islands are popular. There are no motorised water sports.

The atmosphere at Laguna is a little formal, rather than casual and laid back, but it's still a good choice for top-end comforts at a reasonable price.

Vadoo Island Resort (*Vaadhoo island; ☎ 443976;* w *www.vadoo.net; singles/doubles US$180/230; airport transfer dhoni 1hr US$30, speedboat 20min US$80; 33 rooms*) appeals mainly to divers. One reason is the location, as it's right beside Vaadhoo Kandu, with access to great dive sites in both North Male' and South Male' Atolls. The house reef is great for snorkelling, and qualified divers can make unguided dives here. Most dives will be in areas with medium to strong currents and are perhaps not ideal for beginners. The dive centre is geared to the needs of experienced divers, and does not provide rental wetsuits, dive computers or cameras. A single boat dive is US$45 with tank and weights only, or US$55 with all equipment *except* wetsuit and computer. The six days' unlimited diving deal is quite a bit cheaper. Dive courses feature very personalised instruction, with one instructor per two students, but you should reserve a dive course at least three weeks ahead. An open-water course costs about US$527.

The rooms are all reasonably new, and quite well finished (no TV or minibar) – the cheapest ones are in the Sunrise Wing. The over-water bungalows are delightful. You'll like the glass coffee table that looks down into the water (US$500 a double).

The buildings for the restaurant, office and dive centre are somewhat time-worn, but not without a rustic charm. Most meals follow a set menu, and can be very ordinary.

Many of the guests here are Japanese but, surprisingly, there's no sushi in sight! Apart from occasional excursions and fishing trips, there are few other activities – Vadoo really is a diver's resort.

Bolifushi (*Bolifushi island;* ☎ *443517;* **w** *www.bolifushi.com; singles/doubles US$175/215; airport transfer dhoni 70min US$53, speedboat 30min US$74; 55 rooms*) is on a very small island with lots of palm trees, two nice beaches and a good house reef close to shore. Most guests are from Italy, with others from Germany, Switzerland and Japan. Some club-style animation is arranged, mainly for the Italian guests, but others can join in – the atmosphere is relaxed and friendly.

It's not really an island that caters for divers, but there are excellent dive sites in the area and good diving on the house reef, including a small wreck. A single dive costs about US$35 with tank and weights, or US$50 with all equipment. An open-water course is about US$480. The island is surrounded by sheltered waters and is well placed for cat sailing and not-too-strenuous windsurfing.

All rooms have been recently renovated, and are well equipped and spacious – most are in two-storey blocks. The 15 over-water bungalows are also very nice, but perhaps not worth the much higher rates. The restaurant serves a basic buffet breakfast, set-menu lunch and a reasonable buffet dinner. If you want to do a little snorkelling, diving and relaxing, and you're not looking for high style or *haute cuisine*, Bolifushi could be a good choice.

Dhigufinolhu (*Dhigufinolhu island;* ☎ *443 599;* **w** *www.dhigufinolhu.com; singles/ doubles US$181/212; airport transfer 45min US$85; 100 rooms*) is a long, narrow island – the name means 'Long Sand Bank' so it's no surprise to find sandy beaches and a wide lagoon. It has the unusual feature of being linked by long wooden walkways to the resorts of Veligandu Huraa and Bodu Huraa – the three resorts are jointly managed, and are sometimes known collectively as Palm Tree Islands Resort. A fourth island, Bushi, has the dive base, staff quarters, workshops, generator and desalination plants for all three resorts. This means an 800m walk to and from the dive base, but the advantage is the access to several resorts

and a complete absence of service buildings and machinery noise.

The food here is exceptionally good – every meal is a buffet feast of superbly prepared and presented dishes. The 'soft animation' policy provides for a little entertainment and plenty of relaxation. Rooms are comfortable and attractive, with tile floors, timber ceilings and all mod cons except TVs. This is a well-run resort, and the service is first class.

The **Scuba Sub** dive base is also well-managed – a single boat dive is US$50 with tank and weights only, or US$65 with full equipment rental, but costs are a lot less for frequent divers. An open-water course is US$450. Numerous top dive sites are accessible, and a resident marine biologist helps divers appreciate the environment. The wide lagoon is unsuitable for snorkelling, but there's a snorkelling platform at the reef edge, and regular boat trips to good sites.

Guests are a mix of Italian, Swiss, German, British and French, and the atmosphere is very sociable. For eating, diving and relaxing, Dhigufinolhu is hard to beat.

Veligandu Huraa (*Veliganduhuraa island;* ☎ *443882;* **w** *www.veliganduhuraa.com; singles/doubles US$221/258; airport transfer 45min US$85; 56 rooms*), not to be confused with Veligandu resort on Rasdhoo Atoll, is a smaller island than Dhigufinolhu, with slightly better rooms and the same high standards of food and service. Guests are welcome to cross the walkway and use facilities on the bigger island, and both resorts use the same dive centre and water-sports facilities. They're both fine resorts, but Veligandu Huraa is a little quieter and more intimate.

Bodu Huraa (*Boduhuraa island;* ☎ *440172;* **e** *boduhuraa@palmtree.com.mv; singles/ doubles US$240/281; airport transfer 45min US$85; 36 rooms*) is a relatively new resort; all accommodation is in over-water bungalows. The resort is 100% booked by the Italian Hotelplan group. It wouldn't be much fun staying here unless you speak Italian, but from other resorts you can go over to this little Italy for an evening of pasta, pizza and pizzazz.

Biyadoo (*Biyadhoo island;* ☎ *447171;* **w** *www.biyadoo.com.mv; singles/doubles US$155/165; airport transfer 1hr US$75; 96 rooms*) and the nearby resort of Villivaru (see opposite) have been managed by the same company for years, but the lease is due for renewal, and both islands will probably come under new management. It's likely that these resorts will get a major renovation and become more expensive. The island itself is very attractive, with several fine beaches and an excellent house reef.

Villivaru (*Viligilivaru island; ☎ 447070; singles/doubles US$155/165; airport transfer 1hr US$75; 60 rooms*), sister resort of Biyadoo (see opposite), is also due to be re-leased, refurbished and repositioned further upmarket.

Olhuveli Beach & Spa Resort (*Olhuveli Island; ☎ 441957; w www.olhuveli.com; singles/doubles US$150/180; airport transfer 50min US$80; 125 rooms*) has recently been upgraded and really makes the most of this small island. The big saltwater swimming pool is an attraction, and landscaping has really improved the appearance of the resort. The cavernous main restaurant serves mountains of exotic food at buffets for breakfast, lunch and dinner – Maldivian dishes are a regular highlight, along with Japanese, Chinese and continental classics. Most rooms are in two-storey blocks – the older, less expensive ones are plain, white and well equipped with air-con, bathtub, phone and TV; the newer ones have wooden floors, four-poster beds, top-quality furnishings, and cost only US$15 more. The water villa suites are especially swish, for about US$315.

Guests are mostly Italian, with others from Japan, the Netherlands, Germany and the UK. There's some animation for the Italian guests, but it's not a big part of the resort.

The new Serena spa is popular for its Ayurvedic treatments, aromatherapy and massage. Although narrow, the beaches are attractive, and the wide lagoon is good for sailing, windsurfing and being towed around behind a motorboat. This is one of the first resorts to offer kitesurfing lessons and equipment. Snorkelling is excellent off the end of the jetty, at the edge of the reef. The first-class **Sea-Explorer dive centre** (w www.sea -explorer.net) does lots of drift dives in nearby channels, as well as doing wreck and night dives. A single boat dive costs about US$33 with tank and weights, and US$39 with all equipment. An open-water course is about US$500. Nitrox training is available (US$135); nitrox dives cost US$3 extra.

Overall, Olhuveli offers excellent value. What it lacks in luxury and size, it makes up for in the quality of its facilities and services, and in its friendly, fun ambience.

Rihiveli Beach Resort (*Mahaana Elhi Huraa island; ☎ 441994; w www.rihiveli -maldives.com; singles/doubles US$216/354; airport transfer 1hr US$135; 48 rooms*) was very much the personal creation of a Frenchman who lived here for 20 years. He has now moved on, and a legion of loyal guests are hoping that the resort will retain its natural, informal charm and quality. So far, so good.

The rusticated rooms are made of coral stone and have thatched roofs, hot water and natural ventilation – there's no air-con, fridge, phone or TV. The open-air bar has a sand floor and shady trees overhead, while the restaurant is built over the lagoon and has a lovely view as well as truly mouthwatering cuisine.

The usual water sports (windsurfing, sailing, canoeing, even water-skiing) plus tennis are all included in the room price. You can wade across to two other, uninhabited islands where the resort organises regular barbecue lunches. Regular boat trips to other reefs make up for the lack of snorkelling sites next to the resort. The main diving destinations are around nearby Hathikolhu Kandu, and there's a small wreck to explore. A single boat dive costs about US$38 with tank and weights, US$45 with all equipment. An open-water course is about US$500.

With its relaxed ambience, French style and natural appeal, Rihiveli is a unique and special resort for those who appreciate the simple things.

Top-End Resorts

Taj Exotica (*Embudhu Finolhu island; ☎ 442200; w www.tajhotels.com/maldives; singles/doubles with breakfast only US$525/ 550; airport transfer 20min US$75; 64 rooms*) is one of the latest, super luxury resorts. Part of the concept is to offer all à la carte dining, so the price might appear lower than the full-board rates at other deluxe Maldivian resorts. When you add in the cost of those superb meals, the total bill will be up there with the best of them.

This is a narrow little island with a fine, wide beach on one side, facing a broad, shallow lagoon. Handsome pavilions house the reception area, bar and main restaurant, and just eight elegant villas overlook the beach, four with private plunge pools. Fifty-six villas are built over the lagoon on the ocean side, all spacious, stylishly designed and beautifully finished (US$650 to US$700). The details are done to perfection, from silk-covered cushions and goose-down pillows to designer toiletries and private sun decks. The facilities include an entertainment system (CD, TV, DVD), personal safe, teak sun bed and tasteful artwork. The look is modern and understated, with natural materials that blend in with the island environment.

The sumptuous over-water spa is a serene setting for a full range of Balinese-style massages and beauty treatments, while the gym is a very contemporary glass cube above the lagoon. If you're fit enough, you can try a full range of water sports and excursions, or just relax beside the infinity pool (an almost obligatory feature in luxury resorts). For snorkelling, a small boat will take you to a pontoon on the edge of the house reef, a long way from shore. The dive centre, Delphis, looks as elegant as a hotel lobby, and runs small group trips to the many great dive sites accessible by speedboat. A single dive with all equipment provided costs US$70; an open-water course is US$675.

The main restaurant offers an imaginative à la carte menu of eclectic Asian-fusion cuisine. At the other end of the island, built over the water, another fine restaurant features Mediterranean cuisine, fresh seafood and grills. Meals can also be served in your room, by the pool or on the beach. Most main courses are from US$10 to US$30, and wines from the well-stocked cellar start at US$40 a bottle.

In its first year, Taj Exotica hosted guests from the UK, Japan and 23 other countries, and was internationally acclaimed as a top resort hotel. For fine food, high style, and sheer indulgence, this is as good as it gets.

Cocoa Island (*Makunufushi island;* ☎ *443713;* **w** *www.cocoa-island.com; singles/ doubles US$615/690; airport transfer 1hr; 30 rooms*) has been closed for redevelopment for some time. It is due to reopen soon as an exclusive, expensive resort with accommodation in over-water bungalows designed in the style of traditional dhonis.

Ari Atoll

A vast oval lagoon dotted with reefs, plus a couple of outlying coral reefs and islands, make up the administrative district of Alifu, commonly called Ari Atoll. The geography is dramatic if seen from above, as many visitors will see if they take a seaplane flight to their resort. The reefs, thilas (coral formations like underwater hills), sandbars, lagoons and channels form brilliant blue-green-turquoise rings and swirls, and the scattered islands are tiny green dots or streaks edged with bright white.

To the east, Ari Atoll is separated from South Male' Atoll by a 40km-wide channel, perhaps 500m deep; to the west, the sea floor drops precipitously to over 2000m. Abundant marine life in the atoll creates nutrient-rich water that flows out through channels, attracting large creatures from the open sea and divers from all over the world.

Some 26 resorts in the atoll run the gamut from small and simple to large and luxurious. Ari resorts don't offer excursions to Male' because it's too far away – if you want to see the Maldives' capital, arrange to spend a day there at the start or the end of your trip. This may be unavoidable if your flights cannot connect directly with a transfer to your resort – seaplanes and fast boats don't operate at night. Most cruises and diving safaris include Ari Atoll on their itinerary. A typical trip might start in Male' and go up through North Male' Atoll, west across the channel to Rasdhoo, south through Ari Atoll, east across to South Male' Atoll and back to the capital.

THODDOO ISLAND

Though administratively part of Alifu/Ari Atoll, Thoddoo is actually a single, separate, oval island about 20km from the northern edge of the main atoll. It's about 1km across, and has a population of nearly 1100. The principal activity is fishing, but Thoddoo is also known for its market-garden produce (watermelons and betel leaf especially) and its troupe of traditional dancers, who sometimes perform in tourist resorts.

There is evidence that Thoddoo has been occupied since ancient times. A Buddhist temple here contained a Roman coin minted in 90 BC, as well as a silver bowl and a fine stone statue of Buddha, the head of which is now in the National Museum in Male'.

Safari boats can shop here, but usually don't because of the lack of sheltered anchorages. You could also arrange a day trip here from one of the Rasdhoo Atoll resorts.

RASDHOO ATOLL

The small atoll of Rasdhoo lies off the northeastern corner of Ari Atoll proper. The main island of the atoll, also called Rasdhoo (population 920), is the administrative capital of North Ari Atoll, which was formerly a separate administrative district. Rasdhoo has an attractive little village with a junior secondary school, a health centre, four mosques and a score of souvenir shops – it's often visited as a day trip from the nearby resorts. The island has been settled for many centuries and there are traces here of a Buddhist society predating the arrival of Islam.

Diving

The medical centre at Kuramathi has a decompression chamber and trained hyperbaric specialists.

Kuramathi House Reef Accessible from the shore, this reef is good for beginning divers and snorkellers. A small dhoni and a 30m freighter have been sunk off the island to provide an attraction for divers. Sea fans and featherstars decorate the reef wall, while sharks, stingrays and turtles might also be seen.

Rasdhoo Madivaru Also known as Hammerhead Point, this is a more demanding dive on an outer reef where hammerhead sharks, mantas and other large pelagics are frequent visitors. Outside this reef the depth drops rapidly to over 200m and the water is exceptionally clear. It's a fine snorkelling site if conditions permit.

Resorts

Rasdhoo Resorts All the Rasdhoo resorts face a sheltered lagoon on one side, which is wonderful for windsurfing and other water sports.

Veligandu (Veligandu island; ☎ 450594; w www.veliganduisland.com; singles/doubles US$199/234; airport transfer by seaplane 20min US$140; 73 rooms), on the east side of the atoll, is a relaxed, mid-range resort.

The rooms have outdoor bathrooms and all facilities (except TV), but are not especially attractive. Deluxe rooms are slightly bigger and closer to the water and cost about US$40 more, while the nicely decorated over-water bungalows cost at least US$40 more again. The reception area, bar and restaurant have sand floors, cane furniture and a delightfully casual feel. The meals are mostly buffets, offering a limited variety of very good quality dishes. Guests are mainly German, Austrian and Italian couples.

There are a couple of excellent dive sites nearby, but when you've exhausted them, you'll have to take longer boat trips. The **Ocean-Pro** (W *www.oceanpro-diveteam.com*) dive base charges around US$53 for a boat dive with all equipment provided, or US$41 with tank and weights only. An open-water course costs US$524. The edge of the house reef is not very accessible and is not great for snorkelling. But Veligandu isn't primarily a diving or water sports resort – the main attractions are the natural ambience, rustic simplicity and fine beaches.

Kuramathi Resorts The island of Kuramathi used to be inhabited, but the population was in decline, so in 1970 the 120 remaining residents relocated to Rasdhoo, leaving Kuramathi available for resort development. The island is about 1.5km long by 500m wide and has three resorts – Kuramathi Village, Blue Lagoon and Kuramathi Cottage Club. This is unique in the Maldives, where there's usually only one resort per island. They're all under the same management and guests can use the facilities and restaurants at all the resorts. The large swimming pool and well-equipped gym are near the centre of the island, and a minibus shuttles between all the resorts. In all, there are 274 bungalows and rooms on the island, which has some fine beaches, lush vegetation and some magnificent old banyan trees.

Rasdhoo Atoll Divers (W *www.rasdhoo divers.com*) serves all three resorts, charging about US$49 for a boat dive with all equipment, US$42 with tank and weights only, and US$490 for an open-water course. A resident marine biologist gives lectures and slide shows and accompanies dives. The lagoon is perfect for learning windsurfing and sailing, and motorised water sports, including wakeboarding, are available. Stingrays come into the shallows on the beach every evening.

The speciality Thai restaurant, Indian restaurant, grills and coffee shops are excellent eating alternatives, but are not included in full-board packages at any resort (though a nominal discount is offered). If you want to eat around, or you're not a big eater, a half-board package may suit you better. Regular disco nights and special shows are held at the Cottage Club. Deals including basic beer, wine and spirits, use of windsurfers and snorkelling gear, and a couple of excursions cost about US$35 to US$40 extra per day and could be good value if you like windsurfing and/or drinking.

Airport transfer for all the Kuramathi resorts is by fast boat (two hours, US$88). All of them are operated by **Universal Enterprises** (☎ 323080; W *www.unisurf.com; 39 Orchid Magu, Male')*.

Kuramathi Village (☎ 450527; *singles/doubles US$133/161; 144 rooms*) is the largest and least expensive Kuramathi resort. Standard rooms are pleasant, thatched cottages set among luxuriant vegetation, and there are larger and fancier rooms available too. The main restaurant alternates between buffet and set menu for lunch and dinner, with Italian, Chinese or Maldivian special buffet dinners. This end of the island has younger patrons, many of them British and German, on all-inclusive deals and ready to party.

Blue Lagoon (☎ 450579; *singles/doubles US$145/180; 50 rooms*) is at the quiet end of the island. The 20 over-water bungalows (costing US$65 extra) are favoured by honeymooners while quite a few families stay in the beach cottages.

Kuramathi Cottage Club (☎ 450532; *singles/doubles US$145/180; 80 rooms*) is in the middle of the island, and the guests tend to be older and intent on relaxation. The 50 water bungalows here are extra attractive (and cost US$75 extra), but the beach cottages don't have much of a beach.

ARI ATOLL

The geographic entity of Ari Atoll (as opposed to the administrative region of Alifu, also called Ari Atoll) is about 80km from north to south and 30km wide. The most populous island is **Mahibadhoo**, the capital of Alifu, with some 1700 people. Fishing and fish processing are the main

Weighing anchor

Hawksbill turtle

Napoleon wrasse greets diver

Snorkeller swimming near whale shark

Dhonis at sunset

Typical sunset behind a Maldivian island

Romantic stroll along a beach resort at dusk

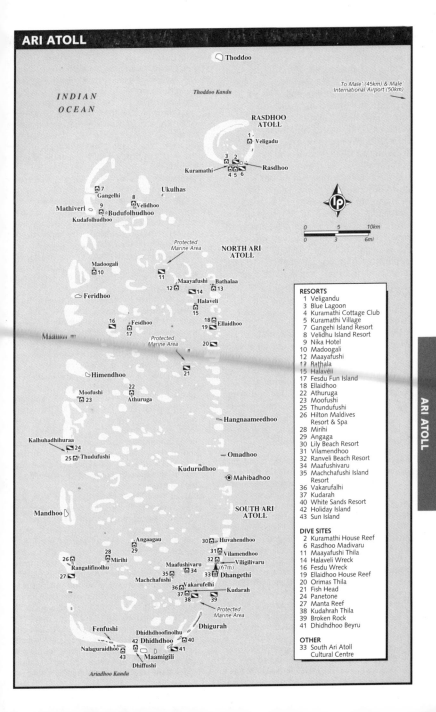

ARI ATOLL

Thoddoo

INDIAN OCEAN

Thoddoo Kandu

To Male' (45km) & Male' International Airport (50km)

RASDHOO ATOLL

1 ☐ Veligadu

3 2
☐ ☐
Kuramathi ☐ ☐ ☐ Rasdhoo
4 5 6

☐7 Gangehi   Ukulhas

8
☐ Velidhoo
Mathiveri ☐   9
☐ ☐ Budufolhudhoo
Kudafolhudhoo

Madoogali
☐10

Protected Marine Area

NORTH ARI ATOLL

11 ☐   Maayafushi   Bathalaa
12 ☐   ☐ 14   ☐ 13
Halaveli
15 ☐

18 ☐
19 ☐ Ellaidhoo

☐ Feridhoo

16 ☐   ☐ Fesdhoo
17 ☐

20 ☐

Maamos ☐

Protected Marine Area

21 ☐

☐ Himendhoo

22
☐
Moofushi   Athuruga
☐ 23

☐ Hangnaameedhoo

Kalhuhadhihuraa
☐ 24
25 ☐ Thudufushi

☐ Omadhoo

Kudurudhoo
◉ Mahibadhoo

Mandhoo ☐

SOUTH ARI ATOLL

☐ Angaagau   30 ☐ Huvahendhoo
28   29
26 ☐   ☐ Mirihi   31 ☐ Vilamendhoo
Rangalifinolhu   32 ☐ Viligilivaru
27 ☐   Maafushivaru   ▲(67m)
35 ☐ 34   33 🏛 Dhangethi
Machchafushi   36 ☐ Vakarufelhi
37 ☐   ☐ Kudarah
38   39

Protected Marine Area

Dhigurah

Fenfushi

Dhidhdhoofinolhu   42 Dhidhdhoo ☐ 40
Nalaguraidhoo ☐   ☐ ☐ ☐ 41
43   Maamigili
Dhiffushi
Ariadhoo Kandu

0 ___ 5 ___ 10km
0 ___ 3 ___ 6mi

RESORTS
1 Veligandu
3 Blue Lagoon
4 Kuramathi Cottage Club
5 Kuramathi Village
7 Gangehi Island Resort
8 Velidhu Island Resort
9 Nika Hotel
10 Madoogali
12 Maayafushi
13 Bathala
15 Halaveli
17 Fesdu Fun Island
18 Ellaidhoo
22 Athuruga
23 Moofushi
25 Thundufushi
26 Hilton Maldives
   Resort & Spa
28 Mirihi
29 Angaga
30 Lily Beach Resort
31 Vilamendhoo
32 Ranveli Beach Resort
34 Maafushivaru
35 Machchafushi Island
   Resort
36 Vakarufalhi
37 Kudarah
40 White Sands Resort
42 Holiday Island
43 Sun Island

DIVE SITES
2 Kuramathi House Reef
6 Rasdhoo Madivaru
11 Maayafushi Thila
14 Halaveli Wreck
16 Fesdu Wreck
19 Ellaidhoo House Reef
20 Orimas Thila
21 Fish Head
24 Panetone
27 Manta Reef
38 Kudahrah Thila
39 Broken Rock
41 Dhidhdhoo Beyru

OTHER
33 South Ari Atoll
   Cultural Centre

ARI ATOLL

industries – there's a cold storage and processing plant here. Safari boats might stop here, but there are no resorts nearby.

Other inhabited islands, typically with a population of a few hundred, are dotted around the edges of the atoll. Few of them are accessible from resorts, but safari boats may be able to stop at some of these islands, which are little visited by tourists. Quite a few islands have ruins or artefacts of ancient Buddhist and Hindu settlements.

Maamigili, in the south of the atoll, has over 1500 people, many of whom work in nearby resorts, or in tourist shops that cater to island-hopping visitors. The island of **Fenfushi** (population 550), on the southwest corner of the atoll, supplies sand and coral-stone for buildings in Male' and elsewhere, and is noted for coral carving. **Dhangethi** (population 700), on the southeastern edge of the atoll, is worth visiting for its Cultural Centre (see the boxed text 'South Ari Atoll Cultural Centre' later in this chapter.)

Diving

All of the resorts have diving operations and some are known as destinations for serious divers. During peak season some sites may have several groups diving on them at one time, but good divemasters will know how to avoid the crowds at popular sites and where to find equally attractive but less popular sites. The following is a brief description of some well-known sites (from north to south) to give an idea of the possibilities.

Maayafushi Thila This is a classic round thila known for the white-tip reef sharks that circle it. Caves and overhangs around the thila have lots of gorgonians, soft corals and schools of reef fish. It's a Protected Marine Area.

Halaveli Wreck This well-known site was created when a 38m cargo ship was deliberately sunk in 1991. It's famous for the friendly stingrays enticed here by regular feeding – keep your fingers away from their mouths.

Fesdu Wreck This 30m trawler has a good covering of corals at a depth of 18m to 30m. Moray eels and groper live inside the hull, which is easily entered and has good growths of soft corals and sponges. Divers can also check the adjacent *thila*, which has hard and soft corals and lots of fish.

Ellaidhoo House Reef Only accessible to Ellaidhoo's guests, this excellent house reef has a long wall just 25m from the beach. It has a row of caves with sea fans, whip corals, schools

of bannerfish, Napoleons, stingrays and morays, and even a small wreck. This reef is popular with night divers.

Orimas Thila Overhangs, caves, crevices, canyons and coral heads make this Protected Marine Area an exciting dive. Marine life includes good growths of soft corals, seafans, anemones and clown fish. The top of the thila is only 3m down, and can be easily enjoyed by snorkellers if the conditions are calm.

Fish Head Also called Mushimasmingali Thila, this Protected Marine Area is one of the world's most famous dive sites. Its steep sides are spectacular, with multilevel ledges, overhangs and caves supporting many seafans and black corals; its top is heavily encrusted with anemones. Beware of stonefish. The prolific fish life includes fusiliers, large Napoleons, trevally and schools of hungry barracuda. The main attraction, however, is the numerous grey reef sharks, which can be seen up close. Strong currents can make this a demanding dive, and extreme care should be taken not to damage this superb but heavily used site.

Panetone The north side of Kalhuhadhihuraa Faru is subject to strong currents, so the caves and overhangs are thick with soft coral growth. As well as the many reef fish, there are giant trevally, sharks, barracuda and turtles. From December to April, mantas feed around the outside of the channel; March to November are the best months to see sharks. Excellent snorkelling in light currents.

Manta Reef Also called Madivaru, this dive is at the end of a channel where powerful currents carry plankton out of the atoll during the northeast monsoon (December to April) – fast food for manta rays. Mantas also come to be cleaned. Reef fish include Napoleon wrasse, snapper and parrotfish, while pelagics such as turtles, tuna and sharks visit the outer reef slope. For advanced divers only, but great for snorkellers in the right conditions.

Kudarah Thila This Protected Marine Area is a very demanding but exciting dive – if there is a current running, this is strictly for experienced divers. There are gorgonians, whip corals, black corals and a whole field of seafans swaying in the current, surrounded by sharks and trevally from the open sea. In the gaps between large coral blocks, bluestriped snapper, tallfin, batfish, goby and other unusual small fish can be seen.

Broken Rock In the mouth of the Dhigurashu Kandu, this thila is bisected by a canyon up to 10m deep and only 1m to 3m wide. Swimming through the 50m canyon is unforgettable, but extreme care is needed not to damage the coral formations on either side. Rock formations around the thila are decorated with seafans and superb corals, and inhabited by abundant marine life.

Dhidhdhoo Beyru From May to September, whale sharks cruise almost continually along the 10km-long reef on the southwestern edge of the atoll, from Ariyadhoo Kandu north to the tip of Dhigurah island. There's plenty of fish life on the reef, and mantas also cruise the area. The reef drops off steeply into deep water, and it's quite exposed and subject to ocean currents.

Resorts

Ari Atoll has a variety of resorts, from exclusive rustic hideaways for rich Robinson Crusoes to slick new places with every modern convenience. Airport transfers are by seaplane or speedboat. Resorts are listed here from north to south.

Budget Resorts

Bathala (Bathalaa island; ☎ 450587; W www.aitkenspenceholidays.com/bathala; singles/doubles US$130/150; airport transfer by seaplane 20min US$160; 45 rooms) is ideally located for divers. Not on the prettiest island, it is nevertheless a nice little low-key tropical hideaway, with its 37 circular thatched cottages (all with air-con and hot water) and reliably good buffets three times a day. An immaculate beach goes right around the island, as does the house reef. Guests are mostly Italians, with a mix of British, German and assorted independent travellers and dive groups.

Dive costs are relatively low if you only need a tank and weights (US$38 for a single boat dive), but costly if you need to rent full equipment (US$55-plus for a single boat dive). Multi-dive packages are much better value. Bring your own wetsuit if at all possible. The edge of the house reef drops off steeply all around, accessible from the beach or more readily from the jetties – it's a good dive site in itself. A couple of rooms have recently been converted into an Ayurvedic spa. Still a popular divers' island, Bathala has broadened its after-dark appeal with some guests on all-inclusive packages and some Italian animation.

White Sands Resort (Dhidhdhoofinolhu island; ☎ 450513; W www.maldiveswhitesands.com; singles/doubles US$90/125, water bungalows US$355/390; airport transfer by seaplane 20min US$220, by speedboat 2hr US$110; 141 rooms) is like two resorts on one island, and the combination works. The older rooms at one end of the island are a

reminder that this resort was once called Ari Beach, a very casual, inexpensive place with a reputation as a party island. At the other end, a long jetty leads to a restaurant and 47 water bungalows perched over the lagoon, all in sophisticated-rusticated nautical style. In between, in price and geography, are the 'superior' rooms, the dive school and a new, Balinese-style spa.

Standard rooms are basic boxes and somewhat worn, but quite OK – they have air-con and a phone, but no hot water. Standard family rooms have space for extra beds. Superior rooms are bigger, with hot water and an outdoor bathroom, while the superior A-frame rooms are bigger again, and have cathedral ceilings, hot water, minibar and better beach frontage (singles/doubles US$165/200). The circular, sand-floored restaurant at this end of the island does buffet meals of a very high standard, in a cool, casual ambience. The Sunset Restaurant and Lounge serves snacks and light meals for those not on full board. The Nagali Bar is the liveliest place at night, with a variety of entertainment – live music, disco nights, cultural shows, and slide shows and videos by the dive school.

The over water bungalows are among the most charming and unusual in the Maldives. The sloping walls, wooden finishes, white fabrics and uninterrupted water views make you feel you're in an old yacht, but all the modern accessories are provided, from hair dryers to cable TV. The over-water bar and restaurant also have a shipboard feel, as you eat and drink on shaded decks with water on every side. The meals here are also excellent, all served buffet style, with quality ingredients and dishes that are not too elaborate but perfectly prepared.

The island itself is long and narrow with natural, somewhat scrubby, vegetation and long, white sandy beaches. The lagoon is wide on all sides, and a good place to learn windsurfing or catamaran sailing – hourly rates are quite high (US$15 and US$25) but courses and 10-hour rentals are a better deal. Water-skiing, wakeboarding and fun rides on the banana are also available. For snorkelling, take one of the free boat trips to the reef edge – these go every afternoon. The island has always been popular with divers, especially for the whale sharks that cruise the outside edge of the atoll here from May to November, and the mantas on the west side of the atoll

ARI ATOLL

from December to May. The very efficient **Euro-Divers** (w *www.eurodivers.com)* dive centre is involved in whale shark research. A single boat dive is US$39 with tank and weights only, US$54 with full equipment. An open-water course costs about US$350. Nitrox courses (US$60) and nitrox diving (US$5 extra) are available.

The food is of the same high standard at both restaurants, and drinks are the same low prices (a beer is US$2.50, and house wine US$3.50 a glass). Guests staying in the inexpensive rooms can indulge in the classy surroundings of the bar and restaurant at the 'water village'; those in the luxury over-water bungalows can enjoy the lively atmosphere and natural style at the 'island village', and take advantage of the relatively cheap diving costs. White Sands has very friendly and efficient management, and the mixed clientele makes it an interesting and fun resort.

Holiday Island *(Dhiffushi island;* ☎ *450011;* w *www.villahotels-maldives.com; singles/doubles US$135/155; airport transfer by speedboat 2½hr US$110, by seaplane 35min US$210; 142 rooms)*, a modern mid-range resort, is now a predominantly Italian resort, though it has a few fully independent travellers (FITS). The rooms are in blocks of two (some with interconnecting doors for families), surrounded by cultivated gardens and fitted out with everything from satellite TV to hot water in the bidet. All meals are served buffet style in the main restaurant – the selection is limited, but the quality is good. The Italian animation includes disco nights, karaoke and fitness sessions.

Recreational activities like table tennis, badminton, billiards, tennis and gym work-outs are included. Windsurfing, catamaran sailing and motorised water sports are available, at a price. The beaches are lovely around most of the island, but snorkelling is not good in the lagoon, and boat trips out to the reef edge and beyond are charged as an extra. Diving is not hugely popular, though there are lots of good dive sites around – a single boat dive costs US$50 with tank and weights, US$65 with all equipment.

Holiday Island is good value for the quality of its accommodation and meals, but it doesn't have any natural character and those who don't fit in with the Italian ambience will miss out on a lot of the fun.

The modern style is typical of Villa Hotels (☎ 316161; Villa Building, Male').

Sun Island *(Nalaguraidhoo island;* ☎ *450088;* w *www.villahotels-maldives.com; singles/doubles US$135/155; airport transfer by speedboat 2½hr US$110, by seaplane 35min US$210; 350 rooms)*, the biggest resort in the Maldives, is also the last word in slick, modern developments with every imaginable service and facility. Opinions are divided about this resort – many feel that it's not in keeping with the Maldives' 'natural' image. The sandy beaches and many of the original trees have been retained, but the island is manicured from end to end, surrounded by bungalows and crisscrossed with paved paths. Riding round it on a bicycle is particularly enjoyable (US$3 per day) but the resort vehicles (minibuses and golf carts) make it look like a Florida retirement village.

The rooms themselves are large and have quality indoor–outdoor bathrooms, bidets, minibars, mini-safes, and TVs that can show in-house movies (US$10 per day) or access the Internet (US$6.80 per half-hour). The water bungalows are even bigger, but don't have a lot of style or privacy; they cost about US$85 more.

The reception area is cavernous and the main dining room is vast. The meals are all buffets and the food just keeps on coming. It's pretty good, but for gourmet fare try one of the three speciality restaurants – Thai-Chinese, barbecue-seafood and Italian-Japanese(!). Allow at least US$15 to US$25 for a main course, with a 20% discount if you've paid for that meal on a full- or half-board package. Various cafés and bars sell snacks and light meals (hot dogs US$5.50) and there's 24-hour room service. Evening entertainment, in the main bar, might be karaoke, disco, cultural show, crab races or live band – sometimes it's a real party, sometimes not. Water is US$3.50 a bottle, beer US$4 to US$6, house wine US$6.50 a glass, imported wine US$22 to US$44 a bottle.

The huge swimming pool features fake waterfalls and a horizon edge that blends into the lagoon. For amusement there's a video arcade (at US$1 a game), billiards (US$14 per hour) or darts (US$3.50 per hour). Squash, badminton, aerobics, spa, gym and tennis are all available at a price (and there's a scale of charges if you damage the equipment – a dart is US$20). For relaxation try a traditional Thai massage (US$60 per 50 minutes).

The **Little Mermaid Dive Center** (W www .diveatmaldives.com) is quite a big operation. It charges US$43 for a single boat dive with tank and weights only, US$54 with full equipment and US$500 for an open-water course. Most dives are done at nearby sites, and groups can be quite large. Snorkelling is OK at the reef edge off the end of the main jetty. Elsewhere the lagoon is wide, and only good for swimming and water sports – from windsurfers at US$18 an hour to jet skis at US$200 per hour.

Guests come from Germany, Britain, Italy, Japan, Korea, Russia and elsewhere. Advertised package prices are often very low, but allow for quite a bit more to pay for the extras that make Sun Island enjoyable. A bewildering number of add-on packages cover the cost of various sports facilities, drinks, restaurant meals and so on. A basic 'all-inclusive' deal may be worthwhile (US$25 per day), but it's hard to imagine getting value out of a 'platinum card' at US$1775 per week, even if it does include unlimited eating, drinking and diving.

Mid-Range Resorts

Gangelhi Island Resort (Gangelhi island; ☎ 450505; W www.clubvacanze.com/ourresorts .html; singles/doubles €323/440; airport transfer by seaplane 20min €143; 25 rooms) is an upmarket Italian resort offering all-inclusive packages – the price covers all meals, drinks (except champagne and liqueurs) and a daily excursion. Two dives per day are included for qualified divers; an open-water course is available for about US$400 extra. The intimate restaurant specialises in seafood and fine Italian cuisine. The island is pretty, with lots of palm trees, but unfortunately has suffered from sand movements, so the seafront rooms have no beach and the over-water bungalows are surrounded by a sandbar.

Velidhu Island Resort (Velidhoo island; ☎ 450551; W www.johnkeellshotels.com; singles/doubles US$168/186; airport transfer by seaplane 20min US$200; 100 rooms) is a sizable island with great beaches and a good house reef. It's not the best-looking resort, with uninspired architecture, haphazard landscaping and rooms with very ordinary interiors, but the food and service are quite good. The new over-water bungalows are the classiest accommodation here (US$75 extra). The **Euro-Divers** (W www.eurodivers.com) dive centre is very professional and enthusiastic about the diving in this part of the atoll. A single boat dive is US$51 with tank and weights only, US$61 with full equipment. An open-water course costs about US$510. The six-day no-limit package is a good deal if you dive a lot. Nitrox courses (US$60) and nitrox diving (US$5 extra) are available. Velidhu could be a good choice for keen divers who aren't looking for luxury, and its low-season prices can be very good value.

Madoogali (Madoogali island; ☎ 450581; W www.skorpion-maldives.com; singles/ doubles US$228/326; airport transfer by seaplane 20min US$220; 56 rooms) blends into its lush island setting and is encircled by perfect beaches. The air-con rooms all face their own stretch of white sand, and feature coral walls, thatched roofs and well-finished interiors. The cuisine is Italian, as are most of the guests, many of whom are repeat visitors. Entertainment and animation is provided in the evening, but this isn't a full-on club-style resort. The Indian-Ayurvedic spa is a new feature.

The house reef is excellent for snorkelling, and as Madoogali is the only resort in this part of the atoll, there is easy access to lots of little-used dive sites. The **Albatros dive centre** charges about US$50 for a boat dive with tank and weights, or US$50 with all equipment. An open-water course costs about US$480. Madoogali is a natural-style resort with a European atmosphere and all-round appeal.

Maayafushi (Mayafushi island; ☎ 450588; e maaya@dhivehinet.net.mv; singles/doubles US$120/170; airport transfer by seaplane 25min US$210; 60 rooms) offers very good value for an unpretentious island holiday. The island is small and quite intensively developed; soft sandy beaches surround it, and the house reef is a beauty. The 60 rooms all have basic furnishings, air-con, hot water, TV, phone and beach frontage. Most of the guests are divers from Germany, Switzerland or Austria, but there are a few families with young children who get on well here. Most meals are set menu (with Indian dishes and lots of fresh fish), but there are a couple of buffet nights each week.

The dive school offers a wide range of courses, night dives and trips to the famous dive sites nearby. A single dive with a boat and all equipment will run to about US$58, and an open-water course is US$450. Once a low-cost divers island, Maayafushi has been upgraded and its rooms improved, but it's still a pretty laid-back resort.

Halaveli *(Halaveli island;* ☎ *450559;* ⓦ *www.halaveli.com; singles/doubles US$140/ 190; airport transfer by seaplane 20min US$173; 56 rooms)* is mainly an Italian resort booked by Gran Viaggi, but it gets quite a few keen divers and FITs from elsewhere.

The rooms are individual coral-and-thatch bungalows with outdoor bathrooms, air-con, phone and heavy wood furniture. The restaurant and bar areas aren't especially appealing, but no-one seems to mind, as a full animation program is provided every afternoon and evening, and the Italian guests are into it with enthusiasm. The breakfast and lunch buffets are a pretty fair selection of tasty dishes with an Italian bias. Dinner is partly à la carte.

The house reef is accessible for snorkelling at several points and it has a variety of fish, but not much coral regrowth. Some of the Maldives' most famous dive sites are in easy reach, and the **TGI dive centre** *(*ⓦ *www.tgidiving.com)* is keen to show them off. Prices are about US$36 for a boat dive with tank and weights, or US$46 with all equipment. An open-water course costs about US$420.

A broad sandspit provides plenty of beach space for volleyball, fun and games, while other beaches are narrower and more intimate. A new Japanese massage centre offers another way to relax. Halaveli has a split personality – it's half divers island; half Italian club resort, and it keeps everyone happy.

Ellaidhoo *(Ellaidhoo island;* ☎ *450586;* ⓦ *www.travelin-maldives.com; singles/doubles US$125/163; airport transfer by seaplane 20min US$180, by speedboat 80min US$100; 78 rooms)* has a reputation as the most hardcore diving destination in the Maldives – over 100 dive sites are within a half-day trip. Recently it has upgraded its facilities and added extra services to broaden its appeal, but divers still predominate. One reason is the Ellaidhoo house reef, only a few metres offshore and offering some great snorkelling and diving with a 750m wall, lots of caves, corals, rich marine life (turtles, sharks, mantas and eagle rays) and even a small wreck. The **Sub-Aqua**

dive centre charges US$44 for a boat dive with tank and weights only, US$50 with full equipment. An open-water course costs about US$500, and Sub-Aqua also runs courses in marine biology.

The rooms have all been rebuilt or refurbished in the last few years, and feature air-con, hot water and even satellite TV. The main restaurant now serves all meals as buffet style, and there's a coffee shop as well. A new sports centre has a gym, sauna, spa and facilities for billiards, squash, tennis and tension-relieving Thai-style massage. Water sports (like windsurfing, jet skiing and wakeboarding) are provided on a neighbouring island with a wider lagoon.

It looks like Ellaidhoo will continue to attract real diving enthusiasts, but non-divers will now find it's a more enjoyable, all-round destination.

Fesdu Fun Island *(Fesdhoo island;* ☎ *450541;* ⓦ *www.visitmaldives.com/resorts/ is_fesdu.html; singles/doubles US$150/170; airport transfer by seaplane 20min US$170, by speedboat 2½hr US$110; 50 rooms)* is a pretty little island with good beaches and a house reef. The thatched bungalows are nestled in palm trees, and the natural finishes inside give them a cosy feel – they have air-con and hot water, but no phone or TV. The main restaurant serves a mix of buffet and set-menu meals that are filling, but not exactly gourmet fare.

For divers, Fesdu is a well-located and economical choice. The **Fesdu Diving Centre** *(*ⓦ *www.fesdu-diving.com)* charges about US$41 for a boat dive with tank and weights, or US$46 with all equipment. An open-water course costs about US$404.

Most guests are from Germany and Britain, on all-inclusive packages that include most drinks and some activities. Some are here for mainly the diving, while others just enjoy an economical and relaxing holiday on an attractive, natural-style island.

Moofushi *(Moofushi island;* ☎ *450598;* ⓦ *www.moofushi.com; singles/doubles €133/ 210; airport transfer by seaplane 20min €250; 60 rooms)* has spacious, natural-style, thatched rooms and 15 water bungalows, all of them filled by Italians. It's a pretty island, but the beach is suffering from erosion and some of the breakwaters are unsightly.

The dive centre charges about US$48 for a boat dive with tank and weights, or

US$55 with all equipment. An open-water course costs about US$460. Nearby Moofushi Kandu has some good dive sites and makes a great snorkelling trip. The main attractions of Moofushi are the low price, the Italian-style animation and the diving.

Athuruga (*Athuruga island;* ☎ *450508;* W *www.planhotel.ch/maldive2.html; singles/ doubles US$335/470; airport transfer by seaplane 25min US$210; 46 rooms*) is marketed on an all-inclusive basis – most drinks, excursions and unmotorised water sports are included in the daily rate. The air-con rooms are spacious and comfortable and all face onto the nice but narrow beach. Guests are mostly from Italy, Germany and the UK, in that order, and the atmosphere is casual. The meals are consistently very good.

The house reef offers easy snorkelling and a lot to see, and there are some good dive sites nearby, though it's an hour by boat to the exciting dives on the western rim of the atoll. The **Crab dive base** charges about US$45 for a boat dive with tank and weights, US$60 with all equipment and US$480 for an open-water course.

Athuruga is quite densely developed, but it still has lots of palm trees and a good beach all round – it's a good value resort with a mainly Italian ambience.

Thundufushi (*Thudufushi island;* ☎ *450597;* W *www.planhotel.ch/maldive1.html; singles/ doubles US$300/410; airport transfer by seaplane 25min US$210; 47 rooms*), also spelled Thudufushi, is a sister resort to Athuruga with the same management and similarly high standards of food and service. The buildings and the style may be a little more formal (no sand floor in the bar), but the island itself is just beautiful, especially the beaches. In high season the majority of guests are Italian, but at other times there are also Germans and Brits. The dive centre management and prices are the same as at Athuruga, but Thundufushi may be better placed for dives on the atoll edge. The house reef is superb, and accessible for snorkelling and diving. If you're happy to pay the all-inclusive rates and enjoy the Italian flavour, Thundufushi is a good choice.

Mirihi (*Mirihi island;* ☎ *450500;* W *www .mirihi.com; singles/doubles US$274/347; airport transfer by seaplane 25min US$215; 35 rooms*) has been redeveloped in classy, contemporary style. It's a tiny island, but 30 of the rooms are built over the water so it's not too crowded. A first-class beach and house reef are easily reached on one side of the island, and there are plenty of palm trees.

The beach villas have eye-catching decor, polished timber finishes, white linen furnishings, rich red accents and every facility, including a CD player, TV and espresso machine. The over-water rooms have all this plus water views and very private sun decks (they cost about US$30 more). The main restaurant presents a lavish gourmet buffet for nearly every meal, usually eaten on a sun deck or on the sand. Some nights feature à la carte specials or theme dinners. Another restaurant, on a jetty over the water, specialises in grills and seafood. A selection of fine wines runs from US$15 to US$70 a bottle.

Use of the gym is free of charge, as are activities like board games, windsurfing and kayaking. The small spa has a range of massage and holistic treatments. Serious divers come here for the house reef and the access to dive sites all over South Ari Atoll. The **Ocean-Pro dive centre** (W *www.oceanpro -diveteam.com*) charges around US$52 for a boat dive with all equipment provided, or US$41 with tank and weights only. An open-water course costs US$520.

Mirihi is remarkable for making the most of a small island without overdeveloping it. It's equally attractive as a stylish resort, romantic retreat or quality dive island.

Hilton Maldives Resort & Spa (*Rangali island;* ☎ *450629;* W *www.maldives.hilton.com; singles/doubles US$364/446, water villas US$847/913; airport transfer by seaplane 35min US$220; 152 rooms*) actually occupies two islands – the heart of the resort, with the main lobby, restaurant, bars, water sports, dive centres and 100 beach villas, is on Rangalifinolhu; on a second island, Rangali, are two other restaurants, a bar, a separate reception area, and 52 over-water villas that really belong in the luxury-resort class. The two islands are connected by a walkway bridge across a broad blue lagoon.

One of the most luxurious resorts in the country, Hilton has tennis courts, a swimming pool, excellent beaches, gorgeous gardens and two spas offering massages (Thai, Balinese, aroma, for US$70), Ayurvedic treatments (US$140) and beauty salon service. The over-water spa is especially serene, with a glass floor looking into the lagoon.

All the public areas are superbly finished with natural materials and an understated island feel.

There's a wide variety of room types and prices, with standard beach villas costing as little as US$200 in low season for room only. These rooms are large and handsome, and equipped with all the usual amenities (but no TV). Guests can use all the Hilton facilities including the over-water spa, and take their meals at any of the gourmet restaurants on either island. Deluxe beach villas (for US$100 more) have a four-poster bed, stereo system, espresso machine and better beach frontage. But for real fabulousness, you need a water villa, with all wooden finishes, terracotta tiled bathroom, ocean view bathtub and private sundeck (around US$700); or deluxe water villa with private spa (US$950). For the last word in wow! appeal, each sunset water villa suite has a glass-floored sitting room, rotating circular bed, large-screen plasma TV, remote control Roman blinds, private boat, butler, and a specially excavated lagoon swimming pool (around US$2500).

Fine dining is a Hilton highlight and the buffet feasts for half-board and full-board guests are presented as a veritable theatre of international cuisine. A half-board or bed-and-breakfast package will let you try the other four restaurants – the Sunset Grill for fresh seafood (check the live lobster pond); Vilu Restaurant, serving creative Euro-Asian fusion dishes; Koko, an outdoor teppanyaki grill; and the Wine Cellar, an epicurean education hosted by the ebullient resident *sommelier* in a climate-controlled cave surrounded by some 5000 bottles of selected wines.

Diving, water sports, excursions and light entertainment are all on offer, but the real attractions at the Hilton are the unobtrusive, efficient and friendly service, the incredible food and wines, and (for those paying luxury room rates) the ultra-attractive water villas. For extra pampering, ask about wedding and spa packages.

Angaga (Angaagau island; ☎ 450510; e an gaga@dhivehinet.com; singles/doubles US$151/185; airport transfer by seaplane 25min US$195; 50 rooms) has especially fine, white beaches round most of the island, and a house reef that's great for diving and snorkelling – the corals are recovering well here. The thatch-roofed bungalows, with a

traditional swing seat (or *undholi*) out front, show a little more character than many of the mid-range resorts. They're fully equipped with air-con, hot water, phone, TV and heavy bamboo furniture.

The spacious sand-floored bar and restaurant also show some style – they're built in a distinctive fish shape. All meals are buffet, and include a good selection of Asian and European dishes – seafood barbecues are a regular event. The house wines are inexpensive, but all-inclusive packages are still good value if you indulge. Entertainment is nothing elaborate, but there are plenty of water sports and excursions on offer. Nearby Angaga Thila is a top dive site, but others are some distance away on the edge of the atoll. The **Sub-Aqua dive centre** charges US$44 for a boat dive with tank and weights only, US$50 with full equipment. An open-water course costs about US$465. Angaga is popular with Germans, Swiss, Brits and other Europeans who like to relax on the beach, dive a little and have a few drinks in the evening.

Lily Beach Resort (Huvahendhoo island; ☎ 450013; w www.lilybeachmaldives.com; singles/doubles US$170/219; airport transfer by seaplane 25min US$185; 85 rooms) has all its guests on an all-inclusive price plan, which includes all meals, snacks, coffee, beer, wine, whisky, gin, vodka, rum, water sports (except diving), tennis and one island-hopping excursion. If you're keen on windsurfing or drinking, this plan could save you US$10 or US$20 per day compared with other resorts. Most guests are European, including a strong British contingent, and quite often families with children (there's a children's play area).

This is an unpretentious resort and the architecture is neat but nothing fancy – squarish white buildings with green tiled roofs. The vegetation is a bit sparse, but there are good beaches on two sides of the island – the main drawback is the circle of ugly breakwaters that protect the beaches. Facilities include a good swimming pool, tennis court, gym and games room. Sand floors in the bar and restaurant go with the friendly and informal atmosphere. All meals are buffets, with a varied selection including pasta and some very tasty Chinese dishes. The standard rooms have air-con, phone and outdoor bathroom with hot water. The water villas are much bigger and cost about US$40 more.

The house reef is very good (turtles are common) and easily accessible for snorkelling – you can do night snorkelling here too. Keen divers come for the many South Ari dive sites, especially in the whale shark season. The **Ocean-Pro dive base** (W *www.oceanpro-diveteam.com*) charges around US$53 for a boat dive with all equipment provided, or US$40 with tank and weights only. An open-water course costs US$520.

Lily Beach is a well-managed resort that offers great value for those who want to eat, drink, dive and relax.

Vilamendhoo *(Vilamendhoo island;* ☎ *450637;* W *www.aaa-resortsmaldives.com/ vilamendhoo; singles/doubles US$185/276; airport transfer by seaplane 25min US$189; 141 rooms)* is on a very lush, well-vegetated island that still has some sense of space. The beaches are narrow around most of the island, but there's a big sandy area at one end, or both ends, depending on the season. The house reef is particularly good

for snorkelling, and marked channels make it easy to reach the reef edge.

The rooms are all air-conditioned, spacious, clean and comfortable, with a thin toupee of thatch as a concession to natural style. The restaurant has a tiled floor, a timber ceiling and no walls, so it's cool and breezy. All meals are buffet style, and offer a wide choice of satisfying dishes, with theme nights for variety and several options for vegetarians. The main bar is the heart of the resort, and the guests on all-inclusive packages make sure it keeps beating.

Plenty of top dive sites are in this corner of the atoll, and many of the guests are divers. The **Werner Lau dive centre** (W *www.wernerlau.com*) charges US$60 for a boat dive with all equipment provided, or US$48 with tank and weights only. An open-water course costs about US$560. For nondivers there are numerous excursions, a tennis court, windsurfing and water-skiing.

Vilamendhoo is efficiently managed, but friendly and informal, and it attracts a good

South Ari Atoll Cultural Centre

On the island of Dhangethi, on the lower eastern side of Ari Atoll, is one of the few attempts to depict and display the traditional Maldivian way of life. The centre comprises three dwellings and several other structures typical of those in which the various activities of an island community were carried out. The buildings are all reproductions, but they have been made using traditional construction techniques and local materials, and they are furnished with authentic artefacts and tools.

The finest house is of a type that might have been occupied by an island leader and his family, and is partly designed as a place to formally entertain guests. It features large lacquerware bowls for serving food, and raised platforms for guests of the highest status. Specific areas of the house are reserved for men and women, whose roles were largely segregated in traditional Maldivian communities.

The house of a fishing family is similar in its basic layout, though smaller and less well finished. The veranda has an assortment of nets, fish hooks and other tools for fishing in the traditional way.

The smallest house comprises a single room, with an outside bathing area and a separate kitchen. The kitchen is made from loosely woven palm fronds, to allow smoke from the cooking fires to clear. It displays the utensils and ingredients that were used to smoke or dry fish – the dietary staple and an important trading commodity.

The largest building is the *haruge*, the boat-building shed, where you can see the tools and techniques of dhoni construction, and also an ingenious machine used to make coconut fibre rope. Another working building is the weaving shed, where screwpine leaves are woven into mats, and coconut fibre is turned into coir products such as nets and bags.

Dhangethi is handy to at least seven resorts in South Ari Atoll, and accessible on longer island-hopping trips from several others – if you don't see a trip advertised, ask your resort if it can arrange one. The cultural centre conducts demonstrations of traditional crafts such as weaving, rope making, blacksmithing and cooking, and ideally your visit should coincide with these (US$5, minimum 10 visitors). At other times you can have a guided tour of the exhibits (US$3, minimum four visitors). The cost of the visit is much less than the resorts charge for an excursion, and proceeds support the local school and education fund. Additional donations are appreciated.

mix of visitors, mostly from Germany, Italy and the UK. It's recommended for divers and relaxers.

Ranveli Beach Resort *(Viligilivaru island; ☎ 450570;* W *www.ranveli-maldives.com; singles/doubles US$240/320; airport transfer by seaplane 25min US$185; 56 rooms)* seems distinctly overbuilt with too many rooms on a small island. The main restaurant is offshore, in an elegant pavilion on a pier over the lagoon, and serves a rich variety of quality meals. The house reef is good for snorkelling, excellent dive sites are nearby, and there's lots of white sandy beach. The guests are all from Italy, and Ranveli offers lots of animation and club-style activities.

Maafushivaru *(Maafushivaru island; ☎ 450596;* W *www.turisanda.it; singles/doubles €202/308; airport transfer by seaplane 30min US$210; 38 rooms)* is entirely booked through the Italian company Turisanda. It's a modern-style resort crowded onto a rather small island. The beaches are attractive, but the circle of sea walls, which protects them, is not. The rooms are boxy and modern, with distinctive blue tiled roofs, but comfortable and well furnished. All meals are buffets, well prepared and presented. The house reef is good for snorkelling and lots of fine dive sites are close by. But the main attraction at Maafushivaru is the sociable atmosphere and the lively Italian crowd.

Machchafushi Island Resort *(Machcha-fushi island; ☎ 454545;* e *info@mach chafushi.com;* W *www.machchafushi.com; singles/doubles US$130/185; airport transfer by seaplane 25min US$180; 64 rooms)* is on a small island with fine beaches and a good house reef, suitable for diving as well as snorkelling. In fact, this is pretty much a divers island, with an almost entirely German clientele. A single boat dive is US$47 with tank and weights only, US$59 with all equipment provided, and an open-water course is about US$504.

The rooms have air-con and nice furnishings; the 10 over-water bungalows cost US$30 or so more. The restaurant does breakfast and lunch buffets and a set meal for dinner – nothing special, but good food for hungry divers. There's a swimming pool and tennis court too, but they seem to be little used, like the water sports equipment. Keen divers with limited means could do a lot worse than Machchafushi.

Vakarufalhi *(Vakarufalhi island; ☎ 450004;* W *www.vakaru.com; singles/doubles US$211/ 247; airport transfer by seaplane 25min US$195; 50 rooms)* has one of the best beaches anywhere – it's wide, white, soft and surrounds the island. The bar and restaurant also feature sand floors, in keeping with the natural style. The individual bungalows are clean and modern inside, with tiled floors, air-con, hot water and open-air bathrooms; on the outside, they have thatched roofs and a canopy of palm trees. Breakfast and lunch always offer a big buffet selection, while dinners alternate between à la carte and theme nights featuring Maldivian specialities (expect fish and curries) or a beach barbecue.

The house reef has caves, overhangs and lots of fish life, sometimes including large visitors from outside the atoll. It's accessible for snorkelling and diving, off the jetties or off the beaches, by day or night. The **Pro-Divers dive centre** is in fact very professional, and charges US$51 for a boat dive with all equipment provided, or US$44 with tank and weights only. An open-water course costs US$565.

A good range of excursions is on offer, along with a little low-key evening entertainment. Vakarufalhi would suit anyone who wants a comfortable beach holiday in a natural environment, with great diving and snorkelling as a bonus.

White Sands Resort – see the earlier Budget Resorts section for information about this resort (it has wonderful water bungalows as well as budget-priced standard rooms).

Top-End Resorts

Nika Hotel *(Kudafolhudhoo island; ☎ 450516;* W *www.nikamaldive.com; singles/doubles US$510/570; airport transfer by seaplane 20min US$220; 26 rooms)* is possibly the finest old-style, natural resort in the country. It has just 26 individual villas, each one spacious and imaginatively designed in a seashell shape. Tastefully decorated with thatched roofs and handcrafted timber furniture, the villas have private gardens and preserve a rustic image – cooling is by natural ventilation through wooden louvre windows. The only air-con here is in the wine cellar! The meals are Italian/international style and excellent, served in the sand-floored dining room or outside on a seaside deck.

Dive costs here are much higher than at other resorts, but groups are small, attention is personal, and the guests can afford it. Fishing, windsurfing, tennis and most other activities are included. Guests are mostly European or Japanese, and value the privacy that Nika provides. Though several new luxury resorts are more sumptuous and have fancier features, Nika is still doing the designer desert island thing to perfection.

Kudarah *(Kudarah island;* ☎ *450610;* ⓦ *www.clubvacanze.com/ourresorts.html; singles/doubles €314/448; airport transfer by seaplane 25min €220; 30 rooms)* is a small luxury resort catering exclusively to the Italian market. With white walls, columns, arches and tiles, even the buildings look Italian. Rooms are large with conservative, quality furnishings, and resort facilities include a tennis court and swimming pool. The dive centre provides personal service with basic dive costs included in the price. It's a Club Vacanza resort, and has a sociable atmosphere, but entertainment and animation are very understated.

ARI ATOLL

Northern Atolls

The northern tourism zone includes Lhaviyani, Baa and Raa Atolls, which have 10 resorts in total, including some of the newest and most interesting in the country. The atolls further north (comprising four administrative districts) are infrequently visited by tourists, but a few safari boats and whale-watching trips now venture up this way, and visiting yachts sometimes stop in the northernmost atoll. The potential for diving is as great as anywhere in the Maldives, and there are known to be wrecks along the western fringe of the atolls, but divers require special permits for these.

This chapter covers the Maldive's northern atolls from north to south. It's worth noting, however, that about 200km further north, the Lakshadweep Islands have had a long association with the Maldives. Formerly known as the Laccadives, these islands are now Indian territory, but geologically they are part of the mostly submerged Laccadive-Chagos ridge that underlies all of the Maldives and extends down to the Chagos Archipelago. On Minicoy, the largest island of the Lakshadweep Islands, people speak a language very similar to Divehi.

IHAVANDHIPPOLHU & NORTH THILADHUNMATHEE ATOLLS

It's a confusing fact that Maldivian administrative districts are often called atolls, but do not always coincide with geographical atolls. So the northern end of the Maldives is commonly called **Haa Alifu Atoll**, but this refers to an administrative district that actually comprises the small, trapezoid shaped Ihavandhippolhu Atoll and the northern tip of Thiladhunmathee Atoll, which together have 16 inhabited islands and a population of just over 14,000.

The second northernmost island, **Uligamu** (population 326) is the 'clear-in' port for private yachts – it has health and immigration officers as well as National Security Service (NSS) personnel, so yachts should be able to complete all formalities here (AMSCO, the port agent, has an office here; see the Getting There & Away chapter). The Sailor's Choice store (on VHF) has basic supplies and some diesel (US$0.50/L). Following a feasibility study, the government has

decided to establish a yacht marina in the northern atolls, but Uligamu has been ruled out for financial and environmental reasons. A number of other islands are being considered by development companies who will bid for the contract. If an uninhabited island is chosen, it will probably get a small hotel and a permit to serve alcohol, like a miniresort.

The capital island is **Dhidhdhoo** (population 2766), which offers good anchorage for passing yachts. **Huvarafushi**, the next largest island (population 2221), is noted for its music, dancing and sporting activities, and it also has a fish-freezing plant.

The island of **Utheemu** (population 584) is the birthplace of Sultan Mohammed Thakurufaanu who, with his brothers, overthrew Portuguese rule in 1573. A memorial to this Maldivian hero, with a small museum and library, was opened in 1986. Thakurufaanu's wooden palace has been restored and Maldivians come to pay homage to the great man (see the boxed text 'The Legend of Thakurufaanu' in the Facts about the Maldives chapter).

Kelaa (population 1196) was the northern British base during WWII, mirroring Gan at the other end of the archipelago. The mosque here dates from the end of the 17th century. Yams and *cadjan* (mat made of coconut palm leaves) are the island's products.

SOUTH THILADHUNMATHEE & MAAMAKUNUDHOO ATOLLS

South Thiladhunmathee Atoll is actually the central section of an elongated reef and lagoon formation extending over 150km north to south, while Maamakunudhoo Atoll is a much smaller, narrow oval of reefs, about 20km to the west. Together they comprise the **Haa Dhaal** administrative district, with about 17,000 people living on the 17 inhabited islands. **Kulhuduffushi** is the capital island and also the most populous, with 6581 people. It has been chosen by the government as the Maldives' northern regional centre, and has a hospital, a secondary school with classes to A level (matriculation), and a telecommunications centre and cyber café. The traditional specialities here are

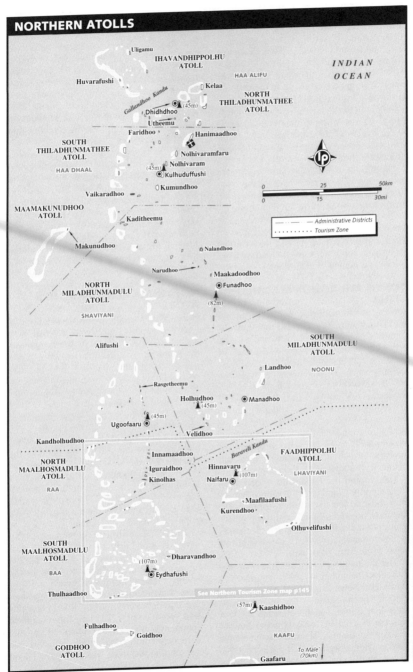

NORTHERN ATOLLS

Uligamu

IHAVANDHIPPOLHU
ATOLL

HAA ALIFU

INDIAN
OCEAN

Huvarafushi

Kelaa

NORTH
THILADHUNMATHEE
ATOLL

Gallandhoo Kandu

Dhidhdhoo (45m)

Utheemu

Faridhoo

Hanimaadhoo

SOUTH
THILADHUNMATHEE
ATOLL

HAA DHAAL

Nolhivaramfaru

Nolhivaram

(45m) Kulhuduffushi

Vaikaradhoo

Kumundhoo

Kaditheemu

MAAMAKUNUDHOO
ATOLL

Makunudhoo

Nalandhoo

Narudhoo

Maakadoodhoo

NORTH
MILADHUNMADULU
ATOLL

Funadhoo

(82m)

SHAVIYANI

Alifushi

SOUTH
MILADHUNMADULU
ATOLL

Landhoo

NOONU

Rasgetheemu

Holhudhoo

Manadhoo

(45m)

Ugoofaaru (45m)

Velidhoo

Kandholhudhoo

Innamaadhoo

Baraveli Kandu

FAADHIPPOLHU
ATOLL

NORTH
MAALHOSMADULU
ATOLL

Iguraidhoo

Kinolhas

Hinnavaru

Naifaru (107m)

LHAVIYANI

RAA

Maafilaafushi

Kurendhoo

Olhuvelifushi

SOUTH
MAALHOSMADULU
ATOLL

Dharavandhoo

(107m)

Eydhafushi

BAA

Thulhaadhoo

See Northern Tourism Zone map p145

(57m) Kaashidhoo

Fulhadhoo

Goidhoo

KAAFU

GOIDHOO
ATOLL

Gaafaru

To Male'
(70km)

0   25   50km
0   15   30mi

— · — · — Administrative Districts
· · · · · · · Tourism Zone

NORTHERN ATOLLS

rope making and shark fishing. The nearest airport is on **Hanimaadhoo** (population 1009). Island Aviation has flights from Male' and back on most days (look for airport code HAQ).

The highest natural point in the Maldives, at about 3m above sea level, is on **Faridhoo** (population 159), where there are ancient Buddhist ruins. On **Kumundhoo** there's a stone circle that seems to be the base of Buddhist stupa, and *hawitta* (artificial mound) remains can still be seen on **Vaikaradhoo**.

The area around Haa Dhaal suffers severe storms, and quite a few vessels have gone down in these waters. Maamakunudhoo Atoll is the graveyard of several ships, including the English ships *Persia Merchant*, wrecked here in 1658, and the *Hayston*, which ran onto a reef in 1819. In each circumstance, survivors were rescued by local people and treated with kindness.

NORTH MILADHUNMADULU ATOLL

Looking at a modern map, Miladhunmadulu and Thiladhunmathee Atolls appear to be part of one elongated atoll enclosing a single very long lagoon. The traditional names of the atolls were probably based on cultural associations as much as geographical features, and depended primarily on what was visible above the sea, rather than a knowledge of the geological connections 100m below the surface. In any case, one section of this long atoll formation is called North Miladhunmadulu Atoll, and it forms the **Shaviyani** administrative district, comprising 15 inhabited islands with a total of 11,406 people.

The capital is **Funadhoo** (population 799), a pretty island with the ruins of an ancient mosque and 13th-century tombstones. The most populous island, with 1606 inhabitants, is **Maakadoodhoo**, which specialises in the production of jaggery, a coarse brown sugar made from palm sap.

The main mosque on the island of **Kaditheemu** (population 1082) incorporates the oldest known example of the Maldives' unique Thaana script – it's an inscription on a door frame, which notes that the roof was constructed in 1588. Another famous island is uninhabited **Nalandhoo**, where the Thakurufaanu brothers hid their boat between guerrilla battles with the Portuguese.

SOUTH MILADHUNMADULU ATOLL

The southern end of the Miladhunmadulu-Thiladhunmathee atoll complex is called South Miladhunmadulu, and it forms the **Noonu** administrative district, comprising 13 inhabited islands with a combined total of 10,429 people. The capital island, **Manadhoo**, has 1239 people, but **Holhudhoo** (population 1562) and **Velidhoo** (population 1866) are more populous.

On the island of **Landhoo** (population 653) are the remnants of a *hawitta* supposedly left by the fabled Redin, a people who figure in Maldivian folklore. The *hawitta* is a 15m-high mound known locally as *maa badhige*, or 'great cooking place'. Thor Heyerdahl writes extensively about the tall, fair-haired Redin in his book *The Maldive Mystery*. He believes them to have been the first inhabitants of the Maldives, as long ago as 2000 BC.

NORTH MAALHOSMADULU ATOLL

North Maalhosmadulu is a reasonably distinct geographical atoll, and together with the island of Alifushi to its north, it forms the **Raa** administrative district, with 14,486 people, 16 inhabited islands and just one resort. Diving safari boats are starting to venture into this area, and new dive sites are being documented.

The sea to the west of Raa has some of the best fishing areas in the country. The capital island **Ugoofaaru** (population 1089) has one of the largest fishing fleets in the country. On the west side of the atoll the tiny island of **Kandholhudhoo** (also spelt Kandoludhu) is the nearest to the rich western waters, and has 2717 people crowded onto it – a candidate for the most densely populated island in the country.

The island of **Alifushi** (population 1737), which is actually in a small, separate atoll to the north of Raa proper, is reputedly the home of the finest dhoni builders in the country. The government-owned Alifushi Boat Yard continues the tradition, producing a modern version of the dhoni. **Iguraidhoo** (population 1274) and **Innamaadhoo** (population 492) are also boat-building and carpentry centres that might be accessible for excursions from Meedhupparu Island Resort.

According to local legend, the now un-inhabited island of **Rasgetheemu** is where Koimala Kaloa and his princess wife landed after being exiled from Sri Lanka and before moving to Male' to found a ruling dynasty. Another important visitor to the atoll was the Arab seafarer Ibn Battuta, who landed at **Kinolhas** in 1343 and then moved on to Male'.

The channel between Baa and Raa, locally known as Hani Kandu, is also named Moresby Channel after the Royal Navy officer Robert Moresby, who was responsible for the original marine survey of the Maldives made from 1834 to 1836 (see the boxed text 'Mapping the Maldives' below). There's good diving on both sides of the Moresby Channel, as it funnels water between the atolls, bringing pelagic fish and promoting coral growth. Mantas abound in October and November. The channels entering the atoll are studded with interesting thilas, and reefs dot the inside of the atoll.

Mapping the Maldives

If you've flown over the atolls by seaplane, you will have seen something of the maze of reefs, channels, sand bars and islands that make up the Maldives. If you've taken a boat trip from your resort, you'll realise that very little of this complexity is visible from sea level. The local boatmen know their way around the atolls from long experience and the tiniest of clues, like a greenish tinge on the underside of a cloud, which can indicate a reef in the water below. Other mariners are dependent on accurate navigational charts, the best of which are published by the British Admiralty.

These charts have their origins in a remarkable marine survey done in the 1830s by three British vessels under the command of Robert Moresby. As British trade with India and the Far East flourished, it became important to chart the shipping routes in the Indian Ocean. In particular it was critical to plot safe passages through the Laccadive-Chagos ridge – a chain of reefs, atolls and islands that extends some 2000km south of India. The Maldives, in the centre of this ridge, form a barrier across the most direct routes between the Middle East and southern India, Ceylon (as it was then) and the Malay peninsula. More than a few ships had foundered on the Maldives because the reefs and passages were not charted with any accuracy.

Moresby started with the Laccadive (now Lakshadweep) Islands in 1828, but was diverted to the Red Sea, where he spent five years surveying and charting. By the time his crews started on the Maldives, in 1834, they must have been a very experienced and highly efficient operation. With only a couple of officers, they worked from north to south, taking hundreds of thousands of depth soundings using a lead-weighted line, painstakingly recording the exact position of each one. This data was plotted precisely on paper, and lines were interpolated to show the extent of every reef, the depth of every channel and the location of every island, shoal and sand bar.

It must have been demanding and exacting work – moving around by sail and oar, calculating position with a sextant and ship's clock, recording pages of data by hand and plotting the charts with pen and ink by the light of an oil lamp. They lived on their tiny ships, worked in oppressive heat and were stricken by dysentery and 'fever' (probably malaria, which was rife at the time). Some had to return to India and at least one died. The survey of the Maldives took two years and two months, and it was another 2½ years before the final charts were drawn and published in England in December 1839.

The accuracy and thoroughness of the charts were immediately recognised, and they were exhibited to Queen Victoria. The charts resulted in an immediate improvement in marine safety and contributed greatly to the scientific understanding of coral reefs. In 1869 the Suez Canal opened and the amount of shipping in the area increased enormously, with mariners relying on Moresby's surveys of both the Red Sea and the Indian Ocean. Today, the Maldives sit on one of the busiest sea lanes in the world, with cargo ships and supertankers plying from Europe and the Middle East to East Asia. The Admiralty charts are regularly updated with the latest satellite-imaging techniques, but still bear the notation that most depth data is based on lead-line surveys from the original Marine Survey of India.

There are not many memorials to Moresby, but if you sit on any resort island in the Maldives, snorkel around any reef, or go diving on any thila, there is every chance that it was once visited by a small British boat under his command. The crew would have surveyed every side of your island, charted your reef and plumbed the depths of your dive site over 160 years ago. They were not on holiday.

Resorts

The southern part of this atoll was included in the tourism zone in the late 1990s, but there were some delays in opening the first resort. Club Med is expected to open a new resort at some stage, but most development plans are on hold until tourism growth returns to pre-2001 levels.

Meedhupparu Island Resort *(Meedhupparu island;* ☎ *237700;* **W** *www.meedhupparu.com.mv; singles/doubles US$110/ 150; airport transfer by speedboat 4hr US$160, by seaplane 45min US$270; 215 rooms)* has about half its guests from Italy, and provides a complete program of activities from a stretching session on the beach in the morning to quiz games at night in the outdoor theatre. Other guests, mainly from the UK and Europe, enjoy the excellent beaches and swimming pool, and the liquid benefits of their all-inclusive packages. The house reef is accessible for snorkelling, but not especially interesting. The island itself has lots of vegetation in a very natural state – it's a bit untidy in places, but may improve with time.

Meedhupparu is a budget resort, and the buffet meals are adequate but unremarkable, catering more to British than Italian tastes. The barn-like restaurant lacks charm and the service isn't always as friendly or as efficient as it could be. Likewise the rooms have all the basic equipment (air-con, hot water, IDD phone), but they don't face the beach, the finishes are rough and the architecture is a bit odd. The massage centre specialises in Ayurvedic treatments in an atmosphere that's more like a clinic than a spa.

The **Crab dive centre** is keen on exploring the potential in the atoll, but it charges more than most resorts – US$57 for a single boat dive with tank and weights, US$72 with all equipment. Multidive packages are better value, and an open-water course is reasonable at about US$460. Diving is the best reason to come to Meedhupparu – the low room rates offset the high cost of dives and airport transfers.

SOUTH MAALHOSMADULU ATOLL

The **Baa** administrative district includes South Maalhosmadulu Atoll and the small Goidhoo Atoll, 10km further south. It has 9612 people in 13 inhabited islands. Fishing is the most important activity, but Baa is also famous for its lacquer work and the fine woven-cotton sarong, called a *feylis*. **Eydhafushi**, the capital and principal island (population 2401), is also the *feylis* centre. **Thulhaadhoo** (population 1941) is the second largest island and the main centre for the production of lacquered boxes and jars. Both of these islands can be visited on excursions from nearby resorts.

Because of its isolation, **Goidhoo** has been a place for castaways and exiles. In 1602 Francois Pyrard, a French explorer, found himself on the island of **Fulhadhoo** after his ship, the *Corbin*, was wrecked. In 1976, a German traveller was banished here for the murder, in Male', of his girlfriend – he refused offers of extradition, converted to Islam and later married a local woman.

Diving

Milaidhoo Reef Strong currents flowing through the Kamadhoo Kandu provide an environment for soft corals, which thrive on the reef on the north side of an uninhabited island, Milaidhoo. The reef top, at 2m, is great for snorkelling, and it drops straight down to about 35m. This cliff has numerous caves and overhangs with seafans and sponges.

Kakani Thila The north side of this thila, at 25m to 30m, retains coral formations in excellent condition, and colourful soft corals fill the overhangs. It's also home to lots of fish, including Napoleons, jackfish and Oriental sweetlips.

Dhigali Haa This small thila, though well inside the atoll, commonly attracts pelagic species (barracuda) and grey reef sharks. Other fish include jacks, batfish and trevally. It's also a good place to see nudibranchs, yellow and orange soft corals and anemones (with clown fish).

Madi Finolhu This sandy reef has large coral blocks on which black corals grow. Stingrays can be seen on the sand, and mantas also pass through. It's a good beginners dive (20m).

Muthafushi Thila Overhangs here are home to soft corals and anemones. Many hard corals are in good condition and very colourful, black corals can also be seen. There are large schools of blue-striped snapper.

Mid-Range Resorts

Reethi Beach Resort *(Fonimagoodhoo island;* ☎ *232626;* **W** *www.reethibeach.com; singles/ doubles US$149/235; airport transfer by seaplane 35min US$220; 100 rooms)* is on a good-sized island with plenty of natural vegetation, soft white beaches, an accessible house reef

Boys playing with a tyre innertube, Mahlos island

Cheeky boy in front of coral-stone wall

Man smoking a hookah

Group of students in Male' where many people go to study

Prow of a dhoni

Tropical beach, Vilamendhoo island

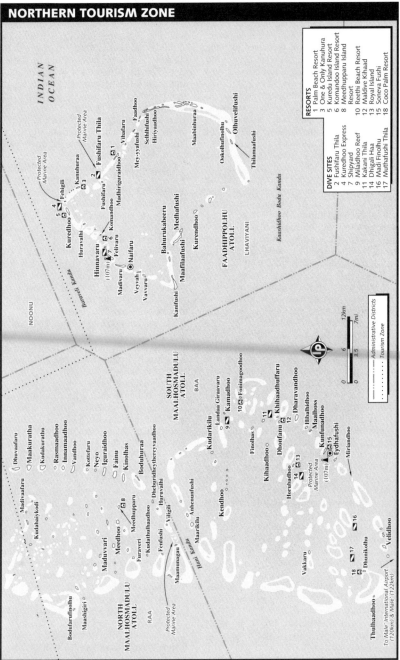

NORTHERN TOURISM ZONE

RESORTS
1 Palm Beach Resort
3 One & Only Kanuhura
5 Kuredu Island Resort
6 Komandoo Island Resort
8 Meedhupparu Island Resort
10 Reethi Beach Resort
12 Maldive Kihaad
13 Royal Island
15 Soneva Fushi
18 Coco Palm Resort

DIVE SITES
2 Fushifaru Thila
4 Kuredhoo Express
7 Shipyard
9 Miladhoo Reef
11 Kakani Thila
14 Dhigali Haa
16 Madi Finolhu
17 Muthafushi Thila

INDIAN OCEAN

Protected Marine Area

NOONU

Kaashidhoo Bodu Kandu

FAADHIPPOLHU ATOLL

LHAVIYANI

Fushifaru Thila
Kanuhuraa
Vihafaru
Faadhoo
Mey-yyafushi
Sethihifushi
Hiriyaadhoo
Maahinhuraa
Fushifaru
Madhiriguraidhoo
Oolohuffinolhu
Olhuvelifushi
Thilamaafushi

Felivaru
Komandoo
Bahurukabeeru
Medhafushi
Maafilaafushi
Kurendhoo
Kanifushi

Fehigili
Kuredhoo
Huravalhi
Hinnavaru
(107m)
Madivaru
Naifaru
Veyah
Vavaru

Baarelli Kanda

Burevvli Kandu

SOUTH MAALHOSMADULU ATOLL

BAA

Landaa Giraavaru
Kamadhoo
Fonimagoodhoo
Kudarikilu
Kihaadhuffaru
Dhonfanu
Dharavandhoo
Kendhoo
Kihaadhoo
Finolhas
Hibalhidhoo
Maalhos
Kunfunadhoo
Eydhafushi
Horubadhoo
Mirandhoo
(107m)
Protected Marine Area

NORTH MAALHOSMADULU ATOLL

RAA

Dhuvaafaru
Maakurathu
Kudakurathu
Rasmaadhoo
Innamaadhoo
Vandhoo
Kottefaru
Neyo
Iguraidhoo
Fainu
Kinolhas
Boduhuraa
Dhebuiridhetherryvaadhoo
Madivaafaru
Kudahaiykodi
Maduvvari
Meedhoo
Meedhupparu
Furaveri
Kudathulhaadhoo
Huravalhi
Fenfushi
Viligili
Maarikilu
Anbenunfushi
Maamunagau

Bodufarufinolhu
Maashigiri
Protected Marine Area

Vakkaru
Dhunikolhu
Thulhaadhoo

Velidhoo

To Malé International Airport
(120km) & Malé (122km)

.... Administrative Districts
.... Tourism Zone

0   3.5   6   12m
0   3.5 7mi

NORTHERN ATOLLS

and an expansive lagoon. The buildings, all with thatched roofs, are designed to blend with the environment, and also incorporate some Maldivian design elements like the deep horizontal mouldings used on the old Friday Mosque in Male'. Rooms are very well finished and have air-con, TV, minibar, IDD phone, quality bathrooms and polished timber floors. The deluxe villas are more spacious and have better beach frontage (and cost US$20 more), but the water villas are not so special (they're another US$20 extra).

Guests are mostly British, German and Swiss, many on half-board packages that let them try the weekly barbecue and the two speciality restaurants (Chinese and Maldivian) as well as the excellent selection in the main buffet. There's some formal entertainment, but most guests seem happy with a few drinks in the well-patronised and sociable bar. It would be a good resort for kids too, though there are no special facilities or programs.

For the sporting guests, there's a swimming pool, gym, squash, badminton and tennis. Windsurfing, sailing and other water sports are popular here, partly because of the wide lagoon and partly because of the enthusiasm of the staff. Kitesurfing is the latest thrill on offer. Motorised activities like parasailing, wakeboarding and jet skis are available only at certain hours. The spa offers a full range of massage and beauty treatments. The **Sea-Explorer dive centre** (**w** www.sea-explorer.net) is very professional and reasonably priced. A single boat dive is US$44 with tank and weights, or US$50 with all equipment. An open-water course costs about US$496. Nitrox diving costs US$3 extra, and a nitrox course costs US$135. Qualified divers can make dives off the house reef, and with few resorts in the area, you'll probably have good dive sites to yourself.

Reethi Beach is an excellent resort all round – attractive, well managed, with great food, where you can relax completely or have a full-on action holiday.

Maldive Kihaad (*Kihaadhuffaru island;* ☎ 236688; **w** www.valtur.it; singles/doubles €220/280; airport transfer by seaplane 35min US$220, by speedboat 3hr US$140; 100 rooms*) entertains Italian guests on packages that include meals, some drinks and lots of activities. The rooms are new, fully equipped (air-con, TV, minibar etc) and

attractively designed; deluxe rooms have hi-fi systems, and water villas are also available. The restaurant serves a rich selection of Italian and international dishes, buffet for breakfast and lunch, table service for dinner. The resort has a first-class swimming pool, disco, spa, kids club and water-sports centre, and the island itself is a delight, with shady palm trees, perfect beaches, a lovely lagoon for sailing and a house reef that's accessible for snorkelling and diving. Bookings are all through the Italian operator Valtur (☎ 39-6-47061, fax 39-6-4706334).

Royal Island (*Horubadhoo island;* ☎ 230088; **w** www.villahotels-maldives.com; singles/doubles US$225/255; airport transfer by seaplane 35min US$230; 152 rooms*) is a new resort – a totally professional, state-of-the-art development in every respect. The island is long and narrow, with long stretches of toothpaste-white beach and a brilliant house reef. Most of the natural vegetation has been preserved, including many coconut palms, pandanuses, screw pines and seven big banyan trees. An old bathing pool and some mosque ruins have also been preserved.

The modern-looking rooms are all nestled in trees and fronting the beach. Inside they have pine walls, hardwood floors and all the gadgets from air-con and IDD phone to electric kettle and satellite TV. The airy main restaurant does a huge variety of styles – Italian, Indian, Mexican, Maldivian and more – all served as buffets. A second restaurant specialises in à la carte Mediterranean meals, while several bars serve snacks and drinks. Alcohol is a bit pricey here (about US$5 for a beer; US$7 for a glass of house wine), but many 'extras' are included in the room rate – mineral water, gym facilities, daytime tennis, windsurfing and snorkelling gear. The Araamu Spa is a luxury facility with a relaxing ambience. Eight therapists perform a range of beauty and 'wellness' treatments from face massage to pedicure.

The **Delphis Diving Center** is keen to have divers explore the many sites in Baa Atoll, and they're very good guides. A single boat dive is US$54 with tank and weights, or US$64 with all equipment. An open-water course costs about US$612. Nitrox courses cost US$250.

Though the style here is much more natural than at other Villa properties, it doesn't have the character of many older, smaller resorts.

But with its high-quality facilities and food, beautiful beaches and fantastic snorkelling and diving, Royal Island represents great value for money.

Top-End Resorts

Soneva Fushi (*Kunfunadhoo island;* ☎ 230304; W *www.sixsenses.com/soneva-fushi; singles/ doubles US$415/550; airport transfer by seaplane 30min US$290; 65 rooms*) has the biggest resort island in the country (more than 1.5 km long), with just 65 luxurious villas. Each one is like a small house built with natural materials, fitted with designer furnishings and finished in rustic style. All the deluxe features are included (air-con, hairdryer, minisafe, CD player etc) but 'modern' items are concealed – no plastic is visible. Villas are well spaced around the edges of the island, affording complete privacy – they're reached by sandy tracks that wind through the lush vegetation, which is kept as natural as possible. There's a range of villas, and prices vary with the season. As you move from low to high season, and from the comfortable to the sublime, the prices move from US$250 to over US$1500 a night for room only.

The reception, bar and restaurant areas all have sand floors and cane furniture, and the chickens are free to wander anywhere. The food is topnotch for the Maldives – nothing too fancy, but with the freshest, finest ingredients, beautifully prepared and presented. It could be called European-Asian fusion cuisine, with a bias towards light and tropical flavours. Lunch and sometimes dinner are buffet style, but the offerings change daily, and the wine list is wonderful. Meals are often served alfresco, and in-room dining is also available.

Picnics on isolated islands are popular, as are the dozens of different massages and treatments offered at the Raison D'Etre spa. The atmosphere is completely relaxed and delightfully unpretentious – leave your jewellery and your dinner jacket at home.

There is the usual range of resort recreations, many of them complimentary. The **Soleni dive school** (W *www.soleni.com*) has years of experience diving the sites around Soneva. A single boat dive is US$64 with tank and weights, or US$74 with all equipment. An open-water course costs about US$665.

For natural style, sheer quality and class, Soneva Fushi is as good as it gets.

Coco Palm Resort (*Dhunikolhu island;* ☎ 230011; W *www.cocopalm.com.mv; singles/ doubles US$411/502; airport transfer by seaplane 30min US$275; 100 rooms*) is one of the most architecturally interesting resorts, with large tent-like thatched pavilions for reception, restaurant and bar areas. The beach villa rooms are circular with high, thatched, conical roofs, quality furnishings and open-air bathrooms, while the deluxe rooms have, in addition, an individual, free-form plunge pool. The 14 over-water bungalows are even more luxuriously appointed, and combine privacy with uninterrupted sea views.

The island itself is quite large with soft, white beaches all around and a very accessible house reef. The vegetation has a very natural look, although a little sparse and scrubby – they're working to thicken it up. Another highlight is the food. All meals are buffet, but the variety, quality and freshness is hard to believe – it's one of the few resorts with perfect avocados.

With no other resorts around, divers here have access to almost untouched sites. Diving is run by **Ocean-Pro** (W *www.oceanpro-diveteam.com*), which offers professional, personal service. A single boat dive is US$44 with tank and weights, or US$59 with all equipment. An open-water course costs about US$539. Nitrox courses cost US$237 and nitrox dives cost US$2 extra.

Whale watching is an option in October and November, when the animals migrate through the channel between Baa and Goidhoo Atolls. Excursions include a visit to Thulhaadhoo, an island well known for producing lacquer work, which you can see and buy. For recreation there's a gym, a spa, tennis courts, and a billiard table, as well as the Mandara Spa for Balinese style massage. Though the rooms here are as romantic as you could want, and Coco Palm has all the ingredients of a top-quality resort, they haven't quite come together yet to create an overall ambience and charm.

FAADHIPPOLHU ATOLL

This single atoll makes up the administrative district of **Lhaviyani**, where fishing is the main industry and tourism is becoming more important. It has a population of about 9400 living on just five inhabited islands. On the capital island, **Naifaru** (population 3707), the people have a reputation for making attractive handicrafts from coral and mother-of-pearl, and for concocting local medicines. **Hinnavaru** (population 3212) is also densely settled and the central government is promoting the development of **Maafilaafushi** as an alternative, but so far only about 100 people have settled there. Maafilaafushi had a much greater population in the 17th century, but it was later abandoned, though remnants of the old mosque can still be seen. It is now being resettled with government support. Day trips from the resorts visit all these islands, as well as **Felivaru**, which has a modern tuna-canning plant.

Diving

The atoll has some very well-known dive sites, which until recently were only accessible from one resort and by the occasional safari boat.

Kuredhoo Express Usually done as a long drift dive through the channel next to the Kuredu resort, this is a demanding dive in strong currents but also offers brilliant snorkelling on the eastern side. Napoleon wrasse, grey reef sharks and trevally frequent the channel entrance, while inside are overhangs dripping with soft corals. Look for morays, turtles and stingrays. It's a Protected Marine Area.

Shipyard This is another demanding dive, with two wrecks within 50m of each other. Strong currents around these ships have promoted rapid growth of soft and hard corals, which now form a habitat for many types of reef fish. Moray eels and sweepers live inside the wrecks, while nurse sharks cruise around the bottom.

Fushifaru Thila When the current is strong, this is no place for beginners, but when the currents are slow the top of the thila is superb for snorkelling. The thila, with lovely soft corals, sits in the centre of a broad channel and attracts mantas, eagle rays, sharks, groper, sweetlips and turtles. Cleaner wrasse abound on the thila, which is a Protected Marine Area.

Resorts

Though Kuredu has been open for over 25 years, the other resorts are more recent (late 1990s), and reflect the upmarket trend in Maldives tourism. The resorts here fit into the mid-range price category.

Kuredu Island Resort *(Kuredhoo island;* ☎ *230337;* ⓦ *www.kuredu.com; singles/doubles US$90/120; airport transfer by seaplane 40min*

US$220, by speedboat 4hr US$80; 300 rooms) now has water bungalows! Established as a diving camp in 1976, Kuredu has long been known as a basic, budget resort, but it has moved upmarket. The beach bungalows are recently renovated with air-con, phone, hot water and minibar, but are still very affordable. The new, all-wood beach villas face the best beach, have an open-air bathroom, stereo and coffee makers, and cost up to US$30 more. Spa beach villas are more expensive again, and the spacious Sangu over-water villas, made with the honeymooners in mind, cost US$150 to US$240, depending on the season.

The spa villas and over-water rooms are at the west end of the island in a quieter precinct with its own attractive restaurant and bar. The restaurant here does first-class buffet meals with live cooking stations as a special attraction. The main reception, restaurant, bar, swimming pool, shops and dive centre are all near the centre of the island, and cater for the generally younger, livelier crowd in the less expensive rooms. The buffets in the main restaurant are pretty good, with a fair selection of Asian and international dishes. In addition there are three à la carte restaurants specialising in Italian pizza, Thai food and grills. There's even a tea shop where you can get typical Maldivian short eats at typical tourist prices (it's more popular with staff than guests). The big Babuna Bar is the busiest place in the evening and hosts movies, discos, cultural shows, games nights and live bands. Other bars offer poolside drinks or a more intimate atmosphere. Most drinks are pretty standard Maldive prices (US$4 beers, US$5 to US$7 spirits) and the house wine is drinkable and affordable (US$7 for a 0.5L carafe). Many guests are on all-inclusive packages and can quaff away without a care.

Recreation facilities include a gym, tennis courts, football field, well-used beach volleyball court and a new, six-hole pitch-and-putt golf course. For water sports there are windsurfing, kitesurfing, catamarans, waterskiing, wakeboards and the ubiquitous banana. A new and palatial spa offers hour-long Swedish, Thai and Oriental massages (US$50) as well as two-hour lessons so you can learn to massage your partner (US$95). Excursions go to a variety of local fishing villages, resorts and uninhabited islands. There's a day cruise on a traditional wooden yacht (US$75) and a choice of fishing trips too.

Excellent dive sites are accessible to Kuredu and just a few other resorts. The **ProDivers centre** (W *www.prodivers.com*) offers a full range of courses, and does a good job matching divers with others of similar experience and interest. A single boat dive costs US$41 with tank and weights, or US$51 with all equipment. An open-water course is US$498. A nitrox course costs US$98, and nitrox dives are available at no extra cost. Rebreather courses and dives are also available. Much of the house reef is accessible, and you can do good dives directly from the shore. ProDivers also runs a complete snorkelling program, with instructors taking groups for fish spotting, photography and wreck snorkelling trips.

It's a well-run resort that has always been popular with young Europeans, giving it a lively, sociable atmosphere. Now it also has more honeymooners, older couples and families. The island is quite large, and has been intelligently developed to cater for a variety of needs. If you want high-style luxury or intimate island atmosphere, this resort may not be for you. But for activities such as diving, snorkelling, relaxing, recreation, families and fun, Kuredu is hard to beat.

Komandoo Island Resort (*Komandhoo island;* ☎ *231010;* W *www.komandoo.com; singles/doubles US$210/220; airport transfer by seaplane 40min US$250, by speedboat 4hr US$100; 45 rooms*) is the smaller and more stylish sibling of Kuredu, and shares the same super-efficient management. The hexagonal rooms, prefabricated in pine from Finland, come complete with air-con, phone, four-poster bed, minibar, safe and CD player, and they all front directly onto a pure white beach.

The house reef is accessible through two channels and has a wide variety of marine life (256 fish species documented) and recovering corals. The very professional **ProDivers** (W *www.prodivers.com*) runs the dive centre, as on Kuredu, but with smaller groups and slightly higher prices – US$49 for a single boat dive with tank and weights, or US$55 with all equipment, US$565 for an open-water course. Nitrox is available.

The island is not lush, but is nicely landscaped. The main restaurant and bar buildings have sea views, sand floors and tropical-island atmosphere. The food and service get rave reviews, and the new Etoile spa adds another opportunity for indulgence. If you want a small, quiet, quality resort, Komandoo is ideal.

One & Only Kanuhuraa (*Kanuhuraa island;* ☎ *230044;* W *www.kanuhura.com; singles/doubles US$413/492; airport transfer by seaplane 40min US$309; 100 rooms*) was called Kanuhura Resort & Spa until it joined the group of One & Only resorts. It's quite new and the rooms and facilities combine natural materials, high style and elegant simplicity. The beach villas have four-poster beds, separate dressing area, fabulous indoor–outdoor bathroom, lots of polished timber and a frontage onto the perfect beach. They're equipped with the works – air-con, safe, stereo, satellite TV, DVD, safe, minibar, bathrobes, umbrellas, slippers... The more expensive suites and water villas are even bigger and feature private spas, sun decks and sea views.

The expansive free-form swimming pool has the main restaurant at one end and the bar at the other – both are high, thatched-roof pavilions with sand floors and open sides, but a table on the deck or the beach may be even more inviting. Also near the pool is the Veyoge Spa, a serene space that's central to the resort's concept. Then there's a second restaurant, gym, aerobics studio, karaoke bar, cigar lounge, games room and library. Other facilities around the island include a disco, boutique, coffee shop, tennis and squash courts, and a kids club. This is a complete resort.

The main restaurant presents an amazing variety of dishes at every meal, and the live cooking stations are lots of fun, though the flavours mightn't be everything you'd hope for – the food is very good, but the wonderful ambience makes you expect something brilliant. The Olive Tree à la carte Mediterranean restaurant does less elaborate but very satisfying pizzas, pastas and salads. A romantic alternative is Coves, an alfresco restaurant on a separate island that you reach by rowboat.

Kanahuraa is a big island, about 1km long, and assiduous landscaping is augmenting the natural vegetation with local species. The environment is a priority here – garden waste is composted, water is recycled, sewage is reprocessed and solar panels provide the hot water. Lovely, squeaky beaches go right around the island, and the wide lagoon makes for smooth sailing – you can follow the reef for 5km and make your own stops at several tiny uninhabited islands along the way. Water skiing is an option; jet skis are not.

The house reef is not suitable for snorkelling, so take one of the special snorkelling excursions run by the **Sun Dive Centre** (w www.sundivecenter.com), a PADI Gold Palm facility that caters for youngsters, beginners and advanced divers. Over 40 dive sites are accessible. A single boat dive is US$57 with tank and weights, US$66 with all equipment, and an open-water course costs US$609. Nitrox dives costs US$6 extra, and a nitrox course is US$256.

While plenty of activities are on offer, the best features of Kanuhura are the pampering service, stylish architecture, romantic rooms and relaxing beaches.

Palm Beach Resort (Madhiriguraidhoo island; ☎ 230084; w www.palmbeachmaldives.com; singles/doubles US$250/320; airport transfer by seaplane 40min US$220; 100 rooms) has one of the largest, lushest islands, and some of the best beaches in the atoll. The bungalows dotted along both sides of the island are quite big and have air-con, phone, TV, in-house movies, minibar and other mod cons, though the white walls, tiled floors and bamboo furniture aren't especially stylish. Most of the resort facilities (restaurant, bar, pool, spa, sports centre) are towards one end of the island, quite a way from some of the rooms. Electric carts and bicycles are available to help people get around.

The main restaurant serves all meals as buffets with an Italian bias, and they're very good. Seven bars are dotted around the island – draught beer is only US$2.50 a litre but wines, and especially spirits, are more expensive. Live music, discos and other entertainment happens in the pool bar. Tennis, squash and most water sports are free, as are some excursions and snorkelling trips (the lagoon isn't good for snorkelling). The **Macana Diving School** charges about US$38 for a single boat with tank and weights, US$58 with full equipment and US$465 for an open-water course.

Palm Beach Resort is operated by Sporting Vacanze and most of the guests come from Italy, but it's not really a club-style resort and the animation is low key. In fact the whole resort has a very casual atmosphere. It attracts all age groups, and quite a few families with children.

Southern Atolls

Until a few years ago, the atolls south of Male' and Ari were isolated and had scarcely seen a foreigner. The exception was Addu, in the far south of the country, where the British had established military facilities in WWII and an air-force base that operated from 1956 to 1976. Now, the tourism zone has been extended to cover five southern atolls (including Addu), a few safari boats are exploring dive sites as far south as the One-and-a-Half-Degree channel, and surfing trips are going to the remotest breaks of Gaaf Dhaal. Despite these forays, the region is almost totally pristine.

Three islands in the southern atolls have domestic airports that are served by daily scheduled flights with Island Aviation. A high-speed passenger ferry is planned to start service between Male' and Addu, with a couple of stops on the way (see the Getting Around chapter). Permits are required for boats to go outside the tourism zones, but these are not difficult for a reputable safari-boat operator to obtain.

Atolls are listed below, from north to south, under their geographical names. Note that Maldivians often refer to atolls by the name of an administrative district, or administrative atoll, which is the basis of local government and official statistics. Atoll and island names have several variant forms and alternate spellings.

FELIDHOO ATOLL

Felidhoo Atoll (also spelled Felidhe and Fulidhoo) and the small, uninhabited Vattaru Falhu Atoll together comprise the **Vaavu** administrative district, the least populous in the country, with 1753 people on five inhabited islands.

The main industry is fishing, and there is some boat-building as well as two tourist resort islands. The capital island is **Felidhoo**, which has only about 323 people, but visitors are more likely to go its neighbouring island, **Keyodhoo** (population 506), which has a good anchorage for safari boats. At the northern edge of the atoll, **Fulidhoo** (population 323) is an attractive island, regularly visited on day trips from the resorts – you may see some impressively large boats under construction here. **Rakeedhoo**

(population 237), at the southern tip of the atoll, is used as an anchorage by safari boats taking divers to the nearby channel.

Diving

There are at least 24 recognised dive sites in the atoll and only two resorts in the area. Some of them are not readily accessible, even from the resorts, and are mostly visited by safari boats. The following sites are rated as amongst the best in the Maldives, and they all offer superb snorkelling.

Devana Kandu This is a not-too-demanding drift dive in a channel divided by a narrow thila; it's great snorkelling area too. There are several entrances to the channel which has overhangs, caves, reef sharks and eagle rays. The southern side has soft corals and lots of reef fish. Further in, the passages join up and there is a broad area of hard corals, the deeper parts being less affected by bleaching. The whole channel is a Protected Marine Area.

Fotteyo A brilliant dive and snorkelling site in and around a channel entrance – it's worth making several dives here. There are numerous small caves, several large caves and various arches and holes, all decorated with colourful soft corals. Rays, reef sharks, groper, tuna, jackfish, barracuda, turtles and even hammerhead sharks can be seen. Inside, the channel floor is known as 'triggerfish alley'.

Rakeedhoo Kandu This is a challenging dive in a deep channel – the east and west sides are usually done as separate drift dives. Broad coral shelves cover overhangs and caves, which have seafans and black corals. Turtles, Napoleon wrasse, sharks and schools of trevally are often seen and the snorkelling on the reeftop is brilliant.

Vattaru Kandu This remote channel dive on the southern edge of Vattaru Falhu is now a Protected Marine Area. It is not too demanding unless the currents are running at full speed. The reef next to Vattaru island is a fine snorkelling area. Around the entrance are many caves and overhangs with soft corals, sea fans and abundant fish life – barracuda, fusilier and white-tip reef sharks. Turtles are sometimes seen here, and manta rays from December to April.

Resorts

Dhiggiri (Dhiggiri island; ☎ 450593; e mmto urs@dhivehinet.net.mv; singles/doubles €198/ 264; airport transfer by seaplane, 20 mins, €168, or speedboat, 1½hrs, €100; 45 rooms)

SOUTHERN ATOLLS

Mahibadhoo ◉ To Male (60km)   KAAFU

ARI
ATOLL
ALIFU   FELIDHOO
                         ATOLL
                         VAAVU

                  Felidhoo ◉

NORTH
NILANDHOO   Vattaru
ATOLL   Falhu
FAAFU   ◉ Magoodhoo

                  Muli ◉
                       SOUTH   ◉ MULAKU
                       NILANDHOO   ATOLL
DHAALU   ATOLL   MEEMU
Kudahuvadhoo ◉
           See Southern Tourism Zone map p154

                              Vilufushi
              Buruni
Kadoodhoo   Dhiyamigili ⛰ Madifushi
                       (72m)
Hirilandhoo   Guraidhoo
Omadhoo   ◉ Thimarafushi
KOLHUMADULU   Veymandhoo   Isdhoo
ATOLL
THAA   Maabaidhoo
           Maavah   Maandhoo ⛰ (67m)
                              Gan
INDIAN   Kadhoo
OCEAN   Kunahandhoo Hithadhoo ◉ Fonadhoo
                  HADHDHUNMATHEE
                  ATOLL
          ⊕   LAAMU

0   25   50km   Huvadhoo Kandu (One-and-a-
0   15   30mi   Half-Degree Channel)

───── Administrative Districts
········· Tourism Zone

                  NORTH HUVADHOO
                  ATOLL
Kolamaafushi   GAAF ALIF
           (30m) ⛰
           Kudhoo ◉ Viligili
        Dhevvadhoo (40m) ⛰ Nilandhoo
SOUTH HUVADHOO   Dhaandhoo
ATOLL   ◉ Thinadhoo
GAAF DHAAL   Kodey
Kaadedhoo   Dhiyadhoo ·
          (120m) ⛰
Hoadedhdhoo   Gadhdhoo ⛰ Kaduhulhudhoo
Rathafandhoo ·   Gan
Fiyoari ·   Vaadhoo   Equator
        Fares
Maadthoda

        Equatorial Channel

          (120m) ⛰
                  FUAMULAKU
          Fuamulaku ◉ ATOLL
                  GNAVIYANI
ADDU
ATOLL   Hithadhoo ·
SEENU (72m) ⛰
Maradhoo ◉ · Hulhumeedhoo
      Feydhoo ⊠ Gan

was completely renovated in the late 1990s
and caters exclusively to the Italian market.
It's a club-style resort, and all guests are on
packages that include activities, a couple of
excursions, all meals (with beer and wine)
and nonmotorised water sports. The rooms
have air-con, TV, phone, minibar and satellite TV; 10 of them are water bungalows.
It's a small island, a little bit cramped,
splendidly isolated, with good dive sites
nearby and a house reef that's accessible
for snorkellers.

Alimatha (Alimathaa Island; ☎ 450575;
safari@dhivehinet.net.mv;   singles/doubles
€188/254; airport transfer by seaplane, 20
mins, €168, or speedboat, 1¾hrs, €100; 102
rooms), like Dhiggiri, was completely renovated in the late 1990s. It's also an Italian
club-style resort with the guests on inclusive packages. It's a bigger, more attractive
island and has a bit more elbow room. The
lagoon is quite wide and more suited to
sailing and windsurfing (included in the
package price) than snorkelling.

MULAKU ATOLL

Also called Mulakatholhu, this atoll is commonly known as Meemu, the name of the
administrative district it comprises. Meemu
has only about 5000 people living on nine
inhabited islands. **Muli** (population 787) is
the capital island, and now gets a few visitors
from the newly established resorts. Nearby
Boli Mulah and **Kolhuvaariyaafushi**, in the
south, are more populous, with about 1200
and 1000 people, respectively. Both these
islands grow yams, which are an important
staple in more fertile islands, and an alternative to rice which must be imported.

The atoll was included in the tourism zone
in the late 1990s, and has lots of sites that are
recently explored and named, both in the kandus on the edges of the atoll, and inside the
atoll around the numerous thilas and giris.

Shark's Tongue As the name suggests, you should
see sharks on this reef slope which is east of
Boli Mulah, in the mouth of the Mulah Kandu.
Whitetips sleep on the sandy plateau, and grey
reef sharks hang around a cleaning station at
20m. In strong currents, blacktip, grey and
silvertip sharks cruise through the coral blocks,
but it's no place for beginners.

Giant Clam An easy dive around two sheltered
giris, where several giant clams are seen
between 8m and 15m, even by snorkellers.

Numerous caves and overhangs are rich with anemones and home to lobsters, gropers and glassfish. Colourful butterflyfish and clown triggerfish are easily spotted, but look hard for well-camouflaged stonefish and scorpionfish.

Resorts

Medhufushi (Medhufushi island; ☎ 460026; W www.aaa-resortsmaldives.com/medhufushi; singles/doubles US$294/458; airport transfer by seaplane, 40mins, US$245; 120 rooms) is stunningly beautiful, unpretentiously elegant and unobtrusively efficient. The island is long and narrow, thick with palm trees and surrounded by soft beaches. The very natural style is reflected throughout in the landscaping, thatched roofs and extensive use of timber finishes. All the beach villas and the 46 over-water villas are fully fitted out with all the basics (air-con, phone), top quality furnishings and extras like a stereo system, TV, minibar, bathrobes and open air bathrooms. Family villas have extra space for kids.

Resort facilities include a semicircular swimming pool, gym, library, billiard room and luxury spa. The poolside restaurant serves a lavish buffet for every meal with theme nights focussing on food styles from around the world – the resort has a reputation for excellent cuisine. You wouldn't come here for the nightlife, but the over-water bar is one of the most agreeable places you'll ever have a sunset drink.

Windsurfers and sailors have miles of lagoon to explore and half a dozen desert islands to discover. Two free snorkelling trips every day make up for the lack of a house reef, while fishing trips and other excursions will get you out on the water. The **Werner Lau** dive centre has pioneered the diving in this atoll – see W www.wernerlau.com for 32 documented dive sites. A single boat dive is US$48 with tank and weights only, US$70 with full equipment, and an open-water course costs about US$565.

For diving, dining, relaxation or romance, Medhufushi is a dream resort. It's run by AAA Hotels & Resorts (☎ 316131; STO Trade Centre, Male').

Hakuraa Club (Hahuraahuraa island; ☎ 460014; W www.johnkeellshotels.com/ hotels/hakuraa/default.html; singles/doubles US$170/195; airport transfer by seaplane, 45 mins, US$240; 70 rooms) caters mainly to British and German guests on all-inclusive packages. All the rooms are over-water bungalows with curious, tent-like roofs and the basic amenities (air-con, hot water, fridge) but no phone, TV or minibar. Across the island from the rooms is a soft beach and a very wide lagoon. It's not good for snorkelling, though snorkelling gear and twice-daily snorkelling trips are included in the package. Use of windsurfers is also included, but at low tide the lagoon is too shallow for windsurfing and sailing.

The restaurant does most meals as buffet style, and English guests are catered to with favourites like bangers and mash. Regular theme nights feature more exotic fare – Chinese, Thai, Italian, Mexican, Mongolian – and there's a weekly beach barbecue with fresh seafood. House wine, beer and no-name brand spirits are included in the package, and the sand-floored, tent-roofed bar is a congenial place to enjoy them.

The **Dive & Sail** dive centre (W www .diveandsail.com.mv) charges US$41 for a single boat dive with tank and weights, US$48 with full equipment, and US$460 for an open-water course. These are some of the cheapest rates in the Maldives. With so many little-visited dive sites in the area, diving might be the best reason to stay at Hakuraa Club.

NORTH NILANDHOO ATOLL

North Nilandhoo Atoll, the administrative district of **Faafu**, has about 3800 people living on its five inhabited islands. The capital island, **Magoodhoo**, is a small fishing village (population 422) with a very traditional Islamic community. On the southern edge of the atoll, **Nilandhoo** (population 1504) has the second oldest mosque in the country, Aasaari Miskiiy, built during the reign of Sultan Mohammed Ibn Abdullah (1153–66). It is made of dressed stone and the interior is decorated with carved woodwork. It's possible that the stones were recycled from the ruins of earlier, pre-Islamic structures.

Thor Heyerdahl's book The Maldive Mystery has an entire chapter about this island. His expedition unearthed many phallic stone carvings, like the lingam associated with the Hindu god Shiva in his manifestation as the creator. Some of these images can be seen in the National Museum in Male'. Heyerdahl's expedition also found ruins apparently from an ancient gate, one of seven surrounding a

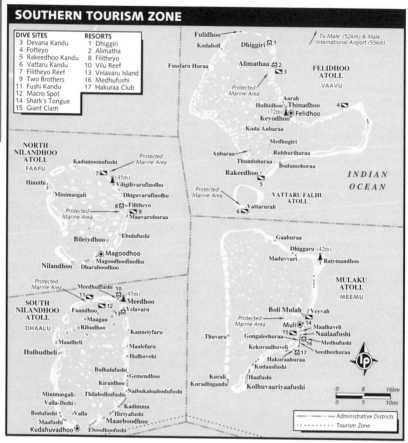

SOUTHERN TOURISM ZONE

DIVE SITES	RESORTS
3 Devana Kandu	1 Dhiggiri
4 Fotteyo	2 Alimatha
5 Rakeedhoo Kandu	10 Vilu Reef
6 Vattaru Kandu	13 Velavaru Island
7 Filitheyo Reef	16 Medhufushi
9 Two Brothers	17 Hakuraa Club
11 Fushi Kandu	
12 Macro Spot	
14 Shark's Tongue	
15 Giant Clam	

great pagan temple complex. You can visit Nilandhoo on a full-day excursion from Filitheyo resort, but the ruins are mostly unexcavated. As Heyerdahl wrote:

Five teams of archaeologists could dig here for five years and still make new discoveries. The magnitude of this prehistoric cult centre seemed quite out of proportion to the size of the island.

Diving

The atoll was little explored by divers until the first resort, Filitheyo, opened in late 2000. The **Werner Lau dive centre** (**w** *www .wernerlau.com*) has documented many of the dive sites, and with only one resort and a few visiting safari boats using them, they are in pristine condition.

Filitheyo Reef The kandu south of Filitheyo resort is now a Protected Marine Area and has several diving possibilities. Only accessible by boat, the house reef on the southeast corner of the resort descends in big steps where great clouds of fish school. Swarms of batfish and several Napoleons are resident, while grey reef sharks, rays and trevallies are frequent visitors.

Two Brothers The brothers are two thilas placed in a narrow channel. The big brother (north), tops out at 3m and is covered with soft corals and sponges, and attracts snorkellers. Many turtles reside here. Big pelagics cruise around both brothers and there are lots of nudibranchs, pipefish, gobies and other small marine life.

Resort

Filitheyo (*Filitheyo island;* **☎** *460025;* **w** *www .aaa-resortsmaldives.com/filitheyo; singles/*

doubles US$240/362; airport transfer by seaplane, 35mins, US$230; 125 rooms) is a beautifully designed and finished resort on a large, well-vegetated, triangular island. The public buildings are spacious, open-sided Balinese-style pavilions with palm-thatch roofs and natural finishes. The main restaurant is especially attractive and serves a wide assortment of wonderful food at buffets for every meal. Even at lunch, expect canapes, soup, several types of fish, chicken, a couple of curries, fresh-cooked pasta and a few vegetarian options. Drinks are very reasonably priced here, and at the main bar and sunset bar (beers US$3 to US$4; house wine US$4 per glass; spirits US$4 to US$6), but all-inclusive options are available.

Most rooms are comfortable timber bungalows facing the best beach, nested amongst the palm trees, and equipped with phone, minibar, TV, CD player, open air bathroom and personal sun deck. Interconnecting rooms are perfect for families. Deluxe villas provide extra space and style, while the water villas have sea views and private balconies. Resort facilities include a gym, small spa, horizon pool, reading room and shops. Some low-key evening entertainment is organised, and an interesting program of excursions and fishing trips.

Beaches are pretty all around, but the lagoon is shallow on the south side, and not suitable for swimming on the east side. The north side has it all – soft sand, good swimming, and an accessible house reef that's great for snorkelling. Qualified divers can do unguided dives off the house reef too. The Werner Lau dive centre charges US$46 for a single boat dive with tank and weights only, US$62 with full equipment, and US$560 for an open-water course. A nitrox course is US$95, and nitrox dives cost US$5 extra.

Filitheyo is a first-class resort with great food, friendly and efficient service and a lovely setting. It's doesn't cater for partygoers or pampering. It suits families and for relaxation, and ideal for diving, snorkelling and other outdoor and water activities.

SOUTH NILANDHOO ATOLL

Another atoll that has only been open to tourism for a few years, South Nilandhoo is the only atoll in the administrative district of Dhaalu, which has about 5000 people living on its eight inhabited islands.

The biggest and most interesting island is the capital, **Kudahuvadhoo** (population 1232), which has an ancient and mysterious mound. The mound is now just sand, but originally this was the foundation of a structure made of fine stone work. The building stones were later removed to build part of the island's mosque. Heyerdahl said that rear wall of this mosque had some of the finest masonry he had ever seen, surpassing even that of the famous Inca wall in Cuzco, Peru. He was amazed to find such a masterpiece of stone-shaping art on such an isolated island, although the Maldivians had a reputation in the Islamic world for finely carved tombstones. Kudahuvadhoo is a long way from the resorts on this atoll, so a visit would be difficult. The waters around Kudahuvadhoo have seen several shipwrecks, including the 1340-ton *Liffey*, which went down in 1879, and the *Utheem*, which hit the same reef in 1960.

In the north of the atoll are the so-called 'jewellers islands'. **Ribudhoo** (population 420) has been long known for its goldsmiths, who are believed to have learnt the craft from a royal jeweller banished here by a sultan centuries ago. Another version is that they developed their skills on gold taken from a shipwreck in the 1700s. The nearby island of **Hulhudheli** (population 524) is a community of traditional silversmiths. Most of the gold and silver work on sale in Male' now seems to be imported, though the gold chains and medallions worn by many children may be made in these islands. Many of the craftspeople here are now making jewellery, beads and carvings from black corals and mother-of-pearl. Ribudhoo is quite accessible from the resorts, but Hulhudheli would be a long day trip.

Diving

Like Meemu and Faafu, Dhaalu Atoll has only recently been included in the tourism zone, and the two resorts here were both opened in the late 1990s. A big attraction of these resorts is their access to infrequently explored dive sites.

Fushi Kandu A channel on the northern edge of the atoll, this site is a Protected Marine Area.

Steps on the east side have eagle rays and whitetip reef sharks. Thilas inside the channel are covered with hard and soft corals, and are frequented by turtles, Napoleonfish and schooling snappers. Look for yellowmouth morays and scorpionfish in the crevices.

Macro Spot This sheltered, shallow giri makes a suitable site for snorkellers, novices and macrophotographers. Overhangs and nooks shelter lobsters, cowries, glassfish, blennies and gobies.

Resorts

Vilu Reef (*Meedhuffushi island;* ☎ *460011;* **W** *www.vilureef.com; singles/doubles US$160/ 220; airport transfer by seaplane, 35mins, US$235; 68 rooms*) is notable for the unusual spiral design of its main restaurant and bar, though both are now covered by lush greenery. The island itself is thick with trees and bushes, though it has a lot of buildings on it and some rooms (the garden villas) aren't near the beach. The rooms are round and have most mod cons (no TV), outdoor bathrooms and a certain romantic appeal, though the finish is not fantastic. The Serena Spa will massage you into sweet oblivion.

The restaurant does big buffets for every meal and they're usually pretty good. The nightlife is not too exciting, but there's a karaoke room for the Italian guests. Some British guests on all-inclusive packages might also be up for the crab races, cultural show and disco. Most guests are from Germany, and many of them are divers with little energy left to party. Tennis, badminton, volleyball and a gym cater for the more sports minded, and there's windsurfing, sailing and motorised water sports.

On one side, a wide beach faces a lagoon that's perfect for sailing and sheltered swimming, while on the other side a nice but narrower beach fronts a house reef that offers excellent snorkelling. Divers are well catered for by **Dive Explorer** (**W** *www.diveexplorer.com*), which offers single boat dives for US$45 with tank and weights, or US$65 with all equipment. An open-water course is US$520. A full nitrox course (US$225) and nitrox diving (US$5 extra) is available.

Vilu Reef is nothing fancy, but it's friendly, informal, and it has character. It's not bad value, especially if you want to dive.

Velavaru Island Resort (*Velavaru island;* ☎ *460028;* **W** *www.velavaru.com; singles/ doubles US$215/250; airport transfer by seaplane, 35mins, US$230; 84 rooms*) has wide sandy beaches where turtles once nested – *velavaru* means turtle island. Now tourists come for the same beaches, and to nest in the comfortable, semicircular rooms. They're a bit unusual, but they're well finished and they have everything you need (you don't need a TV). The public buildings are unusual too, with sand floors and big, thatched, domed roofs (turtle shaped?). The restaurant serves unusually good meals – they're all buffet style, and the selection is not huge, but the dishes are imaginative and very well prepared. The main bar is usually pretty quiet, but it overlooks the beach and is a very pleasant place for a drink. Another quiet place is the Duniya Spa, with Indian, Thai and Swedish massages for various parts of your body and soul.

The wide lagoon is no good for snorkelling, but there are two free snorkelling trips every day. Dive sites in this atoll are not well documented, but the **Ocean-Pro** dive centre (**W** *www.oceanpro-diveteam.com*) knows them better than anyone. It charges around US$53 for a boat dive with all equipment provided, or US$41 with tank and weights only. An open-water course costs US$524. The main attraction here is undoubtedly the diving, but there's also a very nice, relaxed feel about Velavaru – it might be just the sand between the toes.

KOLHUMADULU ATOLL

Kolhumadulu Atoll is a large, slightly flattened circle about 60km across, and one of the major fishing regions of the country. It forms the administrative district of **Thaa**, with 13 inhabited islands and about 9300 people. The capital island is **Veymandhoo** (population 763). All the islands are on the edges of the atoll, mostly clustered around the kandus, and they're quite densely settled. **Thimarafushi** (population 1537), near the capital, is the most populous island, and with two other islands makes up a sizable community. Ruins of a 25m-wide mound on the island of Kibidhoo show this group of islands has been populated for many years.

On **Guraidhoo** (population 1433), in another island group, is the grave of Sultan Usman I, who ruled the Maldives for only two months before being banished here. On

Dhiyamigili (population 484) there are ruins of the palace of Mohammed Imaaduddeen II, a much more successful sultan who ruled from 1704 to 1721 and founded one of the Maldives longest-ruling dynasties.

The northern island of **Buruni** (population 304) is a centre for carpenters, many of whom work elsewhere, building boats and tourist resorts. The women make coir rope and reed mats. Around the mosque are an old sundial and tombstones that have been dated to the late 18th century.

HADHDHUNMATHEE ATOLL

This atoll is more commonly known by its administrative name of Laamu, perhaps because it's easier to spell than the geographical name – Hadunmati, Hadhunmathee, Hadhunmathi etc. The Laamu administrative district has about 11,600 people living on its 12 inhabited islands, and it's one of the major fishing centres in the country. Freezer ships anchor near the former capital, **Hithadhoo** (population 694), collecting fresh fish direct from the dhonis.

The island of **Kadhoo** has an airfield (airport code KDO) that has five flights a week to/from Male'. Kadhoo is linked by causeways to the large island of **Fonadhoo** (population 1740) to the south, which is now the atoll capital. The causeway also goes north to the islands of **Maandhoo** (population 517) and **Gan** (population 2244), forming one of the longest stretches of road in the country – all of 12km. Maandhoo has a government-owned STO refrigeration plant and a fish-canning factory.

There are numerous archaeological sites on Laamu, with evidence of pre-Muslim civilisations on many islands. At the northeastern tip of the atoll, on **Isdhoo** (population 1432), a giant, black dome rises above the palms. Who built the ancient artificial mound, known as a *hawitta*, and for what reason, is not really known. Buddha images have been found on the island, and HCP Bell believed such mounds to be the remains of Buddhist stupas, while Heyerdahl speculated that Buddhists had built on even earlier mounds left by the legendary Redin people. For many years the mound was a landmark for boats navigating between the atolls, but it didn't save the British cargo ship *Lagan Bank*, which was wrecked here on 13 January 1938. The **Friday Mosque**

The Toddy Tapper's Daughter

The Maldives' answer to *Romeo and Juliet* is an old folk tale of star-crossed lovers from the island of Buruni. Dhon Hiyala was the beautiful daughter of a poor but pious toddy tapper, and she fell in love with a local silversmith named Ali Fulhu, who made her gifts of exquisite jewellery. Hiyala's father was known for his eloquence in reading the Quran and this brought the family to the attention of the Male' sultan. The sultan's men noticed the lovely girl with the fine jewellery and, despite her protests, she was taken to the palace in Male'. Ali Fulhu followed, succeeded in finding her, and they escaped from the capital in Ali's boat. The sultan was furious and his guards gave chase. Soon overtaken by the faster boat, the lovers leapt into the sea rather than be captured, and were devoured by a sea monster and never seen again.

on Isdhoo is around 300 years old. It was probably built on the site of an earlier temple because it faces directly west, rather than towards Mecca, which is to the northwest.

Bell also found quite a few mounds on Gan (or Gamu) island, which he also believed to be Buddhist stupas, and he found a fragment of a stone Buddha face, which he estimated was from a statue over 4m high. Almost nothing remains of these structures because the stones have been removed to use in more modern buildings. There are mounds on several other islands in Laamu, including Kadhoo, Maandhoo and Hithadhoo – one is over 5m high.

NORTH HUVADHOO ATOLL

The giant Huvadhoo Atoll, one of the largest true coral atolls in the world, is separated from Laamu by the 90km-wide Huvadhoo Kandu. This stretch of water is also called the One-and-a-Half-Degree Channel, because of its latitude, and it's the safest place for ships to pass between the atolls that make up the Maldives.

Because Huvadhoo is so big, and perhaps as a response to the 'southern rebellion' (see South Huvadhoo Atoll), the atoll is divided into two administrative districts. The northern district is called **Gaaf Alif**, and it has 10 inhabited islands and about 8300 people. **Viligili**, the capital island, is also the most populated with about 2300 people. Just south, the island of **Kudhoo** has an ice plant and fish-packing works. The atoll also has some productive agriculture, much of it on **Kodey** (population 260). This island also has four *hawittas* – evidence of Buddhist settlement. Heyerdahl discovered a limestone carving here, which he believed to be of the Hindu water god Makara. The statue must have been here before the Buddhist period, and is perhaps 1000 years old.

In the centre of the atoll, **Dhevvadhoo** (population 588) is not well placed for fishing or farming, but the islanders are famous for their textile weaving and coir-rope making. There are also and mosques from the 16th and 17th centuries.

SOUTH HUVADHOO ATOLL

Geographically isolated from Male', but strategically located on the Indian Ocean trade routes, Huvadhoo had independent tendencies dating back many years. It had its own direct trade links with Sri Lanka, and the people spoke a distinct dialect almost incomprehensible to other Maldivians. The island of **Thinadhoo** was a focal point of the 'southern rebellion' against the central rule of Male' during the early 1960s (see the section on Addu Atoll, later in this chapter). So much so, that troops from Male' invaded in February 1962 and destroyed all the homes. The people fled to neighbouring islands and Thinadhoo was not resettled until four years later, and it now has a population of 4900. Huvadhoo atoll was divided into two administrative districts with the southern part called Gaaf Dhaal, which now has nearly 12,000 people on 10 inhabited islands and Thinadhoo as its capital.

Though remote from any resorts, Gaaf Dhaal has a small but growing number of foreign visitors who make boat trips around the southeastern edge of the atoll to surf the uncrowded waves that break around the channel entrances (see Surfing under Activities in the Facts for the Visitor chapter). On the island of **Kaadedhoo**, near Thinadhoo, a small airport (airport code KDM) has daily connections to Male' with Island Aviation, and the surfing safari boats meet their clients there.

On **Gadhdhoo** (population 1700), women make superb examples of the mats known as *tundu kunaa*, which are woven from special

reeds found on an adjacent island. Souvenir shops in Male' and on some resorts sell these mats – those from Gadhdhoo are the softest and most finely woven. Gadhdhoo also has one of the Maldives' tallest structures, a 120m-high telecommunications tower that makes the microwave connection across the equatorial channel to an identical tower on Fuamulaku, 60km away in the southern hemisphere.

Just southwest of Gadhdhoo, the uninhabited island of **Gan** has remnants of one the most impressive *hawittas*, originally a pyramid with stepped ramps on all four sides, like many Mexican pyramids. The ruin was 8.5m high and 23m square. Heyerdahl also found stones here decorated with sun motifs, which he believed were proof of a sun-worshipping society even older than the Buddhist and Hindu settlements.

In the south of the atoll, only about 20km from the equator, the island of **Vaadhoo** has two *hawittas*, and a mosque that dates from the 17th century. The mosque is elaborately decorated inside and has a stone bath outside, as well as ancient tombstones carved with three different kinds of early Maldivian script.

FUAMULAKU ATOLL

Just south of the equator, Fuamulaku (also called Foammulah) is not really an atoll, but rather a solitary island stuck in the middle of the Equatorial Channel. It's the only island in the administrative district of Gnaviyani, and has a population of about 7500. About 5km long and 1km wide, it's the biggest single island in the country and one of the most fertile, producing many fruits and vegetables such as mangoes, papayas, oranges and pineapples. Yams grow so well here that they were once a dietary staple, though rice is now preferred. The natural vegetation is lush, and there are two freshwater lakes.

A beach goes around most of the island, but the fringing reef is quite narrow and is pounded by big waves on whatever side is exposed to the prevailing swells. The lack of a safe anchorage has always limited fishing activity and made it difficult to get passengers and goods ashore. With help from the national government, a new harbour is under construction at the eastern tip of the island. The Danish contractor has built a long, curving breakwater made of huge

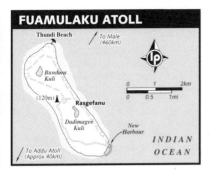

FUAMULAKU ATOLL

Thundi Beach

To 'Male'
(460km)

Bundara
Kuli

0   1   2km

0   0.5   1mi

(120m)

Rasgefanu

Dadimagee
Kuli

New
Harbour

INDIAN

To Addu Atoll
(Approx 40km)

OCEAN

granite boulders imported by the ship load from India. The sheltered harbour will be a boon for Fuamulaku, enabling goods and equipment to be brought in easily and making development of some light industry feasible.

A new road links the harbour and the main village at the island's heart. New roads, wetland reclamation and infrastructure improvements are planned. A 120m-high telecommunications tower in the island's centre is visible from miles away. It makes the microwave connection north to Gaaf Dhaal and south to Addu Atoll, and has reduced the island's isolation, which now has an Internet café and well-used mobile-phone service.

Fuamulaku is officially divided into eight districts, but most of the people live around the north side and across the centre of the island in villages that appear to be a continuous settlement. Sandy roads crisscross the island, and there are lots of motorcycles and small pick-up trucks. Many of the people work in resorts in the tourism zone, and the money they send home partly accounts for the apparent affluence of the island.

Despite Fuamulaku's apparent isolation, the Equatorial Channel has long been used by navigators passing between the Middle East, India and Southeast Asia. Ibn Battuta visited in 1344, stayed for two months and married two women. Two Frenchmen visited in 1529 and admired the old mosque at the west end of the island. In 1922 HCP Bell stopped here briefly, and noted a 7m-high *hawitta*. Heyerdahl found the *hawitta* in poor condition, and found remnants of another nearby. He also investigated the nearby mosque, the oldest one on the island, and believed it had been built on the foundations of an earlier structure built by skilled stone masons. Another old

mosque, on the north side of the island, had expertly made stonework in its foundations and in an adjacent stone bath.

Fuamulaku is not an easy destination for modern travellers. It has no hotels or guesthouses and only a couple of teashops, so you'll need an invitation from a local, and a permit. Daily flights go to Addu Atoll, 50km away, and from there a twice-weekly speed launch carries about 20 people and takes just over an hour if the weather is OK.

ADDU ATOLL

This is the main economic and administrative centre in the south of the country, and the only place to rival Male' in size and importance. The heart-shaped atoll forms the administrative district of Seenu, with some 18,500 people in seven inhabited islands. The airport has a runway suitable for large jet aircraft, and four substantial islands on the southwestern edge of the atoll are linked by causeways and a new road. Hithadhoo is the capital island.

There is an independent streak in the Addu folk – they even speak differently from the people of Male'. Tensions came to a head in the 1960s under the leadership of Abdulla Afif Didi, who was elected president of the 'United Suvadiva Islands', comprising Addu, Fuamulaku and Huvadhoo. Afif declared independence from the Maldives, but the short-lived southern rebellion was quashed by an armed fleet sent south by Prime Minister Ibrahim Nasir. Afif fled the country, but is still talked about on his home island of Hithadhoo. He went to live in the Seychelles, where he ultimately rose to the position of foreign minister.

The biggest influence on Addu's modern history has been the British bases, first established on Gan during WWII as part of the Indian Ocean defences. In 1956, when the British could no longer use Sri Lanka, they developed a Royal Air Force base on Addu as a strategic Cold War outpost. The base had around 600 personnel permanently stationed here, with up to 3000 during periods of peak activity. The British built a series of causeways connecting Feydhoo, Maradhoo and Hithadhoo islands and employed most of the population on or around the base. In 1976 the British pulled out, leaving an airport, some large industrial buildings, barracks and a lot of unemployed people who

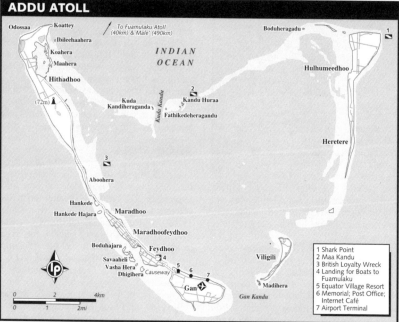

ADDU ATOLL

1 Shark Point
2 Maa Kandu
3 British Loyalty Wreck
4 Landing for Boats to Fuamulaku
5 Equator Village Resort
6 Memorial; Post Office; Internet Café
7 Airport Terminal

spoke good English and had experience working for Westerners. When the tourism industry took off in the late 1970s, many of the men of Addu went to Male' to seek work in resorts and tourist shops. They have never lost their head start in the tourism business and to this day, in resorts all over the country, there's a better than even chance that the Maldivian staff will be from Addu.

Tourism development in Addu itself has been slow to start. The first resort, established in the old RAF buildings on Gan, suffered from irregular flight connections in small planes – luggage sometimes did not arrive until the guests were due to depart! Also, with most Maldivian resorts being marketed in the tropical paradise mould, an old military base didn't hold much appeal to many people.

Now there is a 40-seat jet providing a link to Male' with capacity for tourists *and* their luggage. The Gan resort, now called Equator Village, offers not just sun, sea and the standard attractions, but also unparalleled access to interesting, attractive and unspoiled villages, and the Cold War relic does have nostalgia appeal for some. It's

a very inexpensive resort, and it sometimes gives good deals to fully independent travellers (FITs). If you plan to visit the other islands, don't come during Ramadan.

The island of **Viligili** is also due to be developed for tourism, but commencement of the project has been delayed several times. The central government has taken the unusual step of investing in the proposed resort, because it is keen to promote economic activity in the outer atolls. With concerns about the continued growth in tourist numbers, the new resort may still be some years away. There are also hopes of direct international charter flights to Gan, which would save the time, trouble and expense of transfers from Male'. The old RAF runway is certainly big enough, but work is needed to improve the ground facilities.

Diving

A particular highlight of Addu is the magnificent corals, some of which escaped the widespread coral bleaching of 1998. On the northern edge of the atoll you can see huge table corals that might be hundreds of years old, and fields of staghorns that have all but disappeared in most parts of the country. It's not all good though – corals inside the lagoon suffered as badly as anywhere from coral bleaching.

Other diving highlights are an impressive wreck, and the turtles, sharks, manta rays and other large fish that can be seen at various times of the year. September to December is the best time for whale sharks and January to April is best for mantas. Addu sees vastly fewer divers than any other atoll in the tourism zone.

Wreck of the British Loyalty This oil tanker was torpedoed in 1944 by the German submarine U-183, which fired through an opening in the antisubmarine nets at the entrance to Gan Kandu. The disabled ship stayed in the atoll until 1946 when it was towed to its present location and used for target practice by another British ship. The 140m wreck lies in 33m of water with its port side about 16m below the surface. It has a good covering of soft corals, and turtles, trevally and many reef fish inhabit the encrusted decks. Divers can swim through big holes into the hull, though this may be hazardous.

Maa Kandu The northeastern edge of this channel has a wide reeftop, between 5m and 7m, covered with live acrophora corals – big brain corals, long branching staghorns and table corals 3m across. Whitetip reef sharks, eagle rays and sometimes mantas can be spotted, along with turtles and numerous reef fish. It's an excellent site for snorkelling.

Shark Point Off the northeast corner of the atoll is a plateau at about 30m, sometimes called the Shark Hotel. Grey reef sharks cruise around here, whitetip reef sharks lie on the sand and other sharks can be seen in deeper water further out.

Gan

The Maldives southernmost island was inhabited since ancient times. A large mound here, 9m high, was excavated under the direction of HCP Bell, who believed it to be the ruins of a Buddhist stupa. His expedition made careful measurements of the site, took photos and made precise drawings which are published in his monograph. This was fortunate, as the archaeological sites and almost everything else on Gan were levelled to create the air-force base in 1956.

The British took over the entire island and constructed airport buildings, barracks, jetties, maintenance sheds, a NAAFI canteen, golf course, tennis courts and a 2600m concrete runway. For more about RAF Gan,

check **w** www.rafgan.co.uk. Many of these structures remain, some picturesquely run-down, others used for various purposes. Most of the island's lush native vegetation was cleared, but the British then landscaped with new plants – avenues of casuarina, clumps of bougainvillea, swaths of lawn and even roses. It's much more spacious than most resort islands and it has a slightly weird and eerie atmosphere, but very peaceful and relaxed – like an old, abandoned movie set.

Some of the old buildings have been taken over by foreign-owned garment factories, which employ some 1100 Sri Lankans and a hundred or so locals, mostly women. The Sri Lankans come on contract, work long hours and live in the former barracks. Why do these businesses set up here instead of Sri Lanka or Bangladesh? Because those countries already produce more garments than their US import quota allows, while the Maldives does not. The sweatshop conditions have improved recently, as the buyers are now insisting that work places and living quarters are air-conditioned, and that reasonable safety standards are maintained.

Some other things to see include a memorial to those who served on the base, including Indian regiments such as the 13th Frontier Force Rifles and the Royal Bombay Sappers & Miners. Dozens died here 'in the service of their country', though the atoll saw no action at all apart from the 1944 attack on the *British Loyalty*. Big guns, which were part of the WWII defences, now guard the memorial. Across the road is the post office, some telephones and a branch of the Bank of Maldives. The old Astra cinema, a fixture at all RAF bases, has a few nifty '50s architectural touches. Several times a week it shows Indian and Sri Lankan movies to entertain the garment workers. Also for locals and workers, a small **teashop** serves soft drinks, snacks and light meals for about Rf40. Further east, the not-very-friendly **airport café** also serves inexpensive food.

West of the Equator Village resort is a complex of buildings that used to be the officers' mess and living quarters. It's now the 'Dhoogas', a facility providing accommodation for visiting government officials, and off-limits to foreigners. A small and unimposing building here was once a chapel, but has been converted to a mosque. You can walk or cycle right around the island on narrow dirt roads, crossing the airport runway at each end. You'll see lots of trees and greenery, a couple of graveyards and a few incongruous buildings. There are no decent beaches and no surfable waves – just the Indian Ocean crashing on a broad, shallow reef.

Post & Communications The post office is east of the resort entrance, on the road to the airport, and there are phones outside where international calls can be made with a Dhiraagu card. Across the road behind the memorial is a small **Internet café** *(open 8am to 4pm Sunday to Thursday and 2pm to 5pm Saturday)* that charges Rf45 an hour .

Resort The resort on Gan is about 1km west of the airport terminal, in a compound on the lagoon side of the road.

    Equator Village *(Gan island;* ☎ *588019;* **w** *www.equatorvillage.com; singles/doubles US$80/93; flight from Male' to Gan, 1½hrs, US$240; 78 rooms)* is a budget resort, quite different from any other in the Maldives. The rooms are in long straight lines that are actually the old barracks buildings, thoroughly renovated with bathrooms added. They're spacious and comfortable enough, and have air-con, hot water and a small fridge (no TV or phone). The decor is in pastel colours and the fabrics are floral, but the effect is not romantic.

    The reception, bar and dining areas have been created from the old SNSO (or sergeants) mess, thoroughly redecorated in very unmilitary pink, white and grey (it was Building 21 in the RAF days, and it wasn't the officers' mess). These open-sided spaces with their cane furniture and ceiling fans look out onto a sizable free-form swimming pool and through palm trees to the blue sea beyond. The full-size billiard table is a handsome inheritance from the Brits, as are the first-class tennis courts.

    The meals are all buffets with a limited selection and a British bias – expect fairly good curry, roast beef, mashed potatoes and tinned fruit for dinner; and sausages, eggs and cereal for breakfast. The Maldivian barbecue buffet is the best meal of the week. Most guests are on an all-inclusive package (US$35 a double extra), and can wash it down with beer or house wine. There's not a lot of organised evening entertainment, but the bar is one of the friendliest and most fun in the Maldives.

    Most of the guests are from Germany and the UK, with a mix of Italians, Russians, Japanese and others. More than half are divers, and a few are ex-RAF personnel who were once stationed here – an RAF visitors book at reception has more than 50 signatures, and some books and photo albums are also kept here, available on request.

    Bicycles are available for exploring the neighbouring islands. They're free with the all-inclusive deal, along with an island-hopping excursion, night fishing trip and twice-daily boat to Viligili for snorkelling and beach time. The only beach on Gan is a few hundred metres east of the resort, and it's not great. The house reef is accessible for snorkelling, but it's unattractive and the visibility is poor. The dive centre is a small operation run by **Diverland** *(***w** *www.diverland.com)* and includes the great dive sites in the area. A single boat dive is US$44 with tank and weights only, US$48 with all equipment. An open-water course costs US$425 (minimum of four people required).

Feydhoo, Maradhoo & Hithadhoo

The causeways and the new road goes from Gan to Hithadhoo via Feydhoo, Maradhoo and some former islands to Hithadhoo. There are no spectacular attractions along the way, but the smaller villages are an absolute delight. Local tea shops serve tea, cakes and 'short eats', and some will have a more substantial fish curry. Though you don't need a permit to visit, tourists are supposed to be back at Gan before dark. Please remember that these are Muslim communities. Dress modestly, don't enter mosques uninvited, don't give presents or sweets to kids and don't even think about alcohol. If visitors behave inappropriately, free access to these communities may be restricted in the future.

    Like most Maldivian villages they are laid out on a rectangular grid with wide, straight, sandy streets and white coral-stone houses. A few motorcycles, taxis, trucks and minibuses will be seen, but for most of the day the streets are empty. In the early morning, and especially the evening, locals will be out walking or cycling, sitting outside their houses or leaning against the low front walls. Shady trees overhang the streets and you can usually catch a glimpse of the sea at one end of the street or the other.

Most of the houses have corrugated iron roofs, but are otherwise traditional. Older buildings are made of coral-stone while newer ones are of concrete blocks. There's usually a courtyard or an open space with a shady tree and a *joli* or *undholi* providing a cool place to sit in the heat of the day. Notice the big, square chimney blocks – there are wooden racks inside where fish are hung to be smoked. Another distinctive feature can be seen at street junctions, where walls and buildings all have rounded corners.

You can easily walk from Gan to Feydhoo (population 2829), which has several mosques – a large, new, white one, a small, pretty blue one, and several old ones on the sandy back roads that look a little like tiny churches. On the new lagoon-side road are several new buildings, like the modern petrol station, a big store and a teahouse/café with a Rf20 buffet. Boats to Fuamulaku use the small harbour here.

When the British took over, the villagers from Gan were resettled on Feydhoo, and some of the people from Feydhoo were then moved to the next island, Maradhoo, where they formed a new village. Maradhoo now has a population of 2066 in two villages that have run together – the southern one is called Maradhoofeydhoo. The first thing you'll see as you come up the road is the boat building activity on the lagoon side.

Further north, the road follows an isthmus that was once three narrow, uninhabited islands. One island used to house an ammunition bunker. After a few kilometres of palm-tree-lined road you pass a recycling zone and a sports ground with several football pitches and a grandstand. You're on Hithadhoo, the Maldives' largest town outside Male', with a population currently just under 10,000. The 72m-tall telecommunications mast has a microwave link north to Fuamulaku and the rest of the country, and provides mobile-phone service over most of Addu. The Dhiraagu office near the tower has pay phones and an Internet café. Further up the road are a new mosque and several schools – the high school is one of two outside Male' that teaches up to A level (matriculation).

A power station and several light-industry buildings are near the main road, while a grid of streets with traditional houses extends to

the western sea shore. A few tea shops and some quite big, new commercial premises are appearing here too. Beyond the built up area, the tip of the island bends to the east, and is covered with coconut plantations, swampy lakes and a surprising amount of woodland. The coast is mostly too rocky or shallow for bathing, but there are a some narrow beaches. Rough roads go right to the tip of the island at Koattey, also called Demon Point. It's said there was once a fort here, and later a British gun emplacement, but there's nothing left to see now. It feels like the end of the earth.

Hulhumeedhoo

At the northeast corner of the lagoon, this island has two adjoining villages, Hulhudoo and Meedhoo, both known as Hulhumeedhoo, with a total population of about 3100. Local legend says that an Arab was shipwrecked here in about 872, and converted the islanders to Islam 280 years before the people of Male'. The cemetery is known for its ancient headstones, many of which are beautifully carved with the archaic Dhives Akuru script. A history on this remote little community, can be seen on **w** www.angelfire.com/country/addumeedhoo/gallery/album.html. This island is not connected to Gan by a causeway, so you'll need to charter a dhoni to get here. Equator Village may do a day excursion here.

SOUTHERN ATOLLS

Getting There & Away

Island Aviation flies from Male' to Gan and back once or twice a day. The standard fare for foreigners is US$120/240 one way/return. The views are great from either side of the plane.

Island Ferry Services (☎ 318252, **w** www .ifs.com.mv) were planning to start a fast catamaran service to Addu, departing Male' at 5.30pm Monday, arriving at Hithadhoo at 7am Tuesday. Fares were expected to be Rf495 one way, Rf990 return.

Private yachts should report by radio to the NSS in Gan or Hithadhoo to arrange security and customs clearance, but may have to continue to Male' for health and immigration checks to complete the 'clear-in' process.

Getting Around

The best way to get around Gan and across the causeway to the neighbouring villages is by bicycle – use of a bicycle is included in the Equator Village rates, though the bikes aren't too comfortable for tall people. Taxis shuttle back and forth between the islands and around the villages – a taxi from Gan to Hithadhoo should cost about Rf100. If you need one, call ☎ 583535, 583030 or 582828. The buses you might see on the main road are only for workers in the Gan garment factories.

Language

The language of the Maldives is Divehi, also written as 'Dhivehi'. It is related to an ancient form of Sinhala, a Sri Lankan language, but also contains some Arabic, Hindi and English words. On top of all this, there are several different dialects throughout the country.

English is widely spoken in Male', in the resorts, and by educated people throughout the country. English is also spoken on Addu, the southernmost atoll, where the British employed many of the islanders on the air base for 20 years. On other islands, especially outside the tourism zone, you'd be very lucky to find an adult who speaks anything other than Divehi.

Divehi has its own script, Thaana, which was introduced by the great Maldivian hero Thakurufaanu after he tossed out the Portuguese in the 16th century. Thaana looks like shorthand, has 24 letters in its alphabet and is read from right to left (their front page is our back page).

The Romanised transliteration of the language is a potpourri of phonetic approximations, and words can be spelt in a variety of ways. This is most obvious in Maldivian place names. For example: Majeedi Magu is also spelt Majidi, Majeedhee and Majeedee; Hithadhoo also becomes Hithadhu and Hitadhu; and Fuamulak can be Fua Mulaku, Foahmmulah or, thanks to one 19th-century mariner, Phoowa Moloku.

To add to the confusion, several islands have the same name (there are six called Viligili), and there are names for the 20 administrative atolls that do not coincide with the names used for the Maldives' 26 natural atolls.

There is no officially correct, or even consistent, spelling of Divehi words in official English language publications.

Maldivians are pleased to help you learn a few phrases of Divehi, and, even if you only learn a few words, the locals you meet will be very appreciative of your interest.

The best phrasebook available is *Practical Divehi* by M Zuhair (Novelty Press, Male', 1991). It's available from the Novelty Bookshop in Male' and in a number of the resort shops.

Greetings & Civilities

Hello.	*a-salam alekum*
Farewell.	*vale kumu salam*
Peace.	*salam*
Hi.	*kihine*
See you later.	*fahung badaluvang*
How are you?	*haalu kihine?*
Very well. (reply)	*vara gada*
Fine/Good/Great.	*barabah*
OK.	*enge*
Thank you.	*shukuria*

Useful Words & Phrases

Yes.	*aa*
No.	*noo*
How much is this?	*mi kihavaraka?*
What is that?	*mi korche?*
What did you say?	*kike tha buni?*
I'm leaving.	*aharen dani*
Where are you going?	*kong taka dani?*
How much is the fare?	*fi kihavare?*

I/me	*aharen/ma*
you	*kale*
she/he	*mina/ena*
name	*nang, nama*
expensive	*agu bodu*
very expensive	*vara agu bodu*
cheap	*agu heyo*
enough	*heo*
now	*mihaaru*
little (for people, places)	*kuda*
mosquito	*madiri*
mosquito net	*madiri ge*
bathroom	*gifili*
toilet	*fahana*
inside	*etere*
outside	*berufarai*
water (rain, well)	*vaare feng* or *valu feng*

Some Useful Verbs

swim	*fatani*
eat	*kani*
walk	*hingani*
sleep	*nidani*
sail	*duvani*
go	*dani*
stay	*hunani*

dance	nashani
wash	donani

People

friend	ratehi
mother	mama
father	bapa
atoll chief	atolu verin
island chief	kateeb
VIP, upper-class person	befalu
white person (tourist or expat)	don miha
community religious leader	gazi
prayer caller	mudeem
fisherman	mas veri
toddy man	ra veri
evil spirit	jinni

Places

atoll	atolu
island	fushi/rah
sandbank	finolhu
reef/lagoon	faru
street	magu
lane or small street	golhi/higun
mosque	miski
house	ge

Time & Days

today	miadu
tomorrow	madamma
yesterday	iye
tonight	mire
day	duvas
night	reggadu

Monday	horma
Tuesday	angaara
Wednesday	buda
Thursday	brassfati
Friday	hukuru
Saturday	honihira
Sunday	aadita

Numbers

1	eke
2	de
3	tine
4	hatare
5	fahe
6	haie
7	hate
8	ashe
9	nue

10	diha
11	egaara
12	baara
13	tera
14	saada
15	fanara
16	sorla
17	satara
18	ashara
19	onavihi
20	vihi
30	tiris
40	saalis
50	fansaas
60	fasdolaas
70	hai-diha
80	a-diha
90	nua-diha
100	sateka

FOOD & DRINK

Fish and rice are the staple foods. Any substantial meal, with rice and roshi, is called 'long eats', and might include the following:

mas – fried fish; usually refers to skipjack tuna or bonito
valo mas – smoked fish
mas huni & hana kuri mas – dried, tinned, fried or cold fish mixed with coconut, onion, chilli and spices
mas riha – fish curry
kandukukulhu – a special tuna curry
garudia – the staple diet of fish soup, often taken with rice, lime and chilli
rihakuru – garudia boiled down to a salty sauce or paste
bai – rice
roshi – flat, unleavened bread
modunu – a simple salad
aluvi – potato
paan – bread
bis – egg

'Short eats' or hedhikaa is the selection of little sweet and savoury items that is displayed on the counter of a local tea shop.

gulas – fish ball; deep-fried in flour and rice batter
kuli boakiba – spicy fish cake
bondi bai – rice pudding; sometimes with currants
kastad – sweet custard
foni boakiba – gelatin cakes and puddings

Most fruit is imported, but the following are grown locally:

kurumba – coconut, especially a young or new coconut
donkeo – little bananas
bambukeyo – breadfruit
bambukeyo hiti – breadfruit used in curries
bambukeyo bondibai – breadfruit used in desserts

After dinner, many Maldivians chew betel, a combination of *foah* (areca nut), some cloves and lime paste wrapped in *bileiy*.

The range of drinks is very limited. Tea shops will always serve *bor feng* (drinking water), and of course *sai* (tea). Unless you ask otherwise, tea comes black, with *hakuru* (sugar). Kiru (milk) isn't a common drink, and is usually made up from powder. In local villages you might get *raa* (palm toddy).

Glossary

animator – extroverted person employed in some resorts to promote group activities and good times; the Club Med equivalent is a 'GO'

atoll – ring of coral reefs or coral islands, or both, surrounding a lagoon; the English word 'atoll' is derived from the Divehi *atolu*

atolu verin – atoll chief

bai bala – traditional game where one team tries to tag another inside a circle

bashi – traditional girls' team game played with a tennis ball, racket and net

BCD – Buoyancy Control Device; a vest that holds air tanks on the back and can be inflated or deflated to control a diver's buoyancy and act as a life preserver (also called a BCV: Buoyancy Control Vest)

befalu – upper class of privileged families

bodu – big or great

bodu beru – literally 'big drum'; made from a hollow coconut log and covered with stingray skin; *bodu beru* is Maldivian drum music, often used to accompany dancers

bondi bai – rice pudding

bonthi – stick used for martial arts

BSAC – British Sub Aqua Club

cadjan – mat made of coconut palm leaves

carrom – popular board game, like a miniature snooker; players use their fingers to flick flat round counters from the edges of a square wooden board, trying to knock other players' counters into the four corner holes

chew – wad of areca nut wrapped in a betel leaf, often with lime, cloves and other spices; commonly chewed after a meal

CMAS – Confédération Mondiale des Activités Subaquatiques; French organisation that sets diving standards, training requirements and accredits instructors

Dhiraagu – the Maldives telecommunications provider, it is jointly owned by the government and the British company Cable & Wireless

dhiguhedhun – traditional women's dress, full length with long sleeves and a wide collar, usually in unpatterned fabric but sometimes brightly coloured

dhoni – Maldivian boat, probably derived from an Arab dhow. Formerly sail powered, many dhonis are now equipped with a diesel engine

Divehi – language and people of the Maldives, also spelt 'Dhivehi'

Divehi Raajje – 'Island Kingdom'; what Maldivians call the Maldives

divemaster – male or female diver qualified to supervise and lead dives, but not necessarily a qualified instructor

fahana – toilet

fandhita – magic, wizardry

faru (or faro) – ring-shaped reef within an atoll, often with an island in the middle

feylis – traditional sarong, usually dark with light-coloured horizontal bands near the hem

fihuna – chilli-coated fish pieces

finolhu – sparsely vegetated sand bank

FIT – fully independent traveller; in the Maldives, every effort is made to book these people into a resort as soon as possible!

fushi – island

gazi – religious head of atoll

gifili – courtyard with a well used as an open-air bathroom; a modern version is a popular feature of many resort rooms

giri – coral formation that rises steeply from the atoll floor and almost reaches the surface; see also *thila*

goalhi –short, narrow lane

gulha – fried spicy fish dough balls

hajj – Muslim pilgrimage to Mecca

haveeru – evening

hawitta – ancient mound found in the southern atolls; archaeologists believe these mounds were the foundations of Buddhist temples

hedikaa – selection of finger food

higun – wide lane

hiki mas – dried tuna fillet; a traditional export, especially to Sri Lanka where it is called 'Maldive fish'

hotel – small café or tea shop in Male'; it definitely will not provide accommodation

house reef – coral reef adjacent to a resort island, used by guests for snorkelling and diving; guests from other resorts can't dive on a house reef without permission

hulhangu – the southwest monsoon period, from May to November, which are the wetter months with more storms and strong winds

inner-reef slope – where a reef slopes down inside an atoll; see also *outer-reef slope*

iruvai – northeast monsoon period, from December to March, which are the drier months

jinni – witch or wizard, sometimes coming from the sea

joli (or jorli) – net seat suspended from a rectangular frame; typically there are four or five seats together outside a house

kandiki – sarong worn by women under the *libaas*

kandu – sea channel; connecting the waters of an atoll to the open sea; feeding grounds for pelagics, such as sharks, stingrays, manta rays and turtles; good dive sites, but subject to strong currents

kateeb – chief of an island

keemia – fried fish rolls in batter

kuli boakiba – spicy fish cakes

kunaa – traditional woven mat

laajehun – lacquer work traditionally used as containers, bowls and trays to present gifts to the sultan, now popular as small souvenirs

libaas – traditional dress with wide collar and cuffs, and embroidered with gold thread

madrasa – government primary school

magu – wide street

mas – fish

mas riha – fish curry served with rice and torn strips of *roshi*

MATI – Maldives Association of Tourism; a private tourism industry organisation

miskiiy – mosque

MTPB – Maldives Tourism Promotion Board; the government tourism promotion organisation

mudhim – muezzin; the person who calls Muslims to prayer

mundu – man's sarong, usually made with a chequered cotton fabric with a darker panel at the back

munnaaru – minaret, a mosque's tower

nakaiy – period of about two weeks associated with a specific weather pattern; the year is divided into 27 nakaiy

namahd – call to prayer for Muslims

NSS – National Security Service; the Maldivian army, navy, coastguard and police force

outer-reef slope – outer edge of an atoll facing open sea, where reefs slope down towards the ocean floor; see also *inner-reef slope*

PADI – Professional Association of Diving Instructors; commercial organisation that sets diving standards, training requirements and accredits instructors (also said to stand for 'Put Another Dollar In')

pelagic – pelagics are open-sea species such as tuna, barracuda and whales

Quran – also spelt Koran; Islam's holy book

raa – toddy; the sap of a palm tree, consumed as a fresh or slightly fermented drink

raa veri – toddy seller

Ramazan – Maldivian spelling of Ramadan, the Muslim month of fasting

Redin – legendary race of people believed by modern Maldivians to have been the first settlers in the archipelago and the builders of the pre-Islamic *hawittas*

reef – ridge or plateau close to the sea surface; Maldivian atolls and islands are surrounded by coral reefs

reef flat – shallow area of reef top which stretches out from a lagoon to where the reef slopes down into the deeper surrounding water

rhan – bride price

SAARC – South Asia Association for Regional Cooperation; a regional trade and development organisation which comprises Bangladesh, Bhutan, India, Maldives, Nepal, Pakistan and Sri Lanka

SSI – Scuba Schools International; diver accreditation organisation

STO – State Trading Organisation

Thaana – Divehi script; the written language unique to the Maldives

thila – coral formation that rises steeply from the atoll floor to within 5m to 15m of the surface; see also *giri*

thin mugoali – 'three circles', a 400-year-old game similar to baseball

thileyrukan – traditional jewellery-making

toddy – see *raa*

toddy tapper – person who extracts the sap of a palm tree to make toddy

tundu kunaa – finely woven reed mats, particularly those from Gaaf Dhaal

undholi – wooden seat, typically suspended under a shady tree so the swinging motion provides a cooling breeze

vedi – large *dhoni* used for trading between Male' and the outer atolls

velaa folhi – Maldivian dish using turtle eggs

VSO – Voluntary Service Overseas; British overseas aid organisation

wadhemun – tug-of-war

zileybee – coloured coils of sugared fried batter

Index

Text

Bold indicates maps.

Boxed Text

MAP LEGEND

CITY ROUTES

Freeway .... Freeway	===== Unsealed Road
Highway .... Primary Road	====== One Way Street
Road .... Secondary Road	===== Pedestrian Street
Street .... Street	::::::::: Stepped Street
Lane .... Lane	===== Footbridge

REGIONAL ROUTES

===== Primary Road	----- Unsealed Road
===== Secondary Road	==== 4WD Track
===== Minor Road	

BOUNDARIES

- ─ · ─ · ─ · ─ International
- ─ · · ─ · · · State
- ─ ─ ─ Disputed
- ▬▬▬▬ Fortified Wall

HYDROGRAPHY

.... River, Creek	Protected Marine Area
.... Lagoon	Spring, Rapids
.... Lake	Waterfalls

TRANSPORT ROUTES & STATIONS

-----O-- .... Train	-----🚏 .... Ferry/Dhonis
.... Underground Train	------ .... Walking Trail
.... Walking Tour	.... Path
─╫─╫─🚋 Cable Car/Chairlift	─────── Pier or Jetty

AREA FEATURES

Building	Market	Beach .... Cliff
❀ Park, Gardens	Reef	Cemetery .... Swamp

POPULATION SYMBOLS

✪ MALE' .... National Capital	● Kochi .... City	Meerufenfushi .... Unpopulated Island
◉ Felidhoo .. Regional Capital (Island)	○ Norsup .... Town	Dhiffushi .... Populated Island

MAP SYMBOLS

▪ ⊡ .... Place to Stay, Resort	▼ .... Place to Eat	● .... Point of Interest

✈ ✈ .... Airfield, Airport	⌂ .... Cave	☀ .... Lookout	⚓ .... Shipwreck
✈ .... Airplane Wreck	🏛 .... Church	☾ .... Mosque	🏛 .... Stately Home
⚓ .... Anchorage	🎬 .... Cinema	▲ .... Mountain	⚐ .... Surfing
☒ .... Archaeological Site	🌊 .... Dive Site	🏛 ... Museum/Gallery	▮ .... Telecom Tower
◑ .... Bank	📷 .... Embassy	P .... Parking	☎ .... Telephone
⊡ .... Bar/Pub	✚ .... Hospital	⊙ .... Petrol Station	▣ .... Theatre
▦ ⊡ .. Bus Stop/Terminal	🌐 .... Internet Café	✚ .... Police Station	▪ .... Tomb
☕ .... Café	🗼 .... Lighthouse	✉ .... Post Office	❶ .. Tourist Information

Note: not all symbols displayed above appear in this book

LONELY PLANET OFFICES

Australia
Locked Bag 1, Footscray, Victoria 3011
☎ 03 8379 8000 fax 03 8379 8111
email: talk2us@lonelyplanet.com.au

USA
150 Linden St, Oakland, CA 94607
☎ 510 893 8555 TOLL FREE: 800 275 8555
fax 510 893 8572
email: info@lonelyplanet.com

UK
72-82 Rosebery Ave, London, EC1R 4RW
☎ 020 7841 9000 fax 020 7841 9001
email: go@lonelyplanet.co.uk

France
1 rue du Dahomey, 75011 Paris
☎ 01 55 25 33 00 fax 01 55 25 33 01
email: bip@lonelyplanet.fr
www.lonelyplanet.fr

World Wide Web: www.lonelyplanet.com or AOL keyword: lp
Lonely Planet Images: www.lonelyplanetimages.com